MANAGING CUSTOMER
RELATIONSHIPS ON THE INTERNET

INTERNATIONAL BUSINESS AND MANAGEMENT

Series Editor: **Pervez N. Ghauri**

Published:

The Common Glue
Morosini

Non-Business Actors in a Business Network
Hadjikhani & Thilenius

European Union and the Race for Foreign Direct Investment in Europe
Oxelheim & Ghauri

Strategic Alliances in Eastern and Central Europe
Hyder & Abraha

Intellectual Property and Doing Business in China
Yang

Co-operative Strategies and Alliances
Contractor & Lorange

Relationships and Networks in International Markets
Gemünden, Ritter & Walter

International Business Negotiations
Ghauri & Usunier

Critical Perspectives on Internationalisation
Havila, Forsgren & Håkansson

Managing Cultural Differences
Morosini

Managing Networks in Transition Economies
Johanson

Network Dynamics in International Marketing
Naude & Turnbull

The Global Challenge for Multinational Enterprises
Buckley & Ghauri

Business Network Learning
Hakansson & Johanson

Managing International Business Ventures in China
Li

Other titles of interest:

International Trade in the 21st Century
Fatemi

Globalization, Trade and Foreign Direct Investment
Dunning

International Trade and the New Economic Order
Moncarz

Contemporary Issues in Commercial Policy
Kreinin

Related journals — sample copies available on request:

European Management Journal
International Business Review
International Journal of Research in Marketing
Long Range Planning
Scandinavian Journal of Management

For full details of all IBM titles published under the Elsevier imprint please go to:
http://www.elsevier.com/locate/series/ibm

INTERNATIONAL BUSINESS AND MANAGEMENT   VOLUME 18

MANAGING CUSTOMER RELATIONSHIPS ON THE INTERNET

EDITED BY

ANGELIKA LINDSTRAND
Stockholm School of Economics, Sweden

JAN JOHANSON
Uppsala University, Sweden

DHARMA DEO SHARMA
Stockholm School of Economics, Sweden

Series Editor: Pervez N. Ghauri

ELSEVIER

Amsterdam — Boston — Heidelberg — London — New York — Oxford
Paris — San Diego — San Francisco — Singapore — Sydney — Tokyo

ELSEVIER B.V.
Radarweg 29
P.O. Box 211, 1000 AE
Amsterdam, The Netherlands

ELSEVIER Inc.
525 B Street, Suite 1900
San Diego, CA 92101-4495
USA

ELSEVIER Ltd
The Boulevard, Langford Lane
Kidlington, Oxford OX5 1GB
UK

ELSEVIER Ltd
84 Theobalds Road
London, WC1X 8RR
UK

First edition 2006

British Library Cataloguing in Publication Data
A catalogue record is available from the British Library.

ISBN-10: 0-08-044124-6
ISBN-13: 978-0-08-044124-5

♾ The paper used in this publication meets the requirements of ANSI/NISO Z39.48-1992 (Permanence of Paper).
Printed in The Netherlands.

To Anders Blomstermo, 1963-2003.

Contents

Contributors

Per Andersson	Center for Information and Communication Research (CIC), Stockholm School of Economics, Stockholm, Sweden
Katarina Arbin	Center for Information and Communication Research (CIC), Stockholm School of Economics, Stockholm, Sweden
Enrico Baraldi	Department of Business Studies, Uppsala University, Uppsala, Sweden
Karin Berglund	School of Business at Mälardalen University, Västerås, Sweden
Francesco Ciabuschi	Department of Business Studies, Uppsala University, Uppsala, Sweden
Maria Dahlin	School of Business at Mälardalen University, Västerås, Sweden
Mats Edenius	Stockholm School of Economics, Stockholm, Sweden
Kent Eriksson	Centre for Banking and Finance, Royal Institute of Technology, Graduate School of Infrastructure, Stockholm, Sweden
Mats Forsgren	Department of Business Studies, Uppsala University, Uppsala, Sweden
Daniel L. Grenblad	Department of Marketing and Strategy, Stockholm School of Economics, Stockholm, Sweden

Peter Hagström	Institute of International Business, Stockholm School of Economics, Stockholm, Sweden
Jan Johanson	Department of Business Studies, University of Uppsala, Uppsala, Sweden
Martin Johanson	Department of Business Studies, Uppsala University, Uppsala and Mid Sweden University, Sundsvall, Sweden
Niels Kornum	Department of Marketing, Copenhagen Business School, Copenhagen, Denmark
Angelika Lindstrand	Department of Marketing and Strategy, Stockholm School of Economics, Stockholm, Sweden
Sara Melén	Department of Marketing and Strategy, Stockholm School of Economics, Stockholm, Sweden
Daniel Nilsson	Department of Marketing and Strategy, Stockholm School of Economics, Stockholm, Sweden
Emilia Rovira	Department of Marketing and Strategy, Stockholm School of Economics, Stockholm, Sweden
Dharma Deo Sharma	Department of Marketing and Strategy, Stockholm School of Economics, Stockholm, Sweden
Magnus Söderlund	Center for Consumer Marketing, Stockholm School of Economics, Stockholm, Sweden
Mats Vilgon	Department of Marketing and Strategy, Stockholm School of Economics, Stockholm, Sweden
Alf Westelius	Department of Business Administration, University of Stockholm, Stockholm, Sweden
Antonella Zucchella	University of Pavia, Italy

The Development of Research on Marketing: A Historical Perspective

Angelika Lindstrand, Jan Johanson and Dharma Deo Sharma

Background

Research on marketing is expanding rapidly, which is evident from the large number of books, journals, and journal articles published every year. The increased number of marketing conferences being held each year and the growing number of marketing courses being offered by universities and business schools also emphasize the important role of marketing.

In the beginning, researchers were concerned with the functional aspect of marketing and primarily focused their attention on the exchange and distribution of goods and commodities. This research perspective was followed by the marketing management school, which adopted a more decision-making approach to marketing problems (Sharma, 1993; Vargo & Lusch, 2004). From this thinking, the 4P's model or the marketing mix model emerged (Nicosia, 1966). Early on, researchers investigated marketing as a dyadic exchange process, frequently from the perspective of either a single buyer or a single seller. According to this approach, marketing was considered a decision-making problem. With its emphasis on decision-making, this approach to marketing viewed consumers as passive and advocated active marketing strategy formulation and implementation by the selling firm. The goal of the selling firms was to develop an optimal marketing mix to suit the need of a group or a segment of buyers (Kotler, 1993). The marketing managers analyzed the micro- and the macroenvironments of the firm and developed an optimal marketing mix strategy to attract and serve the consumers.

Development of a New Alternative Paradigm

During the 1980s, a greater emphasis on industrial as well as service markets evolved. Researchers discovered that the volume of sales in the field of industrial goods and services far exceeded the volume of goods sold in consumer goods markets. Following this shift, a critical review of some of the major assumptions of the traditional marketing mix theory was conducted (Webster, 1992). In the early 1980s, Scandinavian marketing scholars developed the interaction model and emphasized the important and active role played by the buyers in achieving marketing exchange (Håkansson, 1982). These researchers stated that buyers are also active in industrial markets. In addition, they advocated the importance of relationships in marketing. This line of thinking also resulted in a number of studies based on power relationships in marketing (Sharma, 1983; Heide & John, 1988). Parallel to the above development was the increase in research being conducted in the field of services (Lovelock, 1983). Studies on professional service markets, for example, found that buyer–seller exchange in the markets shows a degree of stability, indicating that they are loyal to each other (Sharma, 1991).

These changes in the field of industrial and service marketing resulted in the formulation of a number of new concepts in marketing, such as trust, adaptation, and commitment. From these developments, the relational school of marketing or the network approach to marketing was generated. A significant shift in marketing theory and marketing thinking emerged. These researchers pointed out a number of features of markets that are different from those mentioned in the traditional marketing literature. A number of assumptions derived from the traditional marketing mix theory were questioned and then put to the test. An analysis of the network approach to marketing revealed that a degree of stability in buyer–seller relationships exists in markets. Secondly, in contrast to the assumption of the marketing mix model, the network approach emphasized that both buyers and sellers are active in markets. Moreover, both buyers and sellers possess knowledge to initiate exchange. This finding is in contrast to the "assumption" of the traditional marketing mix approach that the selling firm, but not the buyer, possesses knowledge. In addition, researchers found that buyers and sellers interact and adapt in industrial markets. The IMP project, for example, improved our understanding of marketing by contributing a number of new aspects into the analysis, including trust, commitment, and adaptation. This project also convincingly argued that a number of aspects internal to firms are critical to the understanding of marketing. They included aspects such as the organizational structure of the buyers as well as the seller firms, their strategy, and their production technology in the analysis. Moreover, the network approach to marketing stressed that relationships do not exist in isolation but are connected to each other so that every relationship is part of a wider network of relationships in the market. This approach widely enhanced our understanding of marketing as a phenomenon. A new dominant logic in marketing theory thus started to develop.

During the 1990s and thereafter, theory development in marketing continued. Many "new theories" were proposed, but, in essence, most of the fundamental assumptions of the network approach to marketing were accepted and remained unchanged. During these years, researchers in marketing borrowed ideas from the strategy literature, especially from the resource-based view of firms (Penrose, 1959).

Empirical evidences show that buyers and sellers are loyal to each other and that a high degree of stability exists in buyer–seller relationships. An important goal of selling firms in markets is to retain customers and to develop loyal customers. Loyal customers are also profitable. Retaining customers, however, demands that sellers can meet the needs and wants of the buyer, which thus requires two-way communication. It is important for sellers to communicate as early as possible with the counterpart to identify the needs and wants of the buyers. Establishing this two-way communication is also essential from the perspective of sellers so that they can influence the needs and wants of buyers. Moreover, in order for sellers to receive the right signals from the counterpart early in the process, it is important to establish wide areas of contact with the buyer firms, both horizontally and vertically in firms. Timely communication is therefore vital.

Internet, Information Technology Loyalty, and Marketing

The development of the Internet and other types of IT is providing new challenges as well as new avenues of research for marketing scholars. It is well accepted that the modern means of communication are likely to play an important part in facilitating communication between buying and selling firms. Some scholars believe that the Internet may bring about a revolution in marketing and, consequently, in marketing research as well. There is, thus, an increasing need for more research in this field. Specifically, it is believed that the Internet will affect marketing by introducing rapid technical changes and by promoting price competition because of increasing price transparency. It is agreed that the Internet may influence marketing because of its rapid speed, wide and international scope, and low cost. The Internet is also likely to affect marketing because of its impact on information collection, interpretation, and transfer. The speed of communication as well as the cost of communication could be relatively small. The Internet also provides improved interactivity and two-way communication between buyers and sellers. In addition, the Internet permits buyers to manipulate media content. Not the least important of which is the fact that the Internet allows instant connection between media exposure and transaction, thus, the term *hypertext media*. The Internet allows instant presentation of text, picture, sound, light, and animation, hence, the term *multimedia*. It is not surprising that marketers are thrilled by this development. An increasing number of marketers view developments in the field of the Internet with great optimism. They see the Internet as an instrument for exploiting new opportunities, as well as for reaching new customers, in national and international markets. As a reflection of this, marketing researchers are increasingly trying to investigate the new opportunities as well as the threats that the Internet may pose to marketers. Consequently, in recent years, a growing number of articles on various aspects of Internet marketing have appeared. Several academic journals have published special numbers on this topic (Roham & Swaminathan, 2004; Biswas, 2004; Chatterjee, 2002). Sharma and Sheth (2004) write, "The internet creates a fundamental shift in business and consumer behaviours similar to that of the Industrial Revolution" (p. 696). They also state that web-based marketing allows firms to provide information, to communicate, and to conduct transactions.

However, research on the impact of the Internet on marketing has only just begun. A challenge to marketing researchers is the vast number of research issues that require investigation. For example, our knowledge on the use of the Internet in marketing is still limited. What are the potentials and problems in using the Internet in domestic and international marketing? Another important issue is the management of relationships with customers through the Internet. Can it be done? If yes, how? Is it feasible to cultivate relationships with buyers and then convert buyers into co-producers and involve them in delivering goods/services to other buyers? What are the benefits and drawbacks in using the Internet to develop and manage exchange relationships with customers? Moreover, how may the Internet help firms not only to deliver what customers want but also to gauge and monitor their relationships with buyers so that relationships are developed, maintained, and strengthened? Determining the typology of buying and buyer behavior on the Internet would also be of benefit. In addition, there is a need to develop theory and constructs, as well as measurement instruments to operationalize theoretical constructs in this research field. A strategic marketing issue is how to develop loyal, trustworthy, and committed customers and how to determine the impact of the Internet on customer retention.

There may also be research issues related to the introduction and implementation of Internet-based systems in marketing. Such introductions may have far-reaching effects on other systems and activities of the seller firm as well as the purchasing firm. Marketing of Internet-based systems may also be associated with specific problems because they may have unforeseen consequences in the buyer firms. The handling of Internet-based system problems in marketing is certainly a field-requiring research.

The purpose of this book is to investigate some of the above-mentioned research issues. We supply theoretical as well as empirical evidence to enhance our knowledge of Internet issues. The material supplied in this book concerns consumer, industrial, and service markets and covers both domestic and international markets.

Content of the Book

The book contains 14 chapters and is divided into two parts. Many of the contributors to the book have a special interest in international business and marketing, and we, therefore, devote six chapters in the second part of the book exclusively to IT in international marketing. The first part of the book, however, includes eight chapters that deal more with general marketing issues and, as a consequence, do not specially refer to the international dimension of marketing. The first three chapters of this part analyze issues related to the introduction, implementation, and use of IT systems in the purchasing firm.

In Chapter 1, Mats Edenius and Alf Westelius study the consequences of introducing a web-based e-messaging system into healthcare. This chapter focuses on knowledge development in terms of the communication situation and the use of the e-messaging service. They find that the system helps start the process of knowledge development among both healthcare providers and patients.

Katarina Arbin and Per Andersson investigate the effects of mobile solutions in logistics in a hospital. They find that several actors are involved and are affected, which include the following: suppliers (more effective way of receiving orders and order information), the organization as such (reduced lead-time, etc.), end users in the organization (more interesting, social and responsible working tasks), and patients (less exposure to new bacteria).

In Chapter 3, Karin Berglund, Maria Dahlin, and Martin Johanson present research on the link between the planning of IT implementation and the process when the new system is implemented and used. They find that the user firm encountered several unexpected problems. An example with strong marketing implications occurred when the user firm realized that the software supplier had to be replaced by a competing supplier. They also find that discoveries tended to lead to entrepreneurial actions in the purchasing firm, which, in turn, changed the path of the implementation process.

In Chapter 4, Niels Kornum studies the case of the Specialty E-grocer X that establishes a direct channel to consumers. The purpose of the study is to examine whether B2B-based resource dependence is also applicable to the grocery e-commerce business-to-consumer (B2C) setting. This chapter concludes that resource-dependence theory is suited for analysis of grocery e-commerce B2C relationships.

Daniel Nilsson investigates customers' use of the Internet for banking services in Chapter 5. In particular, he studies the importance of customers' Internet knowledge and their acquisition of knowledge. His research shows that knowledge has a strong influence on customers' use of the Internet for banking services and that the social network is crucial to consumers with limited knowledge, whereas consumers with extensive knowledge more actively search for information.

Magnus Söderlund discusses intention variables in empirical research on customer relationships. This empirical study concerns an Internet application and demonstrates that different intention measures give different results. He stresses that analysts must pay attention to how intentions are conceptualized and operationalized. In Chapter 7, Angelika Lindstrand and Kent Eriksson discuss the perceived use of knowledge in relation to IT. In Chapter 8, Daniel Grenblad supplies evidences from IT use in marketing airline services.

The second part of the book starts with two chapters on internationalization. Chapter 9 also investigates the internationalization of firms. Mats Vilgon and Per Andersson examine three interrelated questions regarding the international development of new Internet-based ventures. They started out by finding a number of cooperating companies working in new constellations. Then they discovered that the international ambitions and performances of the ventures differed between two groups. Many of the Born Globals failed to become international, whereas the multinational companies, which appeared later, were more successful in developing a local presence through Internet ventures. A large variation in market approaches over time was also determined.

Born Globals are also the focus of the three following chapters. In Chapter 10, Antonella Zucchella presents a study of 107 born global firms. This study places attention on the use of information and communication technology (ICT) and customer orientation in these firms. One of the main findings of the study is that being a born global firm can be as a result of external conditions. However, success depends on developing an international vision, opening up to world market opportunities, and being able to identify groups of global customers to target with a unique offer.

Chapter 11 by Sara Melén focuses on the process of acquiring foreign market knowledge, which is a crucial and challenging problem for knowledge-intensive small- and medium-sized enterprises (SMEs) selling in international, specialized niche markets. In a case study, she analyzes how a high-tech SME gains such knowledge when interacting with foreign customers and how ICT is used. The findings indicate that ICT facilitates the acquisition of knowledge about existing foreign customers. However, the case study also shows the shortcomings of ICT in terms of the company's ability to initiate new customer relationships.

Emilia Rovira, in Chapter 12, studies a central question in the age of information: How important is face-to-face interaction? Based on case studies of two biotech SMEs, she finds that interactions with customers relates to the levels of customer trust and uncertainty that customers feel about a business relationship. The inducement of customer trust and reduction of uncertainty are, furthermore, specifically important for companies that are in the exploration phase of their international development.

In Chapter 13, Enrico Baraldi and Francesco Ciabuschi develop a model for investigating the role IT plays in the innovation process. In particular, they focus on how the innovation context interplays with IT-solutions during the various phases of the innovation process. Their conceptual discussion is supported using information gained from case studies of two Swedish multinationals, Svenska Cellulosa AB (SCA) and IKEA. They conclude that single IT tools play different roles in each phase of the innovation process and that coordination between the IT tools being utilized is a key issue.

Finally, in Chapter 14, Mats Forsgren and Peter Hagström confront the Uppsala model of internationalization using data and experiences from eight Internet-related firms. They find very little evidence of incremental internationalization behavior among the firms. Stakeholders outside the firm seemed to have a strong influence on their behavior. The study also demonstrated explicit and active internationalization strategies among the firms. Finally, their study indicated that the managerial implications of the Uppsala model are perhaps more relevant than originally intended.

We would like to thank Daniel Grenblad, Department of Marketing and Strategy, Stockholm School of Economics, for his kind assistance in preparing the book.

References

Biswas, D. (2004). Economics of information in the web economy: Towards a new theory? *Journal of Business Research, 57,* 724–733.

Chatterjee, P. (2002). Interfirm alliances in online retailing. *Journal of Business Research, 57,* 714–723.

Håkansson, H. (Ed.) (1982). *International marketing and purchasing of industrial goods.* London: Wiley.

Heide, J. B., & John, G. (1988). The role of dependence balancing in safeguarding transaction specific assets in conventional channels. *Journal of Marketing, 53,* 20–35.

Kotler, P. (1993). *Principles of marketing* (3rd ed.). NJ: Prentice-Hall.

Lovelock, C. (1983). Classifying services to gain strategic marketing insights. *Journal of Marketing, 47,* 9–20.

Nicosia, F. (1966). *Consumer decision processes.* Englewood Cliff, NJ: Prentice-Hall.

Penrose, E. (1959). *The theory of the growth of the firm.* London: Basil Blackwell.

Roham, A., & Swaminathan, V. (2004). A typology of online shoppers based on shopping motivations. *Journal of Business Research, 57,* 748–757.

Sharma, D. D. (1983). *Swedish firms and management contracts.* Ph.D. thesis, Department of Business Studies, Uppsala University, Uppsala, Sweden.

Sharma, D. D. (1991). *International operations of professional firms.* Student Literature, Lund, Sweden.

Sharma, D. D. (Ed.) (1993). Industrial networks. *Advances in international marketing* (Vol. 5). London: JAI Press.

Sharma, A., & Sheth, J. (2004). Web-based marketing: The coming revolution in marketing thought and strategy. *Journal of Business Research, 57,* 696–702.

Vargo, S. L., & Lusch, R. L. (2004). Evolving to a new dominant logic for marketing. *Journal of Marketing, 68,* 1–17.

Webster, F. E. (1992). The changing role of marketing in corporation. *Journal of Marketing, 56,* 1–17.

PART I

Chapter 1

E-Service and Knowledge Formation: The Use of A Web-Based E-Messaging System in HealthCare

Mats Edenius and Alf Westelius

Introduction

Service has, in numerous ways, become a focus of the healthcare sector. There is an increasing interest in employing e-mail or other Internet-based messaging systems to help facilitate communications between patients and healthcare providers. Many different projects have been put into practice. In this chapter, we focus on one such project: the use of an e-messaging system and the knowledge formation resulting from this use.

This chapter presents a perspective in which knowledge is regarded as emerging from the use of an e-messaging system. We assert that the conventional research in this field lacks, to some degree, a discussion of what type of knowledge processes an e-messaging system generates among its users when it is put into practice. These are knowledge processes that the healthcare sector will need to understand and manage if the e-services are to be implemented successfully. We propose an analytical way of thinking about e-service by focusing on the various knowledge processes that are related to an e-service.

Previous studies have concentrated on the content of the communication and how that content is interpreted and given new and different meaning. We, on the other hand, set aside the actual text or message and focus on the knowledge that is developed based on the *communication situation* and *the use of the e-messaging service.* We assert that an e-messaging system should not be seen simply as a tool for performing a specific, well-defined task in a static knowledge domain. Its introduction triggers processes of knowledge development among its users — both healthcare providers and patients.

Background

The Internet has become an important channel for communication, consumption and managing relationships with customers. In symbiosis with this development, the interest in employing the Internet as a means of communication between the healthcare sector and the public has increased (Kapsalis, Charatsis, Georgoudakis, Nikoloutsos, & Papadopoulos, 2004). The number of health-related websites is continually growing, and medical journals contain increasing numbers of articles on Internet use in healthcare. The Internet promises to become an important tool for healthcare service. Patients (healthcare consumers) can log into a web portal to find an appropriate medical treatment and/or find the correct way to get the healthcare they need.

The portal can also be used as a platform and entrance for e-mail or other e-messaging interactions (Hobbs et al., 2003) to increase the service given to the inhabitants. It can increase the use of non-visit care in responding to patients' needs (Sittig, King, & Hazlehurst, 2001). Use of the portal may lead to improvements in physician–patient communication, which in turn could aid in maximising the therapeutic benefits for patients (Lerner, Jehle, Janicke, & Moscati, 2000; Braddock, Fihn, Levingson, Jonsen, & Pearlman, 1997). Another feature of the web as a portal for communication is the ability to use it for administrative purposes. One such attempt is Vårdguiden, the Stockholm County Council's Web portal for healthcare and telephone consultation.[1]

The portal is a non-commercial arena where Stockholm residents can get information about the healthcare sector and get healthcare advice. Vårdguiden offers some interactive services — a type of e-service that is now spreading in the

---

[1]Stockholm County has 1.8 million inhabitants. Within the County Council, there are 26 municipalities of varying size, everything from the City of Stockholm itself, to rural, sparsely populated municipalities. Every inhabitant has the right to choose a doctor and hospital. To be able to offer the best possible care and safeguard the relevant healthcare guarantees, the County Council employs both private and public healthcare providers. Primary care or outpatient medical care is the basis of the County Council's medical care services. This kind of care is organised into health centres. There are a hundred or so health centres with over 800 general practitioners, district nurses and physiotherapists. A typical health centre consists of 4–10 doctors, 3–8 nurses and other administrative staff.

healthcare sector. At the time of our study, the portal included three different communication services. Patients who were registered users could use the system to book, alter and cancel appointments with physicians. They could also renew their prescriptions, and renew their registration on the sick list (for example, when a patient who has had his operation postponed still needs to be on the sick list). In the autumn of 2003, there were six health centres involved in a pilot study where this service was put into practice. Today, a year later, over 40 health centres and hospital clinics offer e-services via Vårdguiden. Vårdguiden offers several different services that utilise e-messaging. From one of the web pages, patients can send messages that will be answered by someone working in the healthcare sector. The name of the system is "My Health Contacts" (MHC). Due to issues regarding privacy and security, the e-messaging function is a proprietary case management solution, where messages are accessible only when you log into the Vårdguiden application. However, you can be notified that a message is waiting for you in MHC by ordinary e-mail.

An increasing amount of research can be found regarding communication services in the healthcare sector and their link to the Internet. In accordance with different service quality models, the research can be divided into two groups. One group focuses on how the system is used (cf. Sittig et al., 2001; Moyer, Stern, Dobias, Cox, & Katz, 2002; Sciamanna, Clark, Houston, & Diaz, 2002; Fridsma, Ford, & Altman, 1994). The other group concentrates on individual characteristics concerning why it is used as it is (cf. Greenspan, 2003; Moyer et al., 2002; Hobbs et al., 2003). These types of research examine important questions in an attempt to improve our knowledge about e-messaging services in the healthcare sector. Naturally, they do not tell the entire story.

In this chapter, we present a study with a divergent perspective from that which is found in the conventional research. What conventional studies have in common is that they either codify different practices (the patients' willingness to use e-mail, how frequently they use it, etc.) or they illuminate the discourse surrounding the use of e-messaging systems in a very descriptive manner. However, few studies provide empirical accounts of how knowledge is produced in concrete practices and day-to-day activities and routines. With this empirical goal in mind, one approach is to discuss the concept of knowledge and when doing this not separate the knowledge from the actual use of an information system.

Our goal is to expand the static realist version of knowledge that is found in the conventional research in this field. We are attempting to do this by emphasising *how* certain forms of knowledge emerge when an e-messaging system is put into practice in the healthcare sector. In this chapter, we examine one of the most utilised of these services to book, alter and cancel appointments with physicians. Our assertion is that an e-messaging system ought not to simply be seen as a tool for performing a specific, well-defined service in a static-knowledge domain. Rather, we posit that its introduction triggers processes of knowledge development among its users. It is a question about knowledge development that may have little resemblance to the task the designer intended the system to support, and knowledge formations that go beyond the instrumental results of an e-messaging system. However, to maintain a high level of service, we must be aware of different knowledge processes and be able to manage them simultaneously.

In the next section, we further explicate the potential benefits and limitations of such a theoretical perspective in the context of an e-messaging system.

Knowledge from a Discourse Perspective

Research about e-messaging systems — in line with the mantra that knowledge is the key entity in modern organisations — demonstrates how people can use computer applications to generate, transmit, store and integrate knowledge (e.g. Venkatesh & Speier, 2000; McInerney, 1999; Miller, Roehr, & Bernhard, 1998; Rao & Sprague, 1998; Edenius & Borgerson, 2003). This is also mirrored in medical informatics literature (cf. Hobbs et al., 2003). The conventional approach in this field coincides with the grand idea of an (almost completely) educated society. This is a concept that could be viewed as an echo of the enlightenment dream: wherein all (health) knowledge is available to each individual. In this chapter, we introduce a view of knowledge that stems from another ontological sphere. In this sphere, utilising an e-booking system is regarded as creating knowledge, rather than simply transferring it. This could appear to be in line with some research in knowledge management (e.g. Nonaka & Takeuchi, 1995; Nonaka & Toyama, 2003) and information systems (e.g. Langefors, 1995; Ngwenyama & Lee, 1997). However, while they focus on the content of the communication and how that content is interpreted and assigned new meaning, we set the actual text or message aside and focus on the knowledge that is developed based on the communication situation and the use of the e-messaging service.

The living act of knowing — making sense of our experience and insights — is partially constituted by the discourse of representations (e.g. Borgerson & Schroeder, 2002). An Intranet (or a similar computer application) intervenes and reshapes the knowledge via diverse modes of representation (cf. Cooper, 1992). Rather than operating as a vessel in which knowledge is assumed to reside as a kind of stable entity or stock of fixed information, the e-messaging system becomes a complex system of discursive practices.

Recognising that knowledge is an ambiguous and multifaceted concept, we adopt the notion of *discourse* proposed by the French historian, Michel Foucault

(1971, see also Edenius & Westelius, 2004). According to Foucault, knowledge-creation can be seen as a discursive practice and formation. In the present study, this means that it is imperative to examine the manner in which the users express their use of an e-messaging system. From this perspective, we put forward how different dividing practices (inclusion/exclusion, inside/outside, etc.) impact discursive knowledge processes, such as what people become and how people act (i.e. Foucault, 1965, 1977).

We thus offer a dynamic view of knowledge by shifting our attention away from a conventional *being-realism* that treats knowledge as a nearly tangible entity, to an ontology of *becoming-realism* that focuses on the *processual* becoming of things (Tsoukas, 1996). In the latter perspective, knowledge is provisional, agreed upon and in a constant process of becoming; it is resisting any closure, it is never definite or absolute. In addition, knowledge is seen as co-production; and, in complex cases, we cannot truly separate what "comes from" the subject from what "comes from" the object; what Castoriadis (1997, p. 345) calls the "principle of undecidability of origin".

One component of our creation of knowledge is our choice of divisions. Foucault (1966, 1971, 1983) shows that we need divisions, because by dividing things we can maintain a vision, get control and ascribe significance to certain aspects of the world, i.e. obtain knowledge. In other words, division serves both the discourse and the learning (the knowledge formation). It accomplishes this by enabling comparison and by singling out aspects of current interest from others that are currently considered irrelevant. Understanding how to act within a domain of action, to refine knowledge, entails learning to make competent use of the categories and the distinctions of that domain (Townley, 1994). When we relate this discussion to our empirical material, we find that by using an e-messaging system, the users, as cognising subjects, re-arrange and re-order what they know from their own context. This creates new distinctions and, therefore, new knowledge.

Hence, the working definition of knowledge we are employing in this text is focused more on what is produced in practices than as a constant property. According to this view, *how* things have come to be constituted and known (becoming-realism) gains precedence over *what* things actually are (being-realism). By asserting this, we do not mean to suggest that practices are self-fulfilling entities for knowledge. Practices are embedded in social settings (networks) and the members of each network share a signifying language. All of us live in varying discursive formations that overlap only partially, if at all.

This returns us to the aim of this study. By examining statements made by various e-messaging users, we will illustrate how an e-messaging service is linked to new knowledge and knowledge processes. We assert that new meaning and knowledge will be generated from the way in which patients and physicians form judgements, distinctions and generalisations when utilising a new e-service. In order to illustrate these issues, we will draw on case study material collected from users of the pilot installations mentioned in the opening of this chapter.

In the next part of the chapter, we will briefly introduce the empirical material being used. Thereafter, we will present different illustrations of the phenomenon "conceptions of e-messaging systems in practice". It is of import to note that this chapter focuses on knowledge related to implementing a new system. We conclude the chapter by stating the implications that this knowledge-formation process may have for the development of e-messaging systems as a healthcare service.

Case Illustration

The empirical material we collected is from qualitative investigations. The quotations are based on tape-recorded and transcribed interviews.

To begin with, 21 patients and MHC users with varying backgrounds and of different ages were interviewed in the autumn of 2003. The structured interviews took place via telephone and lasted approximately one half hour each.

Next, in cooperation with the Vårdguiden project organisation, two focus groups were formed. Each consisted of nine participants, who were asked to discuss their experiences in using MHC. One group consisted of individuals in the lower middle age (35–50) and the other of higher middle age (50–68). Both focus groups were a mixture of men and women (50/50), and a moderator supervised them. The discussions lasted about 2 hours each and took place in the spring of 2003 (see also Edenius & Westelius, 2004).

The interviewees and the focus-group participants were recruited by telephone. They were selected through the answers they provided to a pop-up questionnaire on MHC in Vårdguiden, where they had agreed to participate in evaluating the application.

Finally, we conducted a series of discussions with the Vårdguiden project managers. We discussed the objectives of MHC and its implementation. We then interviewed 10 physicians about their usage and opinions of MHC. In all the groups, general questions were asked about:

- How they currently consumed/administrated healthcare.
- Why they used Vårdguiden/MHC.
- Their experience of using Vårdguiden/MHC.

Our analysis is based on the feedback we received from MHC users. In that respect our chapter does not differ from the conventional theory in the field.

However, we look for different conceptions rather than searching for the "typical conception". We thus have an idiographic rather than a nomothetic intent. Rather than basing our study upon systematic protocol and techniques, our method is based more on the subjective perceptions that arose during our attempts to comprehend MHC usage, and letting the subject unfold characteristics during the process of investigation (see, for example, Burrell & Morgan, 1979). The empirical material in this chapter is intended to serve as a varied basis for examples. It is not intended as an endeavour to develop a clear order from different observations, like a "pure" induction or a complete "case study". The method should be regarded as abductive (see Hanson, 1958; Alvesson & Sköldberg, 2000), i.e. to illustrate and further develop an analytical framework where knowledge is focused upon, not to verify well-defined theories or hypotheses.

Use of the MHC E-Messaging System and Knowledge Formation

In this section, we present a number of quotations from MHC users. We then examine the interpretations of the e-services that these quotations imply. We begin with patient perspectives and then move on to healthcare-provider perspectives.

The Discourse on E-Messaging Systems in Use

The first question to pose is this: what is the aim of the MHC e-messaging system? It is difficult to separate the e-messaging system from the entire web or from the Vårdguiden portal. To quote one physician:

> What is the aim of the MHC application? It is one step in the hope of reaching an ICT Society, where people can capture so much knowledge by the web that they don't have to ask the doctor. I have a dream where physicians can make diagnoses more quickly, to decrease the cycle time and decrease the number of unnecessary treatments. The dream is alive, but we have long way to go. The information could be even better than it is today. It is very popular to talk about finding a language that we (physicians and patients) can share, were we can understand each other in a better way …
> The purpose with the system is naturally to be able to treat patients more efficiently. First, it is better for the patients: it makes it easier for them to reach us.

The stated goal behind implementing the e-messaging system and the portal is echoed in the physicians' statements: the vision of achieving an educated society. Nevertheless, it is necessary to problematise the phenomenon in order to examine what kind of knowledge we can derive from the patients' use of the booking system. From our empirical material, we can identify three different types of knowledge that frequently turned up among the users. Firstly, when the patients began to use the system, they could compare the e-service with the traditional way to get in contact with their healthcare providers. They began to realise how the traditional contact modes had worked when they explored how the new one functioned. Secondly, they began to envisage and demand quicker answers and more developed e-services. Thirdly, triggered by the use of the system, they started to evaluate and discuss administrative process quality in the healthcare sector.

Thinking in Terms of Ways of Communicating

First of all, in line with other studies in the field (see, for example, Harris Interactive, 2002) many users made sense of the application by comparing it with telephone calls, i.e. an older and more traditional way of getting in contact with the healthcare provider. It could be seen as a clear improvement. Appreciative users said they could make contact quicker, thanks to the e-mail system, and it gave them a feeling of being in control. One patient said:

> I can contact my doctor more quickly, not having to spend half a day on the phone and then be disconnected. And I can choose a time for making contact that suits me, and then connect and order a prescription [renewal], an appointment, or whatever. It is on my terms, not on the doctor's.

This statement is a result of comparing two different methods of contacting the healthcare provider. The quotation above demonstrates how people think along these lines: the application is viewed as a form of contact with the healthcare providers and then compared with existing forms of remote contact — typically telephone calls. Making a telephone call took more time and had to be done during business hours. Due to these limitations, the e-mail system appeared to be a better communication tool. What is significant here is not whether the users were actually able to reach the healthcare providers quicker (which indeed seemed to be the case), but to highlight that a new kind of knowledge was generated in the process of using an e-messaging system. The e-messaging system was an alternative to making contact via the telephone. However, in the process of conveniently getting an answer, obtaining control became more important.

Others realised that the free-format communication the telephone offers was missing in the new e-service, and that a combination of the asynchronous character of e-messaging and the free-format possibilities of the telephone would be valuable.

> I think it would be excellent if you could e-mail your doctor directly. Because then you feel you have some kind of contact. This web is all well and good, but, as someone here says, you don't really know when you will receive a reply. If you have a question that is a bit urgent, one that it feels important to have an answer to, then I think it would be super to be able to send an e-mail directly to your doctor.

> I have booked an appointment, I have renewed a prescription and I have written an e-letter. What I wish is that it would have been possible to send an email directly to the doctor. Today I cheat a little, I pretend to book an appointment and then I also write a few sentences. Then the doctor will send an email back in MHC and tell me that I can't get an appointment, but at the same time I will get a written answer and a statement about my health status. That's the way we have used it.

As evinced by the quotations above, some users simply generated the ideas of functionality they wanted to see in the application. Others found ways of realising the functionality they desired by innovatively utilising the system or by other means.

Thinking in terms of a booking system

Several patients we interviewed expressed a desire for more control over finding an appropriate date and time to see a physician. In the system, patients could request an appointment either before noon or after noon, adding a few sentences in free format. The reason for this (limited) selection of options was that the design group, while giving the patient some possibility to specify preferences, had decided to allow the healthcare provider considerable discretion in the booking procedure. However, the ability to request an AM or PM appointment did not decrease the patients' desire for an even more sophisticated time-booking system. Two users said:

> Yes, [I would like to] specify dates. I asked for an appointment, and it took a week or a week and a half. Then the appointment was a further three or four weeks away. It was not a problem for me at the

time, but had the appointment been closer in time, then I would need a greater opportunity to influence the choice of time by specifying dates and time of day. Now you can not specify dates, just days of the week. If you talk on the phone, you find a time that fits, but here it is very awkward. There is a risk that the appointment will be a month into the future, and sometimes you can accept that, but on other occasions, needing an appointment in three or four days … It would help if you could specify dates for two or three weeks.

You could do it like the Motor vehicle inspection site. There, you can decide on the date and the time. You can tick the time you want, and then it's yours.

In this example, the users seem only to be concerned with the functionality of MHC as a booking system. They do not view it as a means of making contact with their healthcare provider. Compared to their previous experiences with booking systems, this appointment booking system seemed rather simplistic and afforded them far less control than other booking systems.

Developing notions of e-service quality

Evaluating the e-service by comparing the user's expectations with alternatives to the e-service affects the notion of quality and efficiency of the e-service.

Yes, I was looking for an appointment, and it took five days to get an answer. I think that is too long. 48 hours, that's the limit; it should not take more than that. It took them five days to tell me that they could not give me an appointment. That's poor performance, I think.

I had to wait for a long time. OK, the woman who took the message replied right away that she would hand it to a doctor. But after that, little happened. Five days passed. Then a doctor answered that she did not have time, but she would hand over to another doctor. Then it was almost a week before I had a note from her, saying that she had time to see me. OK, it was not very important. A health certificate for a driving license; I suppose they know that there is no great rush.

It might seem as if the customers simply become more and more demanding. However, the user demand for quicker service and greater control when utilizing MHC does have a basis. The user's knowledge of the application is created through making generalisations based on other applications they are familiar with.

Developing knowledge of the organisation of healthcare

The manner in which the patient divides information also makes it possible to aquire knowledge about how the healthcare is administrated. The interaction possibilities seemed to enable users to have a clearer view of what was happening in the healthcare administration. It made the healthcare organisation more transparent. Some users began to wonder if their desires for an improved e-service could be reasonably met:

> I realise the kind of problems that are connected to this system. What I had envisaged was to see available appointment times and then book one somehow. But as I said, I realise the kind of problems that would arise if you would allow that.

> I would have wanted to access the calendar and schedule my appointment. But if you could do that, people would perhaps book all the available appointment times, and then nothing would be available anyway, and so on. Nevertheless, I was a bit disappointed.

There were a number of comments regarding how the web service did or did not match the existing routines at the General Practitioner (GP) surgery. These included statements about how different attitudes to, or use, of different channels were seen as indications of irrational practices. The following are three examples:

> I think they do it because they have this automated service. Then they can see when they have vacancies, and schedule you if you book by telephone. Here it is the opposite: that we who book via the web get the appointment times that are left.

> But why can't they reply to an e-mail if they can talk on the 'phone? Then, they would be rid of the call and could attend to the e-mail instead.

> Getting a reply ... I had a letter with an appointment time. I don't know how long it took, but I'm sure that it was a number of days before I received the letter. I also received an e-mail, but it said that I would receive a letter by post. Then I had the feeling that one hand didn't know what the other was doing.

The users do not just interpret the message as such; they conjure images of the process that produces the messages.

The patients' views of the physicians' views   The system also makes the patients more aware of the criticism that is expressed by the medical care providers. There were numerous cases where both patients and physicians were pleased with the system and how it functioned. However, there were also a number of examples of users who began to realise that the image of MHC promoted by the County Council was at odds with the views held by physicians.

> If it would work, it would be super. But according to the information I got at the GP surgery, it is very awkward and means a lot of extra work for them. I don't know if it is more difficult for them to plan, or what. Perhaps, it's when you book an appointment you need some more information regarding what type of appointment is needed — how long it will take and, well, maybe taking tests and suchlike.

> My doctor dislikes the e-messaging system. She says that it doesn't work well. She thinks that MHC just interrupts her in her job. I said to her that next time I will book via MHC, but she said she doesn't like it if the load via MHC increases.

Due to the negative opinions that their healthcare providers express, patients who would like to use the e-service begin to believe that they should refrain from it.

Patient use and knowledge formation   MHC introduces its users to a space where comparison and new distinctions are made possible. These comparisons and new distinctions generate new kinds of knowledge. The web-based e-messaging application can be construed in different ways, which makes it possible to compare it with other communication tools, booking systems, etc. This makes it possible to observe and express things about healthcare provision, which were not previously possible. The users seem, to a large extent, to rely on the distinctions and divisions that they experience in the healthcare setting and in other situations they are familiar with. The distinctions are created from the users' previous context and knowledge. It is also notable that the knowledge they develop is not primarily shaped by interpretation schemes and ideas supplied to them by the County Council and the Vårdguiden project.

The other side of the coin   Some patients have begun to consider how the physicians view the e-messaging system, and have come to realise that the physicians' views sometimes differ from their own. We now develop this further by examining statements made by physicians and other healthcare providers.

The physicians have to base the allotment of appointments on an assessment of medical urgency and their organisational settings. The most pronounced difficulty relates to the triage process — attempting to determine the priority of different patients' requests, and devising ways of responding to them. The physicians apply, and perhaps even construct, a typology. Applying a typology based on oral communication differs from applying it based on short, written communication. If a decision is to be based on a short, written message in MHC, a capacity for doing this will have to be developed. The form of knowledge thus emerging is consistent with the cognitive mode of being a doctor. Discursive practices transform a short text into knowledge that can be used for making a decision. This decision, in turn, has to be represented in text. The physician is partaking in organising a world, and a taxonomy as a discursive practice is giving rise to new (forms of) knowledge. As one physician stated:

> What the patients want is seeing a physician, but not all of the patients need to see a physician; they ask things that could easily be handled by a telephone call or in another way. But, you can't just write yes or no, you have to give them an answer … It is difficult to give a reply without being misunderstood. I can't ask complementary questions, or catch nuances. I think it [MHC] is a little bit too awkward to use.

The e-service for booking appointments is one element of the formal organisation concept. It is a gaze that arrests the flux of phenomena, which in turn makes organising as well as manipulation possible. This phenomenon is sometimes used in management literature to describe how unruly organising processes could be frozen and represented in two-dimensional representations like documents, statistics, annual reports (Cooper, 1993), etc. However, the stable text messages in an e-service system, and the decisions that are made in symbiosis with them, are not an indicator of a stable thing. Rather, it is a way to punctuate the flux, to bracket and ignore differences. The purpose is of course to make healthcare more efficient, and, as many physicians pointed out, to make it easier for patients to contact the healthcare providers. One component of the e-service system is that the practices (clinical work) here have taken a more two-dimensional form (a short message and a request for meeting a doctor). The physicians need to begin to work in a more abstract context than they are used to. This was also pointed out as a problem.

Both physicians and patients become what Reich (1991) has coined as the epithet of the contemporary workforce; "symbol analysts". The physicians are forced to turn the patients' problems into a text wherein knowledge has become the capability to de-codify text as a kind of representation. Reality is turned into a texture of representation, and a part of professional knowledge is to de-codify such representations. What we see here is a kind of a melting pot. The constituting of a world in analytical terms required by the messaging system cannot be fully separated from the profession of being a physician. What ought to be a quite simple messaging system requires not only new knowledge, but it also embraces questions beyond the logic of the technology. It is also a question of mastering a signifying system. The patient's language is crude and unsophisticated compared with the doctor's. The doctors have for years, as cognising subjects, re-arranged and re-ordered what they know. This has created new distinctions and hence new knowledge regarding medical disorders and the necessity of treatment or further consultation. Or, as one physician said:

> I find it quite difficult to say no to a request from a patient in MHC. If you accept an appointment, everybody is happy. A no is trickier. The patients start to argue and start to distrust the health care, and then I have to write a message to explain, but it is hard to find proper formulations for such a message.

Written language in the form of punctuation can always be transferred and displayed, but is not always sufficient as a mode of communication. Our interviews provided several examples of when the physician will revert to calling the patient on the telephone. Here is one:

> Yes, I am basically positive to these e-services. The main difference to talking on the phone is that it's difficult to book appointments based on what people write. Typically, I end up calling the patient to ask additional questions to determine if an appointment is needed at all (which it is not in about 30% of the cases), and if so, try to determine the type of disorder, to be able to determine how to prioritise the appointment.

The system organises what can be called an analytical space (Edenius, 2002). This type of analytical space gives rise to a number of distinctions in the minds of physicians. Some relate to equality and differences between users of different contact channels:

> This is yet an option for those who are already good at getting in contact with us and being served. It comes at the expense of the weak groups.

> Those who have a clear question and want a straight answer use MHC. Those who have less clear-cut thoughts, demanding more space, probably prefer to call. The web is for the technically minded, and it has a strong male dominance. And it's the same in MHC. Almost all those who e-mail via MHC are men.

The explicit nature of the e-messaging system's written, timestamped and counted messages could be seen as enhancing efficiency, but it also works against the system. It draws attention to how long it takes to give an answer, raising questions about whether it is worth spending time e-mailing, etc.

> Yesterday I had 85 patient contacts. That's four minutes on average. If I should write answers to everyone, it would take too long [and I could not see as many patients].

> I can see that people want this channel [MHC], but it is awkward for me. It makes them expect voluminous e-mail conversations, and I just don't have time for that.

Based on the discussion so far, we could conclude that implementing an e-service triggers different knowledge processes. The patients demand even better communication with the healthcare organisations, and they begin to discuss and form opinions about the healthcare sector's organisation and efficiency. Implementing an e-messaging system also sparks different knowledge processes at the health centres. The physicians have to make judgements and new distinctions. They have to prioritise based on a written language. In addition, they are forced to concern themselves with who the users of the e-messaging system are.

The e-messaging system and the organisation   As noted above, not all patients come in contact with healthcare providers who encourage them to use MHC. The healthcare system is divided on this issue. We encounter physicians who encourage their patients to use MHC, as well as others who are irritated by the e-services and try to get their patients to use other means of communication. The division is less clear-cut among the patients in our study. There are those who appreciate the e-services and those who do not think they are efficient. Since we have only interviewed active users, we do not know the attitudes among non-users.

Our interviews indicate that, at present, the physicians spend extra time using the system, rather than saving time. The physicians are also required to log into this system — in addition to the ones they are currently using. They have to think about how to reply to the incoming messages, who to call instead, which requests to decline, etc. The new knowledge that arises from practicing the e-services is certainly not guaranteed to increase enthusiasm and activity. On this account, the responses we received from the physicians diverge from those given by patients.

The lack of enthusiasm for MHC among doctors is not only of concern to the County Council MHC proponents. The way doctors react creates some irritation at the GP surgery level. This is an account given by a nurse:

> So far the doctors have not changed their routines and incorpo-
> rated the use of MHC. It is new, and I have had my hands full, try-
> ing to see to it that the doctors read the incoming messages I have
> assigned them, and that they take the responsibility for attending
> to them. You have to keep reminding them, because they do not log
> in and check routinely. It is not that well established yet. I really
> want to be able to stop nagging. But I think I will with time, as
> MHC becomes part of the established routines.

The new routines the system calls for are not viewed as a neutral change. In some instances they are perceived as a type of discipline that the doctors resent. As one of the physicians said:

> The right to decide over my own calendar is one of the few liber-
> ties I have in an otherwise stressful, highly regulated and not very
> well-paid job ...

The fact that the physicians are divided on this issue should be emphasised. Some are proponents, while others actively resist the system. The majority can be found in-between.

There are also numerous examples of when the physicians' goals and knowl-edge differ from the patients' knowledge of the system. Healthcare providers view MHC as a separate channel and try to make its terms of use as explicit as possible. However, they do not seem to note that patients see the channel as a part of the communication repertoire, and use it only to the extent that it meets their expectations. A typical example is the gap between the patients' expectations of receiving an answer via the e-messaging system and the healthcare's capacity to meet these expectations.

> The advantage of IT-mediated communication is that you can
> request an appointment or book an appointment when you can find
> the time to do so. The drawback is that feedback is not very fast.
> We started out by promising to respond within a week. Then we

reduced it to three days and now further to two. Today I had an irritated patient who had not received an answer the same day that he sent his request. I was absolutely certain that our terms are clearly visible, but obviously they are not. And then, some people have called the next day to ask if they have received "my" email without noticing. They want to double check. It would be good if we had a routine to check that they have opened their email and that this is stated even more clearly in the terms of use. They should not [feel that they] have to call and check.

I thought that the number of email would increase, but now it is down to three per day. Now they call instead. They don't read the terms saying that it takes three days to get an answer [in MHC], and then they call and get an answer right away.

We have provided many illustrations of how the implementation of e-services can be seen as discursive practices that are linked to different knowledge formations. We will end this chapter by employing slightly more normative argumentation. To achieve this goal, we will claim that healthcare practitioners need to understand and manage these knowledge formations in order to maintain a good level of service for their patients.

Further Reflections and Conclusions

In this chapter, we have examined several different knowledge processes that are the outcome of using an e-messaging system. We have presented examples of the ways in which patients and physicians make distinctions, generalise based on their previous experiences and construct ideas and opinions about the application and its impact on the healthcare sector. The conventional focus is on *what* things are. Our focus, on the contrary, has been on *how* things have come to be constituted and known by using an e-messaging system. In brief, the question of what a thing *is* has primarily become a question of how different e-messaging users have come to know this thing (MHC).

We have also demonstrated how investigating different knowledge processes makes it possible to begin a discussion about how to evaluate such processes and their results. The patients write e-messages, the physicians read them, make new distinctions, prioritise, etc. A user who has attempted to use an application has begun to develop elaborate ideas about the application. This is not the case for a prospective user who is asked to describe the functionality they would like to see in an application that has yet to be constructed. With attempted use, knowledge has begun to develop, partly based on the functionality the application provides, and partly based on the functionality that it does not provide. Foucault emphasises that the power to provide others with divisions and categories creates a basis of power over the discourses and values in a society. We note how an objectivist approach to the introduction of the e-messaging service leaves users to form their own distinctions, possibly to the detriment of the intentions behind the introduction of the e-service. Given the authority generally ascribed to the medical profession in relation to patients, this may seem surprising. The healthcare institution has failed to wield power over the discourse formation taking place among users of the e-service. This calls for attentiveness on the part of the developers. They must be aware of the knowledge the users develop, akin to the prototyping tradition. It is also important that they are mindful of the multiple understandings of the application that may develop. With the aim to improve the e-service, such a method could provide an opening for a more intricate exploration of what could be done to the mismatch between the patients' demands and knowledge and the physicians' "life-world". Our text also opens up a picture that makes it possible to manage a relationship with a single patient or a single physician.

There are several available possibilities. The system provides transparency in contacting the healthcare provider, and generates reflections on how the healthcare provision works, while simultaneously decreasing the perceived transparency. In the strictly task-oriented communication that is encouraged by the present design of the system, many users experience a lack of metadata. This metadata includes: what options were available to the healthcare provider booking the appointment, what the reasons behind setting up an appointment with another doctor than the one requested were and why the request was not granted. The patients are left to wonder about what determined the healthcare provider's decision. The physicians, on the other hand, have to prioritise from a thin material. To cope with an increased use of the new channel, they must improve their ability to act on limited information and to communicate in a terse medium without appearing brusque. They must grapple with deciding who they will treat and how to appropriately formulate their decisions into a written language. At the same time, they are highly involved in developing the use of the e-services. They are potential ambassadors for the system, both directly by utilizing it, and indirectly by encouraging their patients to use MHC. When they do, they find that they are a part of a changing organisation with different goals and restrictions.

Even a "simple" e-messaging system raises users' expectations. They desire increased access and service, as well as clarification of how the healthcare sector is operated. In addition, they desire increased control. To some extent, these expectations can be met by the efficiency advantages of the new tool compared with existing modes of communication. However, the more transparency increases and the more control the user demands, the less control will be in the hands of the healthcare providers.

In the section above, we have presented a framework and a theoretical background that will perhaps enable conclusions to be drawn in advance; regarding how people will react to this new technology and how they will use it in the long run. Installing an e-messaging system in the healthcare sector makes it possible to draw a multitude of distinctions. In order to be sufficiently prepared for users' reactions, it may be beneficial to speculate in advance about what the users will do, what generalisations and distinctions they will make and what schemas they will activate. By doing so, healthcare providers can attempt to sketch cognitive maps of how users will try to use the messaging system and how they would like it to be developed.

What is conspicuous in our study is that the patients who use MHC, are, to a large extent, left to their own speculations. It might be valuable to provide them with more of an "inside picture". This would provide the users with a sense of what the healthcare providers' perspectives are. The National Health Service (NHS) website in the UK has attempted to provide some important aspects of an "inside view" on accident and emergency services.[2] It would behove a healthcare provider that offers its customers a computer-based communication tool to incorporate some aspects of this "inside view" into their system. Attending to the formation of knowledge and views is an important aspect of achieving successful use, but it is neither easy nor straightforward. One cannot assume that the more the healthcare providers try to fulfil the demands of the patients who use the e-booking system, the more pleased the patients will become. The more transparent the system becomes, the more thoughts, opinions and ideas the patients will develop, and these will need to be unveiled and addressed. We have also illustrated how putting the system into practice generates knowledge among the physicians that also requires attention. The illustrations presented in the chapter indicate a complex

---

[2]From the NHS website:
"Some myths about Accident and Emergency services:

- Calling 999 for an ambulance gets you to the top of the accident and emergency queue. FALSE. Patients are seen based on medical need not who gets to the hospital first.
- All injuries need x-rays. FALSE.
  The doctor or nurse will be able to assess, on examining you, whether an x-ray is appropriate or not. In many cases x-rays are not needed.
- Accident and Emergency doctors are more expert at dealing with medical problems than your GP. FALSE.
  Your GP is an expert in general medicine. Accident and Emergency doctors are specialists in accidents and emergencies." [40]

process. The more the system is used, the more the physicians will find themselves spending time in front of a computer in an organisation that has to adapt to the new situation. The patients' consumption of healthcare will alter due to new IT-services, and consequently the physician–patient relationship will also be altered. Will these changes be beneficial or will they prove to be detrimental? We cannot definitively answer that question at this point. Our intention is that this chapter will provide a starting point for further discussion of this subject.

References

Alvesson, M., & Sköldberg, K. (2000). Reflexive methodology: *New vistas for qualitative research*. London: Sage.

Borgerson, J., & Schroeder, J. (2002). Ethical issues of global marketing: Avoiding bad faith in visual representation. *European Journal of Marketing, 36,*(5/6), 570–594.

Braddock, C., Fihn, S., Levingson, W., Jonsen, A., & Pearlman, R. (1997). How doctors and patients discuss routine clinical decisions, informed decision making in the outpatients setting. *Journal of General Internal Medicine, 12*(6), 339–345.

Burrell, G., & Morgan, G. (1979). *Sociological paradigms and organizational analysis.* Gower Publishing.

Castoriadis, C. (1997). *World in fragments*. Stanford: Stanford University Press.

Cooper, R. (1992). Formal organization as representation: Remote control, displacement and abbreviation. In: M. Reed, & M. Hughet (Eds), *Rethinking organization*. London: Sage.

Cooper, R. (1993). Technologies of representation. In: P. Ahonen (Ed.), *Tracing the semiotic boundaries of politics*. Berlin: de Gruyter.

Edenius, M. (2002). Discourse on e-mail in use. In: E. Wynn, E. A. Whitley, M. D. Myers, & J. I. DeGross (Eds), *Global and organizational discourse about information technology*. London: Kluwer Academic Publishers.

Edenius, M., & Borgerson, J. (2003). Intranet as a knowledge management technology. *Journal of Knowledge Management, 7*(5), 124–136.

Edenius, M., & Westelius, A. (2004). Patients' knowledge formations through a healthcare e-messaging system. *Journal of Human Resource Costing and Accounting, 8*(1), 21–34.

Foucault, M. (1965). *Madness and civilisation*, New York: Pantheon.

Foucault, M. (1966). *The order of things: An archaeology of the human sciences*, London: Tavistock Publications 1970.

Foucault, M. (1971). In: R. Swyer (Trans.), *The discourse on language*, included as appendix to American edition of *The archaeology of knowledge*. New York: Pantheon.

Foucault, M. (1977). *Discipline and punish*. London: Penguin.

Foucault, M. (1983). *This is not a pipe*. Berkeley: University of California.

Fridsma, D. B., Ford, P., & Altman, R. (1994). A survey of patient access to electronic mail: Attitudes, barriers, and opportunities. In: *Proceedings of the 18th annual symposium on computer applications in medical care* (pp. 15–19).

Greenspan, R. (2003). *Tech-savvy docs resist virtual visits.* http://cyberatlas.internet.com/markets/healthcare/print/0,,10101_1008311,00.html.

Hanson, N. (1958). *Patterns of dicovery. An inquiry into the foundations of science.* Cambridge: Cambridge University Press.

Harris Interactive. (2002). Patient/physician online communication: Many patients want it, would pay for it, and it would influence their choice of doctors and health plans. *Healthcare News, 2*(8), 1–4.

Hobbs, J., Wald, J., Jagannath, Y., Kittler, A., Pizziferri, L., Volk, L., & Middleton, B. (2003). Opportunities to enhance patient and physician e-mail contact. *International Journal of Medical Informatics, 70*(1), 1–9.

Kapsalis, V., Charatsis, K., Georgoudakis, M., Nikoloutsos, E., & Papadopoulos, G. (2004). A SOAP-based system for provision of e-services. *Computer Standard & Interfaces, 26*(6), 527–541.

Langefors, B. (1995). In: Bo Dahlbom (Ed.), *Essays on infology: Summing up and planning for the future.* Lund: Studentlitteratur.

Lerner, E. B., Jehle, D. V., Janicke, D. M., & Moscati, R. M. (2000). Medical communication: Do our patients understand? *American Journal of Emergency Medicine, 18*(7), 764–766.

McInerney, C. (1999) Working in the virtual office: Providing information and knowledge to remote workers. *Library & Information Science Research, 21*(1), 69–89.

Miller, M., Roehr, A., & Bernhard, B. (1998). *Managing the corporate intranet.* New York: Wiley.

Moyer, C. A., Stern, D. T., Dobias, K. S., Cox, D. T., & Katz, S. J. (2002). Bridging the electronic divide: Patients and provider perspectives on e-mail communication in primary care. *American Journal of Management Care, 8*(5), 427–433.

Ngwenyama, O. K., & Lee, A. S. (1997). Communication richness in electronic mail: Critical social theory and the contextuality of meaning. *MIS Quarterly, 21*(2), 145–167.

NHS Direct, http://www.nhsdirect.nhs.uk/SelfHelp/info/advice/emergency4.asp, accessed 2003-07-10.

Nonaka, I., & Takeuchi, H. (1995). *The knowledge creating company: How Japanese create the dynamics of innovation.* New York: Oxford University Press.

Nonaka, I., & Toyama, R. (2003). The knowledge-creating theory revisited: Knowledge creation as a synthesizing process. *Knowledge Management Research & Practice, 1*(1), 2–10.

Rao, R., & Sprague, R. (1998). Natural technologies for knowledge work: Information visualization and knowledge extraction. *Journal of Knowledge Management, 2*(2), 70–80.

Reich, R. (1991). *The work of nations: Preparing ourselves for 21st century capitalism.* London: Simon & Schuster.

Sciamanna, C. N., Clark, M. A., Houston, T. K., & Diaz, J. A. (2002). Unmet needs of primary care patients in using the Internet for health-related activities. *Journal of Medical Internet Research, 4*(3) e19.

Sittig, D. F., King, S., & Hazlehurst, B. L. (2001). A survey of patient-provider e-mail communication: What do patients think? *International Journal of Medical Informatics, 61*(1), 71–80.

Townley, B. (1994). *Reframing human resource management: Power ethics and the subject at work.* London: Sage.

Tsoukas, H. (1996). The firm as a distributed knowledge system: A constuctionist aproach. *Strategic Management Journal, 17,* 11–25.

Venkatesh, V., & Speier, C. (2000). Creating an effective training environment for enhancing telework. *International Journal of Human – Computer Studies, 52*(6), 991–1005.

Chapter 2

Mobile Solutions in Logistics: Effects on Activities in a Hospital Environment

Katarina Arbin and Per Andersson

Introduction

In an increasing competitive business environment organizations have to improve their performance and be cost-effective in order to survive. According to previous research, new technologies are potential tools to use in order to make processes more effective and to cut costs (Huber, 1990). This chapter investigates and discusses different effects when using mobile solutions in logistics. In this chapter, solution is defined as a matching of an offering to a specific customer problem. Mobile solution is defined as an offering to a specific problem, which in some parts, consists of wireless technology. New mobile solutions have the potential to bring changes to businesses and industries, even though changes are expected to come gradually (Gordon & Gebauer, 2001). It has been argued that new mobile technologies have the potential to change the structure of activity links and interactions between actors in different parts of logistics chain, from the suppliers to the customers. Hence, when mobile solutions are implemented, several actors can be involved and affected: the user organization investing in the new solution, the people in the organization using the mobile solution (end-users), the user organization's suppliers and customers and more. Moreover, different actors will perceive the changes in the activities, in the interactions with other actors differently, and also, the effects generated will be perceived differently. This chapter focuses on and investigates changes both in activities and in interactions. An underlying assumption is that effects will be different depending on whose perspective is taken: the user organization's perspective, the individual end-user's perspective, the suppliers' point of view or the customer's perspective.

Aim and Focus

The aim of this paper is twofold: first aim is to describe the effects when improving inventory through using mobile solutions. The chosen case organization is a public hospital that is constantly threatened by lower budgets and reduced working force. In order to be proactive the hospital has started to use mobile solutions to improve their inventory handling, in order to cut costs and create value. The second aim is to discuss effects for different actors (buyers, sellers and other involved actors) when improving inventory using mobile solutions. We also comment on the effects, from the use of mobile solutions, on interactions and relationships in the intra- and inter-organizational networks involved in the inventory and logistics.

Next, the chapter describes previous, related studies focusing on studies of mobile solutions in general, in inventory and logistics and in health care environments. Thereafter, we introduce our framework focusing on various aspects of effects in general, and from a purchasing point of view connecting to our focus on inventory and logistics systems. A few words on methodology are followed by our empirical case study, focusing on two logistics processes, and describing them both before and after the introduction of mobile solutions. The perceived effects from the different actors' point of view are analysed and a set of tentative conclusions is elaborated on.

Some Prior Studies of Mobile Solutions in Organizations

Limited research has been conducted on the use of *mobile solutions in inventory and logistics handling* and on effects when using mobile solutions in organizations. Even though previous research and industry magazines claim a future growth in the use of mobile solutions in organizations (Goodman, 2000; Gordon & Gebauer, 2001), limited research has been conducted on opportunities with mobile solutions in business-to-business environments (Gebauer, Shaw, & Zhao, 2002). Although research has been conducted on, for example, cost benefits and efficiency gains in retailing organizations deploying mobile data solutions (Du Preez, 2002). Sainsbury's deployed a mobile data solution at its stores to improve its order fulfilment system that lead to a streamlining of operations. The result was a rapid, accurate decision-making at the sharp end of business (Du

Preez, 2002). Other studies of mobile solutions used in organizational settings have been presented (Hobday, 2002; Svensson, 2003; Rae-Smith & Ellinger, 2002). Hobday (2002) claims that the efficiencies driven by mobile working mean that operating costs are forced down and the savings passed on to the customer, and that mobile technologies have the capability to enhance the service given to customers by integrating the supply chain. The empirical data in this paper support this, indicating that mobile technologies in fact have the capability to enhance services in supply chains. Other research topics relating to mobile solutions and logistics are balance between companies' inventories and disturbances in logistics flow (Svensson, 2003) and introductions of online logistics service systems (Rae-Smith & Ellinger, 2002). This research however gives limited guidance when investigating effects generated by using mobile solutions in inventory and logistics.

Research has been conducted on the use of *mobile solutions in medical care* (Michalowski, Rubin, Slowinski, and Wilk 2003; Yan et al., 2002; Simpson, 1996; Altimier et al., 2002; Banitsas, Istepanian, and Tachakra 2002; Liang, 2002). For example, Michalowski et al. (2003) have conducted research on the process and methodology of designing and developing a mobile support system to triage abdominal pain in the emergency room of a hospital. Yan et al. (2000) have, for example, been investigating design and evaluation of real-time mobile telemedicine system for ambulance transport. Banitsas, Istepanian, and Tachakra (2002) use a case study to demonstrate that there are important benefits of exploiting the emerging wireless LAN technologies in hospital environments. Their (Banitsas et al., 2002) research gives an overview over potential benefits; for example, they claim that for inventory checks and maintenance schedules, data now on pieces of paper can be streamlined with mobile solutions and wireless LAN technologies as in supermarkets. They do not investigate generated effects with streamlining this process further. Simpson (1996) has investigated what wireless computing is offering when the caregiver goes to the patient, when access to and documentation of on-line patient information is mobile. He (Simpson, 1996) comes up with (1) increased efficiency in writing and sending patient care orders, (2) more efficient utilization of nursing and physician time and (3) more efficient communication among clinicians, departments and administrators. Investigation on how to evaluate an implemented wireless system (each nurse now carried a portable phone that directly sent and received calls, compared to no portable phones before) has been conducted (Altimier, Besuner, Hasselfeld, & Johannemann, 2002). Factors that were analysed in this case before and 3 months after system implementation were: (1) the number of incoming and outgoing calls, (2) how long it took to locate staff by nonwireless phone or intercom and (3) time spent on hold.

Theory: Effects of New Technologies on Activities, Interactions and Relationships in Logistics Systems

This chapter looks at research and modelling on effects of new technologies, in general (Huber, 1990; El Sawy & Bowles, 1997; Anderson & Narus, 1998; Sweet, 2001; Anderson & Narus, 1999), in order to be able to investigate effects generated by mobile solutions in logistics handling. Because of limited previous research on mobile solutions in logistics handling and on effects generated by mobile solutions, the paper will also relate to some previous, general research on effects in logistics handling, drawing, e.g. on purchasing literature (van Weele, 1984; Subramaniam & Shaw, 2002; de Boer, Harink, & Heijboer, 2002). As one of the few covering effects and IT in general can be mentioned from previous studies on value by El Sawy and Bowles (1997), investigating the impacts of an IT-enabled customer support process and its effects in an organization. El Sawy and Bowles divided the impacts into three categories: (i) order direct impacts on transforming the customer support process itself, (ii) order impacts related to integrating customer input into other business areas and (iii) order indirect impacts related to building an IT infrastructure.

Impacts of IT Technologies on Business Relationships

One aim of the study is also to capture some of the effects of mobile solutions on existing intra- and inter-organizational relationships. In the so-called The Industrial Marketing and Purchasing Group (IMP) tradition of studies on business relationships, work has been presented on the impacts of IT on such relationships. In a recent study in this tradition, Baraldi (2003) discusses the interplay between IT and resource structures within and between business organizations (see also his overview of previous studies in this field, pp. 32–33). Previously, Dubois, Gadde, and Håkansson (1989) identified various inhibitors to introducing shared IT systems between organizations. Gadde and Håkansson (1993) identified three central roles of IT in business relationships: the administrative, the coordinative and the commercial role played by IT when introduced into business relationships. In a logistical context, Laage-Hellman and Gadde (1996) also stressed various obstacles to implementing Electronic Data Interchange (EDI) in buyer–seller relationships, due to diverging strategies of the partners. In later studies, in this tradition, the value concept is touched upon by Ryssel, Ritter, and Gemunden (2000), who observed no increased (relationship) value (internally within the selling organization or in the buyer relationship) when new technologies were introduced. This is due to the fact that relationships at the same time are depersonalized. However, in a later study,

Ritter, Muller, and Gemunden (2001) showed that the introduction of new ITs affected the buying organization's evaluation of the buyer–seller relationship. Within this tradition of research, Andersson and Mölleryd (2001) also touched upon relationship changes when buying organizations invested in more advanced mobile systems and technologies. To sum up, the IMP tradition helps us to draw attention to the *contents* of the changes in intra- and inter-organizational interactions and relationships when new technologies are introduced; in this case mobile solutions.

Effects in Purchasing and Logistics Systems

When looking at other approaches of how to measure and investigate effects, the purchasing community has been conducting research on how to measure and evaluate logistics (Monczka, Carter, & Hoagland, 1979; van Weele, 1984; Dumond, 1991; Ellram, 1995; de Boer et al., 2002); however there is limited research on how to investigate effects from different perspectives when using mobile solutions in order to improve inventory and logistics.

A key performance area according to van Weele (1984) is the responsibility of purchasing department for an efficient incoming flow of purchased materials and services. This area includes the following major activities: (1) control of the timely flow of accurate requisitions and bills of material. (2) control of timely delivery by suppliers. (3) control of quantities delivered; and (4) in some cases, purchasing departmentis responsibe for determining and controlling cost-effective inventory levels. In purchasing logistics, according to van Weele (1984), adequate requisitioning and vendor delivery reliability (supplier lead times, quantities delivered) can be measured. When looking at the organization and resources, it is possible to measure changes in personnel resources (van Weele, 1984). van Weele further claims that a danger to avoid is the possibility that the measures may become too complex and too numerous; implicity is the key upto a point .

In Figure 1 we can see purchasing logistics as one of the key areas of purchasing evaluation. Lead times, order quantity, inventories, vendor performance and deliveries (late, on time, early) can be measured. Under the headline purchasing organization we find workload and procedures, which also can be evaluated and measured.

Summing up: Effects from Mobile Technologies and Effects on Relationships

When summarizing potential theoretical guidelines and when investigating effects generated using mobile solutions in logistics handling, we draw on the research introduced above. The IMP tradition helps us draw attention to the *contents* of the changes in intra- and inter-organizational interactions and relationships when new

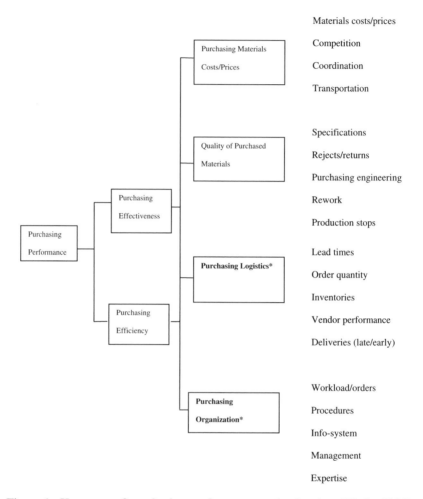

Figure 1: Key areas of purchasing performance evaluation (van Weele, 1984).
* Purchasing logistics is one of the key areas of purchasing evaluation. Lead times, order-quantity, inventories, vendor-performance and deliveries can be measured, as can workload and procedures when investigating and evaluating logistics performance (in bold).

mobile solutions are introduced. Furthermore, we adopt research by van Weele (1984) and Simpson (1996) and their performance discussion above to help us connect the discussion regarding effects to our particular inter-organizational systems in focus, e.g. logistical systems. Without leaving the interactive focus behind, our analytical discussion first approaches the effects created from new mobile technologies, from the perspective of each actor. Thereafter, we comment also on the interaction and relationship effects. However, we give an introduction of our empirical case first.

The Empirical Case Studies and Notes on Methodology

Within Sweden, the case organization, the hospital, is one of the largest university hospitals and is located in Stockholm, the capital of Sweden. It is currently a county hospital, and is closely affiliated with the adjacent university. Approximately 8500 people are working in the organization that has a yearly turnover of approximately 550 million Euro ($630 million).

The two examples on how to use mobile solutions in logistics handling describes processes when handling inventory and laundry at the hospital. Examples on how to use wireless technology in medical care (Michalowski et al., 2003; Yan et al., 2000; Simpson, 1996) are not described or focused on in this paper. The processes that are described in this paper belong to the fields of mobile solutions and logistics.

Empirical data are collected through semi-structured interviews with the purchasing manager, person responsible for inventory, person responsible for logistics at the hospital and with managers at the suppliers. Interviews with these persons were conducted twice, once in February 2002 and once in October 2003. Empirical data have also been collected by using an ethnographic approach (Garfinkel, 1967; Hammersley & Atkinson, 1983; Kunda, 1992; Myers, 1999; Barley & Kunda, 2001), following end-users in their daily work for 1 day. The use of the ethnographic approach aimed at gaining a rich picture of the process when using mobile solutions. How does it actually work, in reality, and what do the end-users (the porters) say of this way of working? These are the questions that the ethnographic methodology helped in answering. Secondary sources have also been used, like statistics and reports regarding the implementation and evaluation of mobile solutions in the organization.

The case introduces two examples on how to use mobile solutions in logistics handling: Process 1 describes an inventory handling process, while Process 2 focuses on the laundry handling operations.

Process 1 — The Inventory Process

Before starting to use a mobile solution for handling inventory at the hospital, there was limited knowledge regarding inventory levels and the need for new material. This resulted in high inventory levels (at the departments they had to be sure that they had enough material to give care to the patients) and a low turnover at a high cost. High costs were because the materials were on the shelf for too long, their best before date expired before use, and hence large losses incurred. There was lack of control and overview over inventories in the hospital. Nurses and doctors from different departments were ordering directly from the supplier without contacting the purchasing department. Large packets with materials were delivered from the goods reception to the departments directly, and then the nurses put them in the inventory cupboard. Normally there was only one large inventory at every department.

The Old Process

The old process without a mobile solution is depicted in Figure 2.

Problems to be Solved? The hospital needed a more JIT (just in time) approach in inventory handling in order to provide the departments with the right material and the right amount of material at the right time. With one large inventory for relatively large departments, doctors and nurses had to spend unnecessary time in running to the inventory obtaining materials. The nurses spent much of their time putting goods in the inventory cupboard instead of attending to the patients. There was a shortage of nurses due to lower budget, and also due to limited supply of educated nurses in the labour market.

The New Process   By using a mobile solution together with an electronic procurement and logistics software solution (called Logistics), the hospital has succeeded in solving the above problems. The current process can be seen in Figure 3.

Information regarding orders is sent to the supplier from the hospital through EDI . The supplier packs the material. The supplier gets detailed information about which department and which inventory cupboard the material is going to through the electronic order, which means that they have the necessary information in order to be able to put all the packets that are going to one inventory cupboard together. The supplier delivers the goods.

The goods arrive at the goods reception in the hospital. The porter (person working with receiving goods and delivering it internally) receives the goods and scans the codes on the goods with a mobile terminal (a PDA) in order to register received goods. He then downloads the information from the terminal to the Logistic system by walking to a room close to the goods reception, where the downloading system is placed together with a computer.

The porter then takes the goods that has to go to a particular department, for example to the children's emergency, delivers the goods through the culvert, underground, with a truck. He then takes the goods up to the department using the

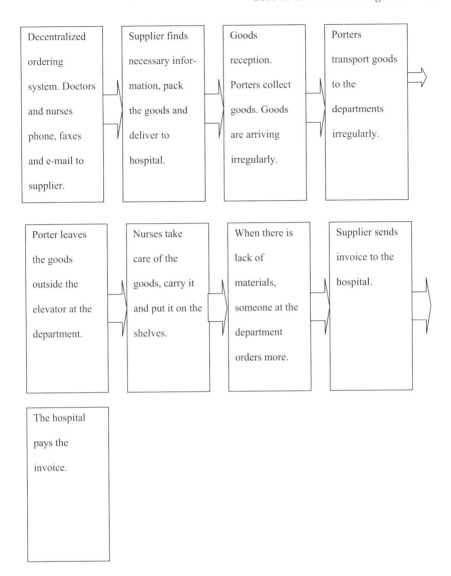

Figure 2: Old process without a mobile solution.

elevators. At the children's emergency there are five relatively small inventory cupboards, instead of one larger one as before. Michel (the name of the porter that was followed and observed in the ethnographic investigation in this paper) first delivers the ordered goods to the different inventory cupboards.

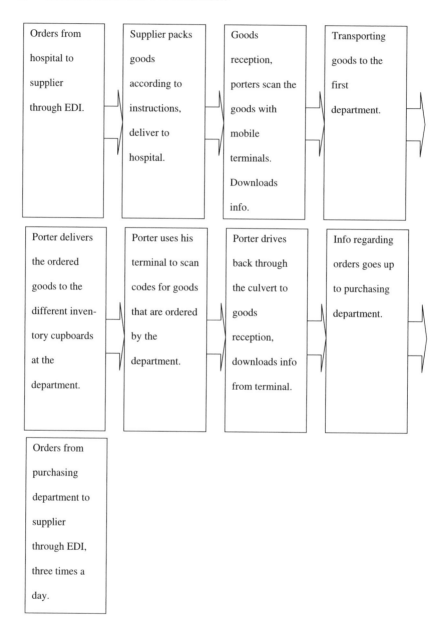

Figure 3: New Process with a mobile solution.

The ordering system works as follows for every inventory locker: in the inventory there are shelves and on the shelves there are two boxes of every item (for example, boxes with tape, cleaning cream, plaster, lamps, paper, flannel cloths, napkins, gypsum). On the shelf there is a badge with a code ; when one box has been emptied, the nurse who took the latest item should place the badge with the code upright on the inventory door. On the door of the cupboard there are four plastic rows. On the top one, badges are placed with the code facing the door, which are the goods that were ordered last time Michel was there, and those are the goods that Michel is delivering to the inventories today. When he puts the goods in their right places, he also takes the badge from the door and places it back on the shelf. He does this for all inventories at the department before he handles new orders. On the second row there are badges that the nurses have put there to order new goods. The code on the badge faces outwards. After delivering all goods, Michel uses his terminal to scan the codes on the badges that are on row two, reading in ordering information into the terminal. He then takes the badge, moves it up to the top row, placing it so that the code faces inwards, against the door. The third row is for goods that have been ordered, but it would take longer time to receive them due to supplier problems. This is to communicate to the department that the goods have been ordered, but it may take a couple of days extra to receive them. The fourth row is a row where they have put extra paperclips. The paperclip is used as a tool to communicate if the department wants to order any extra items; for example, if they need an extra box of tape, they have to place a paperclip on the badge and then Michel knows that he should scan the code on the badge twice.

When the goods have been delivered and scanned for all inventories in the department, Michel drives back, through the culverts to the goods reception, where he gets the goods for the second department and so does the procedure all over again. When all goods are delivered to all departments, Michel downloads the information collected during the day in the terminal to the Logistic system through the computer in the room next to the goods reception. The information about orders made by the departments goes to the purchasing department, and they in turn order the goods electronically from the supplier.

Change with New Process   Now the supplier gets detailed information regarding all orders electronically from the purchasing department. Before using the mobile solution, the supplier recieved orders through phone, fax, e-mail and EDI, from different persons and roles (nurses, doctors, purchasing staff etc.) at the hospital. With the mobile solution, the nurses do not spend time on looking after the inventory at the departments; instead they focus on medical care. Through a mobile solution, it is relatively easy to order the right amount and to keep inventory levels at a satisfying level.

There were now more inventory cupboards at the departments, making it easier for the medical staff to get hold of needed material more quickly when treating patients. The number of inventory cupboards at a department has, on average, increased from 1 to 5. A guaranteed inventory level on all goods is now also in place.

Process 2 — The Laundry Process

Before starting to use a mobile solution for managing the laundering process there were many different actors involved, and there were large problems with the supply of laundered clothes. The laundry process was very similar to the old inventory process. Nurses, doctors and other staff ordered new clothes by phone, fax or e-mail. The laundry supplier delivered the goods to the goods reception, the porter delivered it to the department and the department staff were responsible for managing the inventory. Because of the importance of having clean sheets, patient and staff clothes, departments made up their own large inventories, which resulted in very high inventory levels, low turnover (which when comes to clothes is risky, they need to be washed regularly in order not to spread diseases) and accumulation of old clothes (that had to be thrown away) in the bottom of the inventory cupboards. Since the supply of clean clothes was unreliable, doctors and nurses brought home their working clothes and washed them in cold water (40 degrees), resulting in working clothes spreading bacteria among the already ill and weak patients. There was a very high percentage of losses reported with sheets, blankets and clothes . The hospital estimated at least 10% of losses. There was no control or overview over the supply of laundry at the hospital. For example, last year a department had to close down for a couple of days because of lack of clean clothes and sheets.

The Old Process

The old process can be seen in Figure 4.

Problems to be Solved?   The organization had to have access to clean clothes and other clean fabrics needed. The hospital did not want to have another situation like the previous year, when they had to close down a department because of lack of clean fabrics. It was also important to raise the turnover of laundered clothes, blankets, towels and sheets in order to keep a good hygienic standard and to improve it, and to reduce the inventory level.

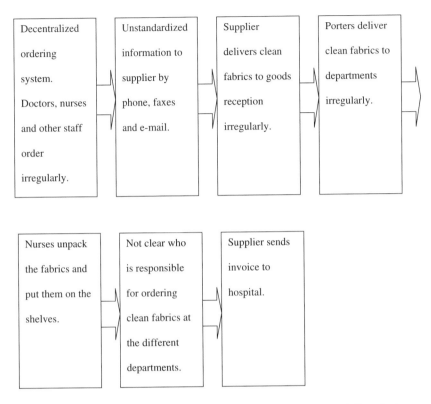

Figure 4: The old process of supplying fabrics without a mobile solution.

The hospital needed better control and overview over the use of clothes, in order to reduce the number of missing clothes. In the old process, nurses and doctors could take as much as they wanted from the clothes inventory without accounting for, and without any demands of returning the dirty clothes to the laundry cleaner and supplier. There were also many cases, where doctors changed their clothes only once a week, which was not hygenic. Another problem that existed was that nurses had to manage the inventory, which demanded time and energy from their medical work.

The New Process   Before there had been several different actors involved in the supply of fabrics, the laundry supplier, the porters, nurses, doctors and other staff, and purchasing staff, but now only one actor managed the whole laundry process, the laundry cleaner and supplier.

The current process can be seen in Figure 5.

The laundry supplier delivers clean fabrics to the goods reception, and his staff delivers the clean fabrics to the different departments through the hospital culvert. It is the laundry suppliers' staff who fills up to the right inventory level. When ordering new clothes, they count the number of towels at the inventory at each department, for example, and after scanning the code with a terminal for, special clothes or towels, for example, they register the number of special clothes or towels at the inventory locker. After conducting this procedure at all departments, they download the information regarding inventory levels from the supplier's office , using the terminal (PDA) into their logistic system. In this way the supplier gets precise information regarding the number of towels, shirts, etc., that should be delivered to the different departments the next day. The hospital pays a

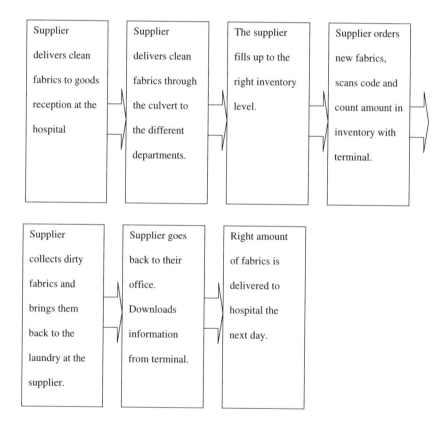

Figure 5: New Process of supplying fabrics with a mobile solution.

weekly fee to the supplier for each item, compared to earlier case when they paid per fabric that was laundered. Together with this solution, they have also installed and implemented three large automatic fabric cupboards (inventories) in order to try to get control over clothes used and delivered to laundry per person at the hospital. Staff at the hospital is allowed to have five items of clothing out. When picking up new clothes at the automatic cupboards they have to return back the dirty ones in order to receive new ones. Information regarding supply of different fabrics in the automatic cupboard is sent automatically to the laundry supplier; this means that the inventory level stays at the decided level. This solution has resulted in less loss of staff clothes.

Change with New Process   With the new process there is one responsible actor instead of many actors involved, and a diffuse responsibility. The mobile solution has resulted in a more secure supply of clean fabrics, and in lower inventory levels. The number of missing fabrics (losses) has been reduced. The hospital now has control and overview over the supply of fabrics.

Analysis: Perceived Effects with New Mobile Solutions

From the empirical description above and with relevant research described earlier in this chapter, effects from different perspectives emerge. In order to structure and analyse generated effects, the framework supplied by van Weele (1984) is used. The factors used to analyse the empirical data are lead times, order quantity, inventory levels, vendor performance, deliveries, workload/orders and procedures.

Effects from the User Organizations' Perspective

Applying van Weele's framework (ibid), we can see that there are effects generated by the use of mobile solutions.

By starting with lead time, we can see that lead time has been reduced through a more effective ordering system. Orders go directly from the hospital through the EDI connection to the supplier, who then gets full information regarding the order, and delivers the goods within 48 h. The right order-quantity is achieved with the mobile solution, and is due to precise and correct order information regarding demanded goods from the hospital and through good electronic communication with the supplier (orders go through the EDI solution).

Satisfactory inventory levels were achieved. During the first year with the mobile solution (2002), the inventory level was reduced by 50%. With the new processes the hospital has secured the supply at the inventories. Earlier, there was often shortage of goods when needed. The new solution contributes to a more secure supply. An example is the department that had to close down for a couple of days, because of lack of clean clothes. With the new laundry process, this is taken care of.

When it comes to vendor performance, the hospital has tied the suppliers' closer, and has decided on a very determined and structured way of working. The hospital, for example, send orders to the suppliers three times a day, at the same time every day, through the EDI connection. And the supplier delivers the goods regularly in the morning at 7 a.m. at least 3 days a week (Monday, Wednesday and Friday). The supplier has strict instructions on how to pack and deliver the goods, collecting all the goods that are going to the same department and inventory together. This creates conditions for a good vendor performance, to demand a good cooperation and work from the supplier through clear and explicit routines.

Deliveries are on time, with the new way of handling inventory- and laundry processes. As said above, deliveries are made three times a week, at 7 a.m., on Mondays, Wednesdays and Fridays; and the supplier delivers within 48 h. The hospital does not have to handle early or late deliveries, which is time-consuming and expensive.

Effects for the organization in the form of more nursing staff have been generated. Nurses who were responsible before for laundry- and inventory supply at the departments now focus on and spend all time on medical care. The hospital estimates that they have hired 40 full-time nurses, who can now concentrate on medical care; however five porters have also been employed .

Because of increase in inventories at the departments, it takes the medical staff less time to get the material and goods needed to give care to patients, compared to earlier times.

There is however more effects obtained than the effects brought up by van Weele (1984). One large cost for all organizations is losses or missing goods; it could be thefts, an old best-before-date, people forgetting to put back goods, etc. Losses have reduced significantly, concerning both goods in the inventory cupboards and fabrics, resulting in reduced costs, after implementing mobile solutions in logistics handling.

Effects from the Individual End-User's Perspective

When asking the end-user (in this case the porters, the people using the mobile solution when conducting their work) about effects from their perspective, they all almost only mentioned effects from the organization's perspective, for example, more time for nurses giving medical care, a better turnover and so on.

There are however effects benefiting the end-users: end-users, said that they thought it was fun to fill the different inventories at the hospital, and being part of a mobile solution. By being in different departments they get to know new people and get closer to the core business.

They now have more different working tasks than before, which they find stimulating and fun. Before they just received the goods and transported it through the culverts, underground, to the department . Now they receive the goods, transport it, fill the inventories and order new goods.

With more deliveries, it is smaller packets that are delivered, which means that the extent of lifting heavy things has reduced dramatically, saving the end-users' backs. Today there are fewer injuries due to less heavy lifting.

Effects from the Supplier's Perspective

Before using mobile solutions in handling inventory and laundry processes, orders were received by phone, fax, e-mail and EDI, and were placed by different persons at the hospital. It was time-consuming for the supplier handling orders in all these different ways. It was also common that orders were placed with lack of important information, resulting in more work for the supplier. With the mobile solution all orders comes through the EDI connection. This has reduced time spent on receiving orders for the supplier. Getting orders in a standardized way, with the necessary information has reduced (almost eliminated) the time spent contacting the hospital asking for missing order information.

Through this new mobile solution process, a regular order receiving flow has been achieved, resulting in lower inventory level also for the supplier, which means lower costs. It is easier for the supplier to forecast customer demand.

Another effect that the suppliers experience is the increased knowledge regarding the use of new technology to improve efficiency and effectiveness that can be transferred to other and new customers. The suppliers are now seen as experts regarding handling inventory and logistic processes in an efficient and effective way, which gives them opportunity to find new customers, and gives them a new competitive selling point.

Effects from theUser's Customers' (Patients') Perspective

Effects from a customer (patients) perspective can be seen as getting care from professionals who are not spreading infections by bacteria, resulting in less risk of new diseases in patients. Also in getting better (optimal) service so that departments do not have to close down due to lack of clean fabrics. These effects are difficult to put in figures , for example, a patient who gets more ill due to infection by bacteria spread by clothes not properly washed can mean much in terms of pain, distress and grief for the patient and his family, though it is difficult to estimate the value of the effect gained in monetary terms.

Discussion

Mobile Solutions as the Main Driver of Change

The mobile solution so far is presented as the sole driver of change and efficiency improvements. However, as can be seen in the empirical data, other factors are also important in order to achieve the effects presented in the analysis section above. New procedures and routines, organizational restructuring and the use of EDI (has been in use for many years) are also contributing to the effects. Mobile solutions are used as a tool together with other tools (EDI and redesign of the internal order collection and delivery processes, for example) in order to increase efficiency. The factors presented above are all necessary for managing the new more efficient processes. Without a mobile solution though, this change of processes had not been possible. The organization itself sees the mobile solution as the main driver of change, as the spider in the system, without the mobile solution there would be no system. Therefore, this chapter views the mobile solution as the main driver of change.

Mobile Solutions and Effects on Established Interactions and Relationships

What are the effects on the existing interactions and relationships of the new mobile technologies? One important dimension of the existing interactions and relationships concern the communication. Gadde and Håkansson (1993) identified three central roles of IT in business relationships: the administrative, the coordinative and the commercial/marketing role . When the mobile technologies were introduced in business relationships, we saw no radical changes as concerning the last of the three. The coordinative and administrative dimensions of the communication were altered, affecting the efficiency. Learning happens on the counterparts in the value constellation, on efficient ways to interact and on existing and emerging modes of exchanging information, services and products in the value constellation. The mobility of the technology seemed in the case to be an important factor, enhancing the mutual learning process. There was more interaction among different actors with the help of the new, more mobile technologies.

Conclusions

The aim of this chapter is to describe effects from different perspectives, when using new mobile solutions in logistics, in a hospital environment.

As has been presented above, other factors than the mobile solution are also important in order to achieve the effects presented in the analysis section. New procedures and routines, organizational restructuring and the use of EDI (has been in use for many years) are also contributing to the effects. The organization however views the mobile solution as the main driver of change, as the spider in the system, without the mobile solution there would be no new processes.

From an empirical point of view, we can observe a number of effects emerging from the new mobile solutions.

(1) Mobile solutions in logistics handling can be a cost-cutting tool that generates positive effects when used in an organization, in this case a hospital.

(2) From our focal organization's point of view, effects can be generated through reduced lead times, improved right order quantity, lower inventory levels, a more secure supply of goods and laundered items, improved vendor-performance, decrease in deliveries that are not on time, increase in available nursing experience and a reduction in losses.

(3) From the end-user's perspective effects can be obtained through more interesting, social and responsible working tasks. End-users who were observed and interviewed thought it was more fun working, having more different working tasks to perform. Increased amount of goods deliveries has resulted in smaller packets, which has resulted in less heavy lifting, resulting in fewer back problems.

(4) Effects perceived by the supplier are threefold, first a more effective way of receiving orders and order information, and reducing time spent on handling orders. Lower inventory levels can also be achieved through a more regular ordering flow. In addition, by using mobile solutions together with their customer, they can increase their knowledge and obtain a competitive advantage.

(5) It is difficult to estimate value gained by the customers from the effects (in this case the patients). Value is though to be gained through less exposure to new infections by bacteria. Doctors and nurses are assured secure supply of clean working clothes, not exposing the already ill and weak patients to new infections . Due to a more secure supply of medical care, departments now do not have to close down because of lack of clean fabrics.

A last concluding remark is that it is possible to improve efficiency and reduce cost by using mobile solutions in logistics. Organizations should to a larger extent try to investigate possible ways to combine organizational routines and other information technology solutions (EDI and e-procurement systems, for example) with mobile solutions, in order to make processes more efficient, reliable and effective.

References

Altimier, L., Besuner, P., Hasselfeld, K., & Johannemann, T. (2002). Go wireless to spark productivity. *Nursing Management*, *33*(7), 43–44.

Anderson, J. C., & Narus, J. A. (1998). Business marketing: Understand what customers value. *Harvard Business Review*, *76*(6), 53–64.

Anderson, J. C., & Narus, J. A. (1999). Business market management: Understanding, creating and delivering value. Upper Saddle River, NJ: Prentice-Hall, Inc.

Andersson, P., & Mölleryd, B. (2001). Buying centre consequences of technological convergence. *European Journal of Purchasing and Supply Management*, 7, 121–132.

Banitsas, K., Istepanian, R. S. H., & Tachakra, S. (2002). Applications of medical wireless LAN systems (MedLAN). *International Journal of Medical Marketing*, 22, 136–142.

Baraldi, E. (2003). *When information technology faces resource interaction. Using IT tools to handle products at IKEA and Edsbyn.* Doctoral thesis No 105, Department of Business Studies, Uppsala University.

Barley, S. R., & Kunda, G. (2001). Bringing work back in. *Organization Science, 12*(1), 76–95.

de Boer, L., Harink, J., & Heijboer G. (2002). A conceptual model for assessing the impact of electronic procurement. *European Journal of Purchasing and Supply Management*, *8*(1), 25–33.

Dubois, A. Gadde, L.-E., & Håkansson, H. (1989). *The impact of information technology on purchasing behaviour and supplier markets — A pre-study.* IMIT report series, Working Paper no. 1989:11.

Dumond, E. J. (1991). Performance Measurement and decision making in a purchasing environment. *International Journal of Purchasing Materials Management, 27*(2), 21–31.

Du Preez, A. (2002). Mobile data matters in lean times. *Logistics & Transport Focus, 4*(9), 51–54.

Ellram, L. (1995). Total cost of ownership. *International Journal of Physical Distribution and Logistics Mangement, 25* (8/9), 4–24.

El Sawy, O. A., & Bowles, G. (1997). Redesigning the customer support process for the electronic economy: Insights from storage dimenstions. *MIS Quarterly, 21*(4), 457–485.

Gadde, L-E., & Håkansson, H. (1993). *Professional purchasing.* London: Routledge.

Garfinkel, H. (1967). *Studies in ethnomethodology.* Cambridge: Polity Press.

Gebauer, J., Shaw, M. J., & Zhao, K. (2002). Assessing the value of emerging technologies: The case of mobile technologies to enhance business-to-business applications. In: *Proceedings for the 15th Bled electronic commerce conference,* eReality: Constructing the eEconomy. June 17–19, Bled, Slovenia.

Goodman, D. J. (2000). The wireless internet: Promises and challenges. *IEEE Computer, 33*(7), 36–41.

Gordon, P., & Gebauer, J. (2001). M-Commerce: Revolution + inertia = evolution. *Information Management & Consulting,* Special issue on M-Commerce, no 2.

Hammersley, M., & Atkinson, P. (1983). *Ethnography: Principles in practice.* Tavistock, London: Tavistock Publisher.

Hobday, A. (2002). Seamless mobile working: Logistics and transport. *Logistics & Transport Focus, 4*(9), 36–38.

Huber, G. P. (1990). A theory of the effects of advanced information technologies on organizational design, intelligence, and decision making. *Academy of Management Review, 15*(2), 47–71.

Kunda, G. (1992). *Engineering culture: Control and commitment in a high-tech corporation.* Philadelphia: Temple University Press.

Laage-Hellman, J., & Gadde, L.-E. (1996). Information technology and the efficiency of materials supply. *European Journal of Purchasing and Supply Management, 2*(4), 221–228.

Liang, T. Y. (2002). Strategic exploitation of information and communication technology in the healthcare sector. *Human Systems Management, 21,* 241–248.

Michalowski, W., Rubin, S., Slowinski, R., & Wilk, S. (2003). Mobile clinical support system for pediatric emergencies. *Decision Support Systems, 36*(2), 161–176.

Monczka, R. M., Carter, P. L., & Hoagland, J. H. (1979). *Purchasing performance: Measurement and control.* The Board of Trustees, Michigan State University, East Lansing, Michigan.

Myers, M. D. (1999). Investigating information systems with ethnography research. *Communications of the AIS, 2*(4), 1–18.

Rae-Smith, J. B., & Ellinger, A. E. (2002). Insights from the introduction of an online logistics service system. *Supply Chain Management: An International Journal, 7* (1), 5–11.

Ritter, T., Muller, T.A., & Gemunden, H.G. (2001). The role of IT in customer satisfaction in inter-organizational relationships. *Proceedings of the 17th annual IMP conference,* 9–11 September 2001, Oslo.

Ryssel, R., Ritter, T., & Gemunden, H.G. (2000). The impact of IT on trust, commitment and value-creation in inter-organisational customer-supplier relationships. *Proceedings of the 16th annual IMP conference,* 7–9 September 2000, Bath.

Simpson, R. L. (1996). Wireless communications: A new frontier in technology. *Nursing Management, 27*(11), 21–22.

Subramaniam, C., & Shaw, J. M. (2002). A study of the value and impact of B'B e-commerce: The case of web-based procurement. *International Journal of Electronic Commerce, 6*(4), 19–43.

Svensson, G. (2003). The principle of balance between companies' inventories and disturbances in logistics flows. *International Journal of Physical Distribution & Logistics
Management, 33*(9), 765–784.

Sweet, P. L. (2001). *Designing interactive value development: Perspectives and strategies
for high precision marketing*. Institute of Economic Research, Lund: Lund Business
Press.

Van Weele, A. J. (1984). Purchasing performance measurement and evaluation. *Journal of
Purchasing and Materials Management, 20*(3), 16–23.

Yan, X., Gagliano, D., LaMonte, M., Hu, P., Gaasch, W., Gunawadane, R., & Mackenzie,
C. (2000). Design and evaluation of a real-time mobile telemedicine system for ambulance transport. *Journal of High Speed Networks, 9*(1), 47–57.

Chapter 3

Technology-Driven Discovery as a Catalyst for Entrepreneurial Action: A Case Study of the Implementation of Information Technology in a Group of Firms

Karin Berglund, Maria Dahlin and Martin Johanson

Introduction

Technological change can be viewed as an important aspect of the entrepreneurial process (Schumpeter, 1934), but it seems that most research on entrepreneurship investigates the process after the technology has been put into use, that is, after opportunities have been discovered (Fiet, 1996; Shane, 2000). An alternative would be to view both the implementation and the use of the new technology as integrated parts of the entrepreneurial process, causing change, both expected and unexpected. The latter view is in focus for this study.

Drawing on Austrian economics, we assume that knowledge is imperfectly dispersed among actors and not given to anyone in a complete package (Hayek, 1936). In a critical note on the governing of economic activities through centralised plans, Hayek (1945) argued that centralised planning systems were limited in their ability to adapt to unexpected discoveries. Often planning is put forward as the most crucial aspect of technology implementation, even though some researchers highlight the importance of balancing planning with improvisation in order to manage the unexpected (Markus & Benjamin, 1997). Implementation of an information technology (IT) represents a non-predictable process, which was even more the case in the 1990s, when IT underwent rapid technical development and when most organisations were ignorant about the nature of the new technology. Moreover, IT often had an extensive impact on large parts of the organisation, which, in turn, made the implementation process complex.

Our point is that discoveries are of crucial importance and that they are to be understood in relation to planning. We take this as our point of departure when studying the process of planning and implementing IT in order to understand its impact on organisations.

Building on these ideas, we explore the relation between the planned process and the handling of unexpected aspects, that is the discoveries, which are made during the process. Further, we do not hide from the fact that entrepreneurship in terms of discovery also can take place within an organisation or between organisations (Amit, Glosten, & Mueller, 1993; Casson, 1982; Shane & Venkataraman, 2000). The IT implementation process is not regarded as linear but rather as an interactive and dynamic process where the employees gradually reduce ignorance, which means that discoveries in terms of opportunities are natural elements.

The paper is organised in the following way. In the next three sections, we discuss the key concepts: discovery, planning and entrepreneurial action. The methodology is described in the fifth section. The sixth section presents and analyses the case, which deals with implementation of a new IT system in an organisation. Finally, we discuss the case and try to highlight some implications for research.

The Discovery Concept

The discovery of the unknowable is likely to be an important element when a new technology is implemented. A discovery is defined as the firm finding "ends or means that it did not know about or was not searching for". This is in accordance with Kirzner's (1973, 1997) view of discoveries as unexpected findings followed by a surprise. Kirzner argues that discovery takes place in a situation of sheer ignorance, that is, when the actor does not have any knowledge, in advance, about the finding she/he makes. This means that the actor is surprised when the non-obvious and non-deliberate discovery is suddenly made (Demmert & Klein, 2003). Consequently, the actor could not have predicted or anticipated what she/he would discover. This seems to be the case when firms implement new IT, and especially if they are ignorant about the process and the potential discoveries that might be made. It is even likely that the less a firm knows about an IT *ex ante* the more discoveries will be made when the technology is implemented and put into use (Shane, 2000). As well as imposing new structures, IT also inhibits the potential to destroy old structures, hierarchies, routines and roles (Orlikowski, 2000) and thereby opens up opportunities for unexpected insights.

Demmert and Klein (2003) stress the role of an interpretative shift in which the unexpected finding is transformed into a discovery. Following Kirzner, some entrepreneurship researchers have developed his concepts. For example, Eckhardt and Shane (2003) suggest that there is a creative element in entrepreneurial discovery, and stress that perception of a new means-ends framework is central. For our purpose, we contend that discovery can be viewed as a process closely interrelated with perception and creation processes. But we keep in mind that the above-mentioned authors discuss entrepreneurial discovery, which concerns discoveries that lead to opportunity recognition, development, and market action. Like Kirzner (1973), we regard discovery as an unexpected finding associated with some surprise, but the objective of our study is narrower, in the sense that we want to examine the role of the unexpected finding in the IT implementation process, and we focus on the discoveries which are caused by the technology.

Planning

Building on the idea that knowledge is imperfectly distributed in the society and that no one has complete knowledge, Shane (2000) observes that the entrepreneur's prior knowledge influences the ability to interpret, recognise, comprehend, absorb and apply new knowledge. Plans are almost always made out of existing knowledge, because it is difficult to construct plans that contain future knowledge. Hence it is impossible to make plans, which capture ends and means we know nothing about. Thus planning itself conserves the *status quo* for several reasons. First, it builds on existing knowledge. It is difficult to include new knowledge in the plans and impossible to include discoveries in the plans. Second, it is usually easier to plan when things are stable and unchanging.

In the case of implementation of IT, several dimensions are important to the planning of the process; resistance among the actors involved (Markus, 1983), the fit of the technology (Klein & Speer Sorra, 1996), the prior knowledge of the actors, the expected goal and use of the system (Leonard-Barton, 1988) and the alignment of the organisation's goals and objectives (Singh & Beyer, 1990). Hence, the planning process defines the expected ends and means of the technology's implementation.

Bearing in mind that IT implementation is a process, where events and episodes take place over time, both the past and the future are of importance (Hayek, 1936, 1945). Consequently, planning is an activity that we must consider.

By planning, the firm defines and specifies what it will do in the future. In the case of new technology, planning can be viewed as activities the firm performs in order to define how it will implement and use the new technology.

Entrepreneurial Action

Discoveries lead to opportunity identification, which is a first and necessary step in the entrepreneurial process (Kirzner, 1973, 1997; Shane, 2003; Shane & Venkataraman, 2000; Davidsson, Low, & Wright, 2001). According to Venkataraman (1997, p. 218), research of entrepreneurship involves:

> the study of sources of opportunities; the processes of discovery, evaluation, and exploitation of opportunities; and the set of individuals who discover, evaluate, and exploit them.

Here we are interested in the processes of discovery of opportunities brought by the implementation of IT *within* an organisation. In order to handle the discoveries, the people in the organisation have to fit them into the regular activities of the firm. The closer the discovery lies to the ongoing activities in the organisation the easier it becomes to exploit it. When an organisation implements new IT, it usually has certain objectives, more or less defined and specified, but since the discovery means unexpected findings and surprises, the new technology usually involves changes in terms of how the organisation acts, thus discovery caused by the implementation of new technology causes a change of action. Butler, Brown, and Charmonmarn (2003, p. 52) state that:

> after entrepreneurs notice an opportunity they need to identify the steps needed to exploit it. This action is what really constitutes entrepreneurial action.

Thus, action that is subsequent to discoveries made is called entrepreneurial.

On Method

The case concerns implementation of new IT in an organisation of about 20 firms. In the discussion that follows, the whole organisation is labelled Alfa Inc., while the centrally located firm, which is owned by all the other firms in Alfa Inc., is labelled Alfa Central. Alfa Local refers to the locally situated firms that get IT support from

Alfa Central. The process, described below, involves a project where IT is implemented in Alfa Inc. The case also concerns the firm that supplied the software, labelled Asterix, and the two consultants, labelled Obelix and Idefix, which were assigned to adjust and implement the purchased software. In Alfa Inc. most business takes place on local markets. Historically, the Alfa Locals have been quite independent and have had a great deal of autonomy working with their own businesses and selling their own products in geographically separate markets.

The purchased IT was developed by an American software firm, Asterix, which has developed one of the largest Customer Relationship Management (CRM) systems for service firms that is available on the market. To implement the CRM system, two IT consultants, first Obelix and, later on in the process, Idefix, were contracted to work with adaptation and implementation. This CRM system makes it possible to create one single source of information in order to enable and/or support multichannel sales, marketing and customer service systems over the web.

The data collection combines two temporal approaches (Leonard-Barton, 1990). While the period 1998–2002 was studied in retrospect, the data collection from 2002 was conducted in real time. Data have been collected through in-depth interviews with seven persons, four of whom were interviewed on two occasions. At each interview respondents were asked open-ended questions about their work and their views on the process. Each interview took about 2 h. The respondents were working at Alfa Central, Alfa Local and at Idefix, and they all have different positions; both managerial and operational levels are represented. Both broad and specific types of questions were asked. The aim of the interviews was to get the respondents' views of the process but also to get more specific facts about the Alfa Locals and their relations to each other, to Alfa Central and to Obelix and Idefix. In accordance with Eisenhardt's (1989) and Yin's (1994) descriptions, case studies combine different sources of data and methods of data collection. Besides the interviews, we have used documentary sources such as annual reports and internal documents.

The Case

The IT implementation process is described by presenting three phases in chronological order, taking place over a period of 5 years. The first phase focuses on the acquisition of a competitor and the need to integrate information by purchasing a CRM system. The second phase concerns the start of the implementation of the new system, and the third phase is characterised by the replacement of Obelix. We begin the discussion of each phase by briefly summarising the main observations made. We subsequently report selected events and activities that took place in each phase.

Phase I — The acquisition of the competitor   This phase is characterised by taut planning of how to handle the inconvenience of having two different IT systems, a problem caused by the acquisition. As a reaction to the problem, Alfa Central was commanded to start searching for a new IT system. Most of the planning was thus carried out at Alfa Central.

The acquisition of the competing firm took place in the late 1990s, which implied a takeover of customers and IT systems. Due to this acquisition Alfa Inc. had to decide whether to manage two different IT systems — their own fairly outmoded system and the system that accompanied the acquisition — or to integrate information by investing in new IT. Several reasons, such as economic decline, the potential to increase efficiency by increased cooperation, increased competition and, not least, the inefficiency of suddenly having two separate systems, led to the decision to search for new technology.

The acquisition thus brought problems, which had to be handled, and Alfa Inc. felt forced to act. Alfa Central was therefore assigned to carry out the project with the intention to integrate a new IT system, which could handle their business relationships more effectively after the acquisition. The planning of the purchase of software led to a decision process where different solutions were discussed, which ended with the choice of one of the largest CRM systems available at the market. Obelix was contracted to implement the CRM system, and, with a focus on technology, the aim was to conduct a smooth and fast shift of IT systems to create a more effective organisation. A 5-year project plan was conducted to secure the project, which gave instructions about how to proceed with activities during the project. The establishment of a 5-year plan can be seen as a sign of how the project, at this stage, still was regarded as fairly simple and easily controlled.

Planning can be seen as taut in the sense that its focus was long-term with no optional scenarios concerning how the technology could be implemented and used. It was not considered important to reflect on how the technique would affect the work processes in the organisation; rather the standardised processes inherent in the technology set the rules of the project process. During the first phase, the project was viewed as a pure technology project, caused by the acquisition. Alfa Inc. entered the project taking a wide range of resources into account, both in terms of employees and in terms of financial resources; it was ignorant about the extent to which the project would affect the whole organisation further on.

Phase II — Transition from purchase to implementation phase   In this phase the Alfa Locals began to take part in the project, and as a consequence, interaction among firms increased. It became clear that the 5-year plan would be difficult to implement. Also, the implementation plan proved to be unsuccessful. More actors became involved in planning the process, which made it more complex but also opened up opportunities for discoveries. Some opportunities are simple and may be taken up immediately, while others are postponed, where there is a lead-time between the event causing the discovery and the moment the discovery is made. In this case, when actors at different firms and at different hierarchical levels discovered difficulties with matching the IT with their work processes, a new project was introduced. This project focused on organisational work processes and can be seen as a response to pressure placed by the Alfa Locals on Alfa Inc. to take action. Also, major adjustments were made to the technology. Implementation of IT seems to have opened up opportunities for discoveries, which in time were reacted to with — sometimes involuntary — entrepreneurial action.

In the first phase Alfa Inc. perceived themselves as being forced to act by handling the problem of incompatible IT systems, and in the second phase they had to take the consequences of that action. Many of the involved actors perceived that they lost control of the project, which instead was driven by the technology. During the purchase of the CRM system the Alfa Locals were quite passive; Alfa Central took most of the responsibility and action. Work processes were not affected by the project, but during the implementation phase the situation changed and action was required. The Alfa Locals could no longer avoid the project.

Many of the Alfa Locals felt abandoned by Alfa Central. At the same time they were anxious to keep their independence and autonomy, which limited the exchange of knowledge and experience among the Alfa Locals. Implementation of the CRM system was intended to increase efficiency and make work processes easier, but instead it caused chaos and slowed down work processes. Frustration grew among the Alfa Locals as they realised that the implementation would require much more time than planned. Most frustrated were the Alfa Locals that were taken by surprise by the complexity of the CRM system and its implementation, and whose existing work processes were fundamentally different from the new ones brought by the CRM system. Alfa Central, being the intermediary between Obelix, Asterix and the Alfa Locals, had a better understanding of why the process was not running as smoothly as planned. They had acquired knowledge about the new IT system during the planning phase, while the Alfa Locals, to different degrees, had a much harder time understanding the problems, and moreover, handling the problems that often occurred on a local level. Problems that arose in the Alfa Locals also became problems to Alfa Central, which had its reputation to defend towards all parties.

Several problems were discovered during this phase. Alfa Central discovered their own ignorance of how operations worked in the Alfa Locals. Moreover, they discovered the differences in expectations for the new IT in the Alfa Locals and differences in work processes among the Alfa Locals, and thus they began to understand the complexity of Alfa Inc. In some cases, several persons had to interact with each other over a period of time before making a discovery and then acting on it. These types of discoveries led to the sense that the IT was driving the process. Also, the Alfa Locals discovered the complexity of their own organisation and the technology, and they started to put pressure on Alfa Central to act and to do something about the difficulties to make the technology fit the work processes. Alfa Central reacted by adjusting the standardised system, which was a compromise, as the Alfa Locals had to adapt to the system. Changes to the system were supposed to make that adaptation somewhat easier.

Because of the passivity of the Alfa Locals in the earlier phase, differences among the Alfa Locals as well as differences between the Alfa Locals and Alfa Central did not appear until the implementation of the new CRM system. When the Alfa Locals started to participate actively in the project it became clear that different actors had quite different requirements of the system and that they also had quite different ways of working, both internally and in their interactions with customers. The project at this stage was not regarded as an organisational project, even though it was closely connected to organisational processes. Instead it was communicated to the Alfa Locals as a technological change project. In order to get as much as possible out of the standardised system the Alfa Locals had to have similar work processes. Alfa Central recognised the gap between the organisation and the purchased technology, which was handled in two ways. First, Alfa Central started to make extensive adaptations to the CRM system to make it better fit the requirements of the Alfa Locals, and, second, Alfa Central introduced a new project which focused on operations and aimed to introduce a uniform way of working in Alfa Inc. This meant that Alfa Central had to handle and synchronise two projects and, at the same time, the Alfa Locals were suddenly being affected by two different projects.

Phase III — The replacement of the IT consultant firm   In this phase, the Alfa Locals and their work processes were affected by the new technology, for example when work processes slowed down. Dissatisfaction was directed primarily towards Obelix. The perceived problems made planning reactive and decentralised. A chain of discoveries made at different firms gave insight into the complexity of the project. Some of these discoveries were postponed (as they were the result of a process over time). Even though this phase to a high degree is characterised by chaos, it is in this context that some firms discover that IT brings about new possibilities. What are perceived as problems by some are, for others, opportunities to act upon.

As frustration grew among the group of firms, much of the dissatisfaction was directed towards Obelix. Alfa Central felt a lack of understanding from the IT consultant and that the consultants too easily "let go" of the project. During the implementation, Alfa Central became aware of their shortage of IT knowledge. They also became painfully aware of their lack of ordering experience and how they, from the start, understood neither the character nor extent of the project. Above all they discovered that the project was not only about purchasing new IT, but also to a large extent about operations and work processes, cooperation between the firms and, not least, interaction with the customers. These insights meant that the project changed character from a pure technology project to an organisational one. This was one explanation of why Alfa Central felt that Obelix let the project go — or slip between their fingers — as they were engaged to implement a technology project, and they realised too late the fundamental need to connect the operations to the new technology.

Alfa Central felt that Obelix basically let go of the project since they continued to concentrate on technology instead of taking operations into consideration. This led to the entrance of another IT consultant, Idefix, into the project. At this point Obelix had spent all the consultant hours committed to the project, but implementation was far from finished. As Alfa Central painfully had become aware of its own shortcomings about the technology and operations among the Alfa Locals in the group, Alfa Central thus commissioned Idefix to evaluate the project so far by analysing it and making recommendations for further action. After conducting the evaluation, Idefix was contracted to address the most acute technological problems, or to conduct "a cleaning project", as they put it.

Instead of letting technology drive the process, some of the Alfa Locals discovered that they could use IT to strengthen their own work processes, giving them new possibilities for action. A new way of working evolved among the Alfa Locals as a result of more and more people starting to act and make use of the technology. Employees in the Alfa Locals were referring to the changing work processes as something that initially seemed like a struggle but which eventually led to new ways of doing things. Cooperation within and between the firms at Alfa Inc. increased, and this interaction enabled individuals to compare their own discoveries with those of others. This interplay caused chain reactions of discoveries, which were added together and made visible, and in time, taken for granted.

Burned by earlier experiences, Alfa Central decided to minimise the influence of external actors. Idefix was not given much access to the Alfa Locals, and when doing the analysis of the project they spoke only to Alfa Central. Idefix had to "jump into" the project without obtaining any information from the earlier implementer, as they were forbidden by Alfa Central to speak to Obelix. However, what was meant to be dissolution of the relationship with Obelix never became reality, because Alfa Central was still dependent on Obelix to support the IT system. Both Obelix and Idefix eventually got supporting functions, and the service firm dealt directly with Asterix. Alfa Central built their own centre of competence regarding IT to decrease dependencies on external actors. Also, the Alfa Locals discovered the problem of Alfa Central having the dual role of purchaser and executor. This discovery started a process, which led to reorganisation at Alfa Central.

Case Discussion

Change of the Nature of Planning

The case demonstrates that implementation and use of a new IT system sometimes is a complex and long-term process, which can be difficult to control and to predict in advance. Nevertheless, the case also clearly shows that planning plays a critical role in that process. Planning can be viewed as taut or loose. Planning usually consists of two sequences: establishment of plans and execution of plans. Taut planning entails considerable lead-time between establishment and execution, whereas for loose planning, establishment and execution take place almost simultaneously. Moreover, the issue of taut and loose planning also contains an organisational aspect, since the establishment and execution of plans can be performed by the same department or organisational entity, but they can also be performed far away from each other, which is typical for taut planning. Taut planning also implies small differences between the content of the plan and the result of the plan's execution. Altogether, this means that the two sequences can be separated from each other in both space and time.

In the case, planning at the beginning was taut. The actors' knowledge about the processes initiated was low, and taut planning seems to have been an attempt to compensate for ignorance. By planning in detail the implementation of the new IT system, and by viewing it as only a technological project, the actors seem to have tried to decrease the perceived uncertainty. In the light of these planning activities the case also reveals that unexpected events were perceived as problems which needed solutions and which required that action be taken.

A second important observation is that when the process produced unexpected results in terms of several discoveries during the first phase, the firms had to change the way they were planning. One example is the failure of the implementation plan. This failure reveals the complexity and the demand for autonomy expressed by the Alfa Locals. The abundance of taut planning in the shift between the first and second phases meant that the firms became open to unexpected events, alternative solutions and scenarios and to the fact that the implementation of the new system was not only a technological project but also an operational and social project.

The movement from taut to loose planning also meant that establishment of plans and execution of plans tended to merge and was no longer two distinct and separate activities. This, in turn, also meant that the hierarchical structure of the taut planning was eroded. To some extent the local firms became more of both establishers and executers of the plan. By changing from taut to loose planning, the firms seem to have discovered that implementing and using an IT system entails more than keeping strictly to the plan.

Different Types of Discoveries

The main reason the firms changed the nature of the planning activities was that during the second phase they made several discoveries which were not expected and which could not be foreseen. These discoveries had to be managed. Discoveries did not stop after the second phase; the firms continued to make discoveries during the third phase. We see that discoveries were an integrated and important part of the implementation of the new IT system and we can also observe that they seemed to be related to the planning activities; that is, the nature of the discoveries were contingent on the plans made and the planning activities performed.

However, among these discoveries we also observed differences. In order to act on a discovery the Alfa Locals had to realise that they had come on something new; they also had to recognise the novelty of what they had found. This was usually combined with a feeling of surprise and, not unusually, frustration. We noticed that sometimes the Alfa Locals acted almost immediately on a discovery, for instant when employees discovered that old work processes and routines could no longer be used. Instantly they had to change their way of working, and as a consequence work processes slowed down. The time between the event causing the discovery and the insight that the Alfa Locals had found something that was largely novel seems short. We label this type of discovery an immediate discovery.

But there are also situations in which there is a lead-time between the event and the insight and awareness that the firm has made a discovery, which, in turn, results in a significant lead-time between the event causing the discovery and the entrepreneurial action. This type of discovery is called postponed discovery, such as the decision to replace Obelix. The decision was preceded by a process of discoveries such as the complexity of IT, the mismatch of IT and work processes, and not least, distrust and dissatisfaction among the Alfa Locals. Eventually these discoveries led to action, the replacement of Obelix, which was not included in the initial plans.

We believe that these two types of discoveries in the case were closely related to the character of the IT and to the actors' prior knowledge about the technology. For most people involved in the case, a new IT system meant a high degree of novelty with high complexity. It follows that several discoveries observed in the case are better characterised as postponed, although individuals in the firms were surprised and realised that an unexpected event had happened for which they could not directly predict the consequences. One can say that the new insight was only a piece or a detail in a bigger whole, and it was only when capturing the relation between the surprise in terms of a piece of knowledge and the remaining body of knowledge that they recognised the effects of the detail found. In the case, the new IT system was something completely new and appeared to be much more than just a technology; that is, prior knowledge about IT systems was low and the technology complex, and so postponed discoveries were rather common.

Different Types of Entrepreneurial Action

We see in the case firms acting on the different discoveries as an important aspect of the implementation process. This type of action often departs from the intention of the established plan and goal. Entrepreneurial action can thereby be viewed as doing something different from what is planned and intended, which, in turn, is a result of prevailing and existing knowledge. Entrepreneurial action is taken when a firm's action differs from action based on plans and prior knowledge and instead is based mainly on the discoveries. We can distinguish three types of entrepreneurial action.

The *first* type concerns how the firms direct and re-direct their action. In the case, this is exemplified by the change of focus from technology to operations. This change partly meant that activities and behaviour departed from what was planned and expected. When discovering the impact of IT on organisations, a new project with a focus on operations was introduced.

The *second* type has to do with the extension of the technology. Thus the firm may, after making a discovery, decide to diminish its use in terms of application. But, the opposite can also happen, that is, after making discoveries firms may extend the use of the system, for instance, by applying the new IT in more areas than had been planned and expected. Another example of an extension would be the case in which a bigger part of the organisation uses the new IT than initially was planned, or using it to produce more products or serve more customers than expected. From the start, the new IT was planned to serve some employees; however, during the project it became clear that, to make use of the IT, access had to be given to a broader category of people. Hence, employees at Alfa Central also implemented the new CRM system, something that was not part of the initial plan.

The *third* type of action is the pace of the process. Discoveries can strengthen the plans and even accelerate the pace of the process and give the firms reason to increase their commitment to the new IT. But, there are also moments in the case when the process was slowed down due to the Alfa Locals. Consequently, changing the pace of the project, that is, accelerating or slowing down the project in relation to the plan, can be viewed as a component in the concept of entrepreneurial action. In the case described, the pace of some aspects of the project slowed down, such as the pace of implementation. Expectations were not fulfilled as implementation turned out to be more complicated and require much more time than planned. Other aspects of the project were accelerated, for instant regarding the extent to which operations were affected by the new IT.

Therefore, we believe that direction, extension and pace are three aspects of entrepreneurial action, which, in turn, follow on discoveries made during the process. Moreover, we maintain that direction, extension and pace concern not only the planning and implementation but also the use of the new IT, even though, in this chapter, we have chosen to focus on planning and implementation.

Final Remarks

In accordance with Demmert and Klein (2003) our study indicates that the relation between planning and discoveries is important in the sense that planning often affects whether discoveries of the unexpected are interpreted as opportunities or problems. In order to determine whether a discovery is a problem or an opportunity, firms must interpret and reflect on what has been discovered. Moreover, firms have to compare the contents of the discovery with their existing plans and knowledge. This process has much in common with a sense-making process. Making sense does not always happen instantly; instead, it can take time, and it follows that some discoveries are immediate while others are postponed. It seems that immediate discoveries are more common when firms quickly make sense out of what has been discovered, and when the discovery is simple and fits into the prevailing plans and prior knowledge. On the other hand, a postponed discovery takes more time to recognise because the discovery concerns more complex issues and does not easily fit into the firm's prior knowledge and existing plans.

This study has observed that there can be a lead-time between a discovery and a subsequent entrepreneurial action, because of the time it takes to make sense of the discovery. Hence, what is perceived as problems and opportunities is often a matter of sense-making. This, in turn, means that discovery as a sense-making process is a more fruitful approach than viewing a discovery as something objective, which is found 'out there' (Weick, 1995; Gartner Cartner, & Hills 2003, Orlikowski & Gash, 1994). Thus, combining a sense-making and a discovery approach to implementation of IT looks like a promising research area.

References

Amit, R., Glosten, L., & Mueller, E. (1993). Challenges to theory development in entrepreneurship research. *Journal of Management Studies, 30*, 815–834.

Butler, J. E., Brown, B., & Charmonmarn, W. (2003). Informational networks, entrepreneurial action and performance. *Asia Pacific Journal of Management, 20*, 151–174.

Casson, M. (1982). *The entrepreneur.* Totowa, NJ: Barnes & Noble Books.

Davidsson, P., Low, M.B., & Wright, M. (2001). Editor's introduction: Low and MacMillan ten years on: Achievements and future directions for entrepreneurship research, *Entrepreneurship Theory & Practice, 25*(4), 5–15.

Demmert, H., & Klein, D. B. (2003). Experiment on entrepreneurial discovery: An attempt to demonstrate the conjecture of Hayek and Kirzner. *Journal of Economic Behavior & Organization, 50*, 295–310.

Eckhardt, J. T., & Shane, S. A. (2003). Opportunities and entrepreneurship. *Journal of Management, 29*(3), 333–349.

Eisenhardt, K. M. (1989). Building theories from case study research. *Academy of Management Review, 14*(4), 532–550.

Fiet, J. (1996). The informational basis of entrepreneurial discovery. *Small Business Economics, 8*, 419–430.

Gartner, W. B., Cartner, N. M., & Hills, G. E. (2003). The language of opportunity. In: C. Steyaert, & D. Hjorth (Eds), *New movements in entrepreneurship* (pp. 103–124). Cornwall: MPG Books Ltd.

Hayek, F. A. (1936). Economics and knowledge. *Economica, n.s. 4*, 33–56.

Hayek, F. A. (1945). The use of knowledge in society. *American Economic Review. 35*(4), 519–530.

Kirzner, I. M. (1973). *Competition & entrepreneurship.* Chicago: University of Chicago Press.

Kirzner, I. M. (1997). Entrepreneurial discovery and the competitive market process: An Austrian approach. *Journal of Economic Literature, 35*, 60–85.

Klein, J. K., & Speer Sorra, J. (1996). The challenge of innovation implementation. *The Academy of Management Review, 21*(4), 1055–1080.

Leonard-Barton, D. (1988). Implementation as mutual adaptation of technology and organization. *Research Policy, 17*, 251–267.

Leonard-Barton, D. (1990). A dual methodology for case studies: Synergetic use of a longitudinal single site with replicated multiple sites. *Organization Science, 1*(3), 248–266.

Markus, L. (1983). Power, politics, and MIS implementation. *Communications of the ACM, 26*(6), 430–444.

Markus, M. L., & Benjamin, R. I. (1997). The magic bullet theory in IT-enabled transformation. *Sloan Management Review, 38*(2), 55–68.

Orlikowski, W. J. (2000). Using technology and constituting structures: A practical lens for studying technology in organizations. *Organization Science, 11*(4), 404–428.

Orlikowski, W. J., & Gash, D. C. (1994). Technological frames: Making sense of information technology in organizations. *AMC Transactions on Information Systems, 12*(2), 174–207.

Schumpeter, J. (1934). *Theory of economic development.* Cambridge: Harvard University Press.

Shane, S. S., & Venkataraman, S. (2000). The promise of entrepreneurship as a field of research. *Academy of Management Review, 25*(1), 217–226.

Shane, S. S. (2003). *A general theory of entrepreneurship: The individual-opportunity.* Nexus, USA: Edward Elgar Publishing.

Shane, S. S. (2000). Prior knowledge and the discovery of entrepreneurial opportunities. *Organization Science, 11*(4), 448–469.

Singh, I. B., & Beyer, R. C. (1990). Information resource planning methodology: A case study. *Systems Integration, '90 Proceedings of the first international conference,* (pp. 634–642), Morristown, NJ, USA. IEEE Comput. Soc. Press.

Venkataraman, S., (1997). The distinctive domain of entrepreneurship research, *Advances in Entrepreneurship Firm Emergence and Growth,* Greenwich, CT: JAI Press.

Weick, K. E. (1995). *Sensemaking in organizations.* London: SAGE Publications.

Yin, R. K. (1994). *Case study research: Design and methods.* Thousand Oaks, CA: Sage.

Chapter 4

Resource Dependence Theory in an E-Grocery BTC Context: The Case of Specialty E-Grocer X

Niels Kornum

Introduction

In recent years, grocery e-commerce has learned some initial and harsh lessons trying to become profitable. The surviving and successful firms might be those who have developed closer connections to their customers. In line with this, grocery e-commerce[1] firms establish a direct channel to reach each consumer individually and use the channel for bi-directional communication via homepages and call centres, delivery of goods and services directly to the doorstep, dialogue with drivers of the delivery vans, etc. The relations are becoming relatively long lasting, with indications of a high degree of customer loyalty (Kornum, 2002). Furthermore, customers are beginning to act as co-producers.[2] Thus, grocery e-commerce may become a new learning space for a relationship-oriented method to interact with consumers.

This calls for studies focusing on BTC exchange from a BTB relationship perspective (Håkansson, 1982; Hägg & Johanson, 1982; Gummesson, 1987; Easton, 1992; Håkansson & Johanson, 1994; Håkansson & Snehota, 1995, Wilkinson,

---

[1]Grocery e-commerce and grocery home shopping is used as synonymous concepts.
[2]An example of this is the selected case of Specialty E-grocer X.

2000), but also from a service marketing perspective, as the offerings of e-grocers involve high levels of service content. Nordic service marketing researchers, especially, have paid much attention to a relationship perspective as opposed to a traditional transactional perspective (Grönroos, 1994, 1995, 1997, 1998; Storbacka, Strandvik, & Grönroos, 1994; Ravald & Grönroos, 1996; Coviello, Roderick, & Brodie, 1998; Grönroos, Heinonen, Isoniemi, & Lindholm, 1999). Earlier contributions from this research suggested that improved quality leads the customer to be more satisfied, which, in turn, leads to higher customer relationship profitability. Storbacka et al. (1994) claim that other constructs should be included in the sequence that influences customer relationship profitability. Especially, structural elements are included: "bonds", "perceived alternatives" and "patronage concentration". When discussing further research in the article, they propose "relationship strength" as an area where research is needed: "As the strength of a relationship is of outmost importance when designing action programmes for customer relationship enhancement, we feel that what is needed first is a good understanding of what constitutes relationship strength and how it can be affected" (*ibid.*, p. 36).

   This chapter will propose that resource dependence theory is a fruitful starting point when trying to enhance the understanding of what constitutes relationship strength in the relation between the e-grocer and its customers. The core of resource dependence theory is preoccupied with the "understanding of what constitutes relationship strength" (e.g. Emerson, 1962; Pfeffer & Salancik, 1978; Stern & Reve, 1980; Arndt, 1983; Heide & John, 1988; Frazier, Sawhney, Shervani, 1990; Gaski, 1992; Hultman, 1993; Wilkinson, 1973, 2000; Buvik & Reve, 2002). They claim that firms engage in external exchange because the exchange partner possesses resources that are valued and that if this resource is also scarce, then this is likely to influence relationship strength/dependence. Thus, analysing dependency includes the study of specific dyad or network configurations and the focal firms' perception of valued resources owned by the exchange partner (Emerson, 1962; Wilkinsson, 1973; Pfeffer & Salancik, 1978; Weber, 2002). Studying *specific* configurations of relationships reveals a dimension that is not considered in the customer relationship profitability model, namely, the balance of a relationship. Presupposing that dependence exists in a relationship, the balance or distribution of dependence between the parties will condition which of the parties that are able to decide the further development of the relationship. Thus, applying resource dependence theory to the e-grocery BTC context includes an examination of which dimensions are necessary to understand not only relationship strength, but also the balance in a relationship configuration.

Against this background, the *purpose* of this chapter is to develop an analytical framework in order to understand which configurations of dependence structures will influence the strength and balance of the relationship between the provider and the customer in grocery e-commerce BTC dyads, and examine to what extent the framework derived from a BTB setting is applicable in a BTC E-grocery setting. The case of Specialty E-grocer X contributes to the evaluation of the applicability of the framework. Thus, the purpose of this chapter is *not* to evaluate the prospects for Specialty E-grocer X to survive and expand.

As already indicated, resource dependence theory is the foundation for identifying the core concepts of how dependence should be analysed. These basic concepts are discussed in a BTB context in the second section. In addition to classic resource dependence theory, the concept of assets stock accumulation (Dierickx & Cool, 1989) is included under the term of "existing resource stock", recognising that "asset stock accumulation" is a slightly different concept, developed in a firm internal context. This section also includes the term "asset specifity" from transaction cost theory (Willamson, 1985), but it is termed "investments in future resource stock". Based on Kornum (2003), the main difference between valuable/concentrated resources and relation-specific assets is related to time scale. The former represents accumulated valuable resources that exist from day zero (when we monitor the phenomenon), whereas relation-specific assets are investments in future valuable resources. In the third section, the analytical framework is applied to a Specialty E-grocer context and it is discussed to what extent the BTB perspective matches this BTC context.

In the fourth section, the use and applicability of the framework is exemplified in a case study of the relation between Specialty E-grocer X and its customers. The relation is analysed in order to identify the strength and balance of dependency. Furthermore, consequences of possible future investments in future resource stock are addressed. The fifth section discusses the applicability of resource dependence theory to the e-grocery BTC context and the sixth section revisits the Storbacka et al. (1994, p. 23) Relationships Profitability Model and suggests an incorporation of resource dependence theory and a separation of the static and dynamic parts of the model.

The Framework in a BTB Context

Important/Valuable and Concentrated Resources

According to Pfeffer and Salancik (1978), firms are interdependent because they, from external sources, need to acquire resources that are important for their activities. Thus, the resource is important[3] because it is valued (Emerson, 1962) or perceived to be *valuable* (Storbacka et al., 1994) by external sources that acquire them. This definition will be used in the rest of the chapter. The perception of which types of resources can be considered valuable will vary considerably dependent on the channel, dyad or firm that is examined (Wilkinson, 1973; Javidan, 1998). It is therefore necessary to identify which specific resources the individual exchange partner perceives to be valuable. This will lead to a firm/customer-, dyad- or channel-specific list of valued resources (Weber, 2002).

Exchange partners may value the resources they acquire from the counterpart. However, only if the valued resource is *concentrated*,[4] this will lead to *dependence*. In such cases, the valued resource possessed by one of the exchange partners is difficult to replace or is not easily available; in other words, it is concentrated (Pfeffer & Salancik, 1978; Kornum, 2003).

Existing and Future Resource Stock

The value and concentration of a resource then represent the basic dimensions needed for an empirical investigation of the dependence in a given exchange

---

[3]Pfeffer and Salancik (1978) suggest two dimensions to the importance of a resource exchange: the relative magnitude and the criticality in the functioning of the firm of a given resource exchange. The dimension of criticality is seemingly difficult to apply empirically and seems to overlap with the concept of "concentration". It may therefore be more appropriate to think of "criticality" as the combination of the importance of a resource and the concentration of this resource. Besides the example by Pfeffer and Salancik (1978, p. 46) of "electric power" as a critical resource, it is seemingly difficult to apply the concept of criticality empirically. The authors mention "the fact that a resource is important to the organization's functioning is, in itself, not the source of the organization's problems". Instead problems derive from changing environments, "so that the resource is no longer assured". This has very close parallels to the availability or concentration of a resource. The second dimension of resource importance is the relative magnitude of an exchange. It ".... is measurable by assessing the proportion of the total inputs or the proportion of total outputs accounted for by the exchange" (Pfeffer & Salancik, 1978, p. 46). The authors exemplify this by suggesting that a firm selling only one or few products or sourcing only one or few raw materials or other inputs will be "more dependent on the sources" or markets than a firm producing several products to distinct markets or purchasing from several sources of inputs (*ibid.*). However, the sum of customers buying a single versus multiple products may be the same and thus leading to no change in the degree of dependency. Relative high inputs or outputs are normally valued by the exchange partner and it is suggested here that the relative magnitude of an exchange can be an element that is valued along with other types of resources.
[4]Storbacka et al. (1994) also discuss dependence, but the underlying constructs are related in slightly different ways in the sequence in the customer Relationship Profitability Model (*ibid.*, p. 23). Relating to this model resource dependence theory proposes that perceived value (same concept as in model) combined with perceived concentration (perceived alternatives and patronage concentration), decides dependence (bonds) and thereby relationships strength (same concept as in model) and the balance of the relationship.

relation. The strength and balance of these dependencies will condition which of the exchange partners will be able to decide the development and configuration of a given relation. Investments in relation-specific assets will, however, also potentially generate dependence. What is then the difference between the dimensions: relation-specific assets and valued/concentrated resources? The most obvious difference is related to time scale (Kornum, 2003).[5] If a given exchange relation is examined, then the firms involved will historically have invested certain resources that the counterpart finds valuable and these resources may also to some degree be concentrated. These historically generated resources that are present at the point in time when we monitor T_0 (today) is the type of resources that resource dependence theory focuses on. The relation-specific assets, which transaction cost theory declares to be an important dimension of their framework (Williamson, 1985), is preoccupied with investments that point towards the future (from T_0). Here, the crucial question seems to be: what are the future lock-in effects of investing certain assets today? Translated into the terms used here, the dependence effect is determined by the projected future value of the invested resources and projected concentration of the same resources (Kornum, 2003).

Introducing a time dimension in the analysis reveals close parallels to the concept of asset stock accumulation (Dierickx & Cool, 1989), although this concept is developed from a firm internal core competence/capability perspective.[6] Using the term *resource stock*, the existing resource stock then consists of the historically generated resources that are present "today" in a given relation. Relation-specific resources (assets), on the other hand, are investments that potentially build future/new resource stocks or transforms existing resource stock. If the resources exchanged are both valued and concentrated, then the party (-ies) that possesses them will to a large extent be able to determine the direction of the

---

[5]The need for investments in relation-specific asset will potentially generate dependence or a lock-in situation giving one or both of the parties in a dyad an incentive to safeguard assets (Williamson, 1985; Buvik & Reve, 2002) in order to reduce the risk of sunk cost, e.g. induced by one of the parties behaving opportunistically. So introducing relation-specific resources will potentially lead to more dependence. The strength and balance of dependence will be influenced by the number of exchange partners investing in the specific assets and on the degree of specifity of the assets. Besides the lock-in dimension, asset specificity also involves an importance (value) dimension (Buvik & Reve, 2002). Relating this to the dimensions of valued and concentrated resources, the value dimension is precisely the same in the two perspectives. The lock-in dimension is clearly derived from the degree of concentration of a valued exchange (Kornum, 2003), but using the economic term of oligopoly or monopoly (Williamson, 1985).
[6]Dierickx and Cool's (1989) definition of "critical or strategic asset stock" include that this asset is nontradable, which is the reason why it is termed "internal". Hereby it differs when compared to the resource stock discussed in this chapter, because it is considered tradable although it may be scarce in supply.

future development of the relation, including decisions regarding investments in future resource stock. This ensures that the investments will be in favour of the party (-ies) that possesses the valued/concentrated resource (Kornum, 2003). If, however, the resources exchanged are not concentrated, then the outcome in terms of creating dependence reveals a more complex pattern depending on the specific dyad and network configurations (*ibid.*).

The Framework Applied to a BTC Specialty E-Grocer Context

The Existing Resource Stock of a Specialty E-Grocer

Valued resources   In Figure 1, configuration of the existing resource stock of a Specialty E-grocer and its customers is discussed. According to this figure, a study of existing resource stock will consist of a mapping of valued resources split into resources relating to the service delivery system and to branding and assortment issues. Furthermore, it is viewed from the perspective of both the provider and the customer, including a discussion of the degree of concentration of these valued resources. Viewing the resources of the firm from a *customer perspective*, the distribution, or service delivery system, seems to be of high value to the customers. Elements like convenience, saving time and money are causing the service delivery system to be valuable. The assortment of the firm is suggested to consist of premium and specialised assortments with low accessibility in supermarkets. The customers may value the corporate brand of such a Specialty E-grocer, because it represents a sense of belonging to a "club" or a "group of privileged people".

From the *perspective of the firm*, the more direct customer contact is suggested to lead to a more precise complaint and quality management, more loyal customers with higher retention rates, and therefore they will also be more profitable. Also, larger order sizes contribute to profitability. To the firm the (core) customer may represent a valued resource, because of the low budget word-of-mouth marketing, in which the customers engage voluntarily. Word-of-mouth promotion may also potentially signal higher credibility, potentially leading to an inflow of more loyal and profitable customers.

Concentrated resources   Viewed from a *customer perspective*, doorstep delivery systems offered by a Specialty E-grocer may be a concentrated resource. This is especially valid for grocery distribution that handles logistically demanding products. Furthermore, if the distribution covers large areas of the potential

	Valuable or valued resources		Concentrated resources	
	Firm's perception of customers	**Customers' perception of firm**	**Firm's perception of customers**	**Customers' perception of firm**
Service delivery system	• Direct customer contact – complaint and quality management easier • Potentially more loyal customer, higher retention rate & more profitable customers • Larger order sizes	• Door-step delivery system and call centre Convenience • Time saving may be used to earn extra money • High accessibility saves petrol • Low level of spontaneous purchase saves money • Direct personal response on complaints	The core segment of loyal, long term customers interested in convenience and time saving, and buying in larger order sizes may be concentrated and represent a very small proportion of the grocery market that is not easily replaced	Doorstep delivery systems may be a concentrated resource- especially grocery distribution with logistically demanding products and when covering large areas, it will take time or demand huge investments to offer the same service right away
Branding / assortment	• Direct customer contact and word-of-mouth marketing • Larger degree of Word-of-mouth promotion – high credibility – lower promotion budget –inflow of potentially loyal and profitable customers	• Premium & specialized assortments product with low accessibility	Same as above	The assortments offered may be accessible as single products, but not as a total assortment that is doorstep available The feeling of belonging to a 'club' or a 'group of privileged people' may be hard to imitate in this specific area and in this specific context

Figure 1: Existing resource stock.

(national) market, then it will take time or demand huge investments in the short term to build a system that can offer the same service. The single products of the assortment of a Specialty E-grocer may be available from different specialty shops, but the assortment in its totality may be concentrated in supply. If, furthermore, the size of the assortment is combined with doorstep availability, then something unique may be at hand. From the *perspective of the firm*, the core segment(-s) of their customers may be scarce in supply and therefore not easily replaced.

The Potential Investments of a Specialty E-Grocer in Future Resource Stock

Investments from individual customers in the future resource stock of a firm selling to BTC customers are seldom substantial in size, e.g. in monetary terms. The customers may invest significant human-specific resources in a relation with a specific firm, e.g. learning specific routines for trade and usage. This may also include investment in specific equipment, e.g. software, delivery boxes, etc. All together, this type of investment potentially causes stronger dependence. Do investments in resource stock that is specific to individual customers have any applicability? In certain parts of the service industry human assets that are specific to individual customers can be found. However, in general, such investments are designed to have as broad an applicability as possible and hereby distribute the risk to a broader basis of customers.

Instead, it may be appropriate to use "customer segment" specific investments in resource stock as the dimension. Consider the following example. A supermarket is planning to open a new channel offering home shopping of groceries. It will be open to the entire customer base within a specific area, but in reality only specific segments will use the service. Investments in web-facilities, extra call-service, handling equipment, education of employees, etc. is then dedicated to this new customer segment.

Figure 2 discusses potential and projected investments of a Specialty E-grocer and customers in resource stock. From the *customers' perspective*, a number of add-on services may be valuable and attractive to specific segments of customers, e.g. more frequent delivery, a wider (or deeper) assortment of selected product categories like milk or specialty products and discounts when the customer buys in larger outlay sizes. The add-on services may cause the total service offering to be more unique and will probably lead to stronger dependence between the customer segments and the Specialty E-grocer. The *firm*, on the other hand, will see these investments from a different *perspective*. The value of such investments in add-on services stems from the prospects of attracting new customers or creating stronger dependence to existing customers, retaining them for a longer period and

	Valuable or valued resources		Concentrated resources	
	Firm's perspective → customers	**Customers' perspective → firm**	**Firm's perspective → customers**	**Customers' perspective → firm**
Service delivery system	• Preferences of high service segment => Investment in infrastructure, e.g. information- and operational management technology, transportation equipment, etc.	• Segment preferring providers with high-frequency service	The invested resources are dedicated / concentrated to the firm, not the customer	The customer prefers the service, but invests only human resources, e.g. learning new system
Branding / assortment	• Wider assortment – low value=> Investments in development and implementation of temperature regulated transport box, human and other assets related to administering return system, etc. • Wider assortment – high value=> Investments related to purchasing, e.g. searching, negotiating, etc. with new suppliers • Large quantity order discounts=> Investments related to accounting, budgeting, etc.	• Segment preferring wider assortment of low value, but high handling relieve effect, e.g. milk • Segment preferring wider assortment of high value, e.g. ethnic specialty food • Segment preferring discounts if larger orders should be submitted	Same as above, however the low value assortment is likely to demand much higher investments than to widen the high value assortment or give large order discounts	Same as above

Figure 2: Potential investment in future resource stock.

motivating them to buy in larger quantities. These prospects should be balanced against the value of the investment in itself. In a BTB setting, both parties often partake in the investments in new resource stock, however this is very seldom the case for BTC customers. Thus, the firm normally unilaterally holds the investments in infrastructure in a BTC setting.

Case: The Relation between a Specialty E-Grocer X and its Customers

Specialty E-Grocer X as Case

Specialty E-grocer X is a Scandinavian firm that has experienced a rapid growth in the past 4 years. Last year (2003), it had around 40 employees and a turnover between 100 and 200 million SEK. The number of customers is between 20 and 40 thousand. The focus of the firm is premium quality specialty grocery products that are not readily available in ordinary supermarkets. The products are delivered to the doorstep. The rapid growth is now declining to more average growth rates; still the firm is now obtaining profits.

Data collection   The case is based on an interview with marketing director Ken Ohlsson[7] from Specialty E-grocer X, February 9th, 2004. Other primary data is based on a survey with 1222 respondents in Denmark; the respondents are representative for the population with Internet access (Hansen, 2003). Furthermore, in-depth interviews with 10 respondents in Denmark are included (Friese, Bjerre, Hansen, Kornum, & Sestoft, 2003). With this data, it is possible to identify the respondents who are customers of Specialty E-grocer X and thereby compare their characteristics with rest of the population of respondents. Detailed methodological considerations can be found in Hansen (2003) and Friese et al. (2003).

It is here important to underline that the purpose of using the interviews and surveys in this chapter is *not* to study the Specialty E-grocer as business format and its prospects of survival and further development. This would generate a need for detailed description of case selection and methodology. Rather, the case of Specialty E-grocer X is selected to exemplify and explore theoretical constructs and how to possibly develop these.

---

[7]The name of the firm and the name of the marketing director are kept anonymous for reasons of confidentiality.

The following three sections will reflect these data and compare it with the configurations proposed in the third section (Figures 1 and 2) of existing and future resource stock for an e-grocery retailer in general, with the mapping of the specific configuration of Specialty E-grocer X. From this specific configuration, the strength and balance of the dyad between Specialty E-grocer X and its customers is identified in the fourth section.

Mapping Existing Resource Stock

Valued resources from the customer's perspective   The marketing director was asked to mention which of Specialty E-grocer X's resources and services he expects is valued by their customers. In summary form, the director underlined:

> The customers value our offerings that is characterized by: a) delivery free of charge b) convenience c) premium quality d) niche product with certain characteristics e) surprise elements when buying products as an assortment pre-packed in different types of boxes f) good conscience when buying politically correct products.

> An assortment as wide and deep as ours is often not available in ordinary supermarkets.

> We clearly have a special brand. People like to identify with us and like to trade with us. The way we do business is different and therefore not easily comparable with ordinary grocery retailing. Customers may also have a sense of belonging; — of being a member. We do not yet know if this includes a sense of 'membership of a club' way of looking at the relation. Furthermore, our appearance in national broadcasting and in weekly magazines is far above the average appearance of similar business in these media. This may strengthen the 'sense of belonging' by the customers. We think the signals from our organization correspond with the way we want to present our brand in general. Also, the delivery boxes, as a physical manifestation of our brand, supports the brand much like a coca-cola bottle does.

The respondents from the *in-depth interviews* value the following aspects of the products and services offered by Specialty E-grocer X. Under each heading, the corresponding results from the *survey* are described. From these results, it is possible to identify to what extent Specialty E-grocer X respondents have attitudes that differ from the rest of the population (n=1222) concerning aspects of grocery online shopping that they value. Thus, the respondents answer questions relating to grocery online shopping in general, not online shopping via Specialty E-grocer X.

Convenience   Respondents of the *in-depth interviews* mention "saving time" and "not needing to carry" the goods as valued offerings. The delivery of a prefixed assortment in a box — "not having to choose the products" is valued as convenience. This is surprising, because a prefixed assortment is a restriction in consumer choices. Still, the consumer may be relieved (convenience), because they do not have to plan and compose the assortment in the box. In the *survey*, 76% of the Specialty E-grocer X respondents (called SEC in the following) (n=71) agree or strongly agree that "Using electronic shopping of groceries saves much time". Of the rest of the respondents (n=1151), only 53% have the same opinion. Thus, there is a higher likelihood of finding a Specialty E-grocer X customer that values the potential time-saving element than in the rest of the population. Furthermore, 73% of the SEC respondents agree or strongly agree that "shopping groceries via the Internet is favourable as it makes me less dependent of opening hours", whereas only 46% of the rest of the population state this. Thus, nearly the same pattern occurs here.

Surprise element   The respondents in the *in-depth interviews* point to the surprise element of not knowing what the composition of the assortment in the box will be in a specific delivery. The situation can be compared to receiving a birthday or Christmas present (X-mas effect). The *survey* does not include questions directly relating this very Specialty E-grocer X specific feature. Still, it includes a question of whether "Electronic shopping of groceries is less exiting than buying in the non-Internet shop"? To that question 31% of the SEC respondents disagree or strongly disagree, whereas only 9% of the rest of the population disagree or strongly disagree.

Delivery (larger time window, high customer satisfaction)   In the *in-depth interviews*, the SEC respondents claim that they are satisfied with the delivery system, although deliveries are scheduled on fixed weekdays within large timewindows. The cause for this may be that the distribution system has a relatively high regularity. Is this attitude towards Specialty E-grocer X's distribution system indirectly visible in the *survey* where the SEC respondents answer general questions concerning delivery of Internet ordered groceries? Sixty-six per cent of the SEC respondents disagree or strongly disagree that "It is difficult to receive groceries purchased via the Internet and home delivered", whereas only 16% of the rest of the population think so. So it is fair to conclude that SEC respondents in general find delivery of e-groceries easy, yet we do not know if it is Specialty E-grocer X or other e-grocers that are generating this positive experience?

Minimal customer perceived risk as damaged or bad items are credited without questions asked   SEC respondents from the *in-depth interviews* experience a minimal risk conducting grocery e-commerce with Specialty E-grocer X, because bad items are credited without further notice. The *survey* does not address the specific valued feature of Specialty E-grocer X, but includes a more general question: "One risk from buying groceries via the Internet is receiving low-quality products or incorrect items". Twenty-seven per cent of the SEC respondents disagree or strongly disagree, but only 7% of the rest of the population feel the same way. It is not a very large proportion of SEC respondents, but if the group that neither agrees nor disagrees is considered (SEC 42% — others 22%), then nearly three fourth of the SEC does not agree to the question. One possible explanation is that the SEC respondents to a minor degree *do* receive "low quality products or incorrect items", but it is not perceived as a risk because it is always credited swiftly. Therefore, they can "neither agree nor disagree". Relating to this, 35% of the SEC respondents disagree or strongly disagree that "Return and exchange opportunities are not as good on the Internet as in the supermarket/non-Internet shop" compared to 7% of the other respondents. This means that many SEC respondents (as compared to other respondents) in general do not consider the return and exchange opportunities worse than in the offline shop; a possible explanation for this is the SEC respondents' (positive) experiences with Specialty E-grocer X's complaint management procedures.

Trust in the Specialty E-grocer's service as distributor (good image)   From the *in-depth interviews*, we know that the SEC respondents underline trust in Specialty E-grocer X as distributor. The promises of Specialty E-grocer X are met in the daily practical operations. Concerning the statements of the SEC respondents in the *survey*, 59% of the SEC respondents disagree or strongly disagree that "The groceries are often damaged when I receive them at home", but only 31% of the rest of the population[8] have the same opinion. Again, it must be underlined that it is not possible to distinguish customers' experiences; — whether they have bought groceries from Specialty E-grocer X or from other e-grocers.

---

[8]Only respondents who have tried to buy groceries online have answered this and the next four questions. Thereby, $n = 186$ for the respondents not being the customers of Specialty E-grocer X.

Packaging (high customer satisfaction, image of delivery box)   The SEC answers concerning "groceries are often damaged" are not only an indicator of keeping promises, but also of packaging quality standards. Packaging and especially keeping satisfactory temperature levels and return flows are of importance when customers assess the value of the offered system. From *in-depth interviews*, we know that the SEC respondent in general value the packaging system of Specialty E-grocer X. The delivery box of Specialty E-grocer X clearly has a better image than boxes from other e-grocers. Thus, the SEC respondents were much less sensitive to the annoyance from storing the boxes between deliveries, when the box was from Specialty E-grocer X than from other providers. This indirectly stresses the Specialty E-grocer X delivery box as an important brand attribute, which the marketing director also noted.

Forty-seven per cent of the SEC respondents disagree or strongly disagree that "I often lack room at home for returnable boxes and so", as compared to 19% for other respondents. To the question "I often have difficulties at home in disposing of non-recyclable packing", the corresponding figures are SEC 54% and 36%. Thus, the SEC respondents in the *survey* also differ from the other respondents in this field. The most obvious explanation for this is socio-economic differences (see Figure 3); that is, the SEC respondents in general live in larger apartments and houses, which reduces the storage problem. However, the special image of

	Specialty e-grocer X	Other consumers
	Percent	Percent
Male	33.8	42.1
Female	66.2	57.9
25-45 years of age	90.1	74.8
Middle and Long-term higher education	69.0	45.4
Household Income Per Year above € 65,000	63.4	42.0
Household Grocery Budget Per Month above € 660	33.8	16.6
Household with 1 or more children	63.4	49.9
2-4 cars per household	33.3	28.9

Figure 3: Socio-economic characteristics of Specialty E-grocer X customers.

the Specialty E-grocer X delivery box may be part of the explanation, because we know from the in-depth interviews that the very same SEC respondents (in the same home) had different evaluations of the boxes from Specialty E-grocer X and other providers.

Additionally, a single respondent from the *in-depth interviews* also mention good quality and the easy access to specialties that you do not get in other places as a valuable feature, which Specialty E-grocer X offers.

There seems to be a good match between the firm's view on their own valuable resources and the respondents' view in the in-depth interviews. Still, the interviews do not ask about corporate branding issues and only some elements of the branding of Specialty E-grocer X are treated. If, however, the elements of trust, high customer satisfaction, good image and the image of the delivery box are considered as a whole, this to some degree supports the firm's perception of the value of their brand.

Valued resources from the firm's perspective   The firm may also value resources possessed by the customers or more precisely by segments of customers. The director describes their customers as

> High income, well educated families normally with resident children. Main part of them live in urban areas.

> Some of our customers have traded with us for a longer period and some of them also represent higher order sizes. We have not yet segmented our customers. We perceive our customers as individual beings and we believe in the dialogue (in the human interaction). So we don't know the distribution of relationship length and order sizes. However we plan to obtain this knowledge. Our customers also participate in focus group arrangements, visits to our suppliers and answer questionnaires from us, resulting in relatively high percentages of answers. Clearly, also a large part of new customers stem from word-of-mouth communication from our existing customers.

This description matches the socio-economic data from the *survey*, but the survey adds new knowledge to this description as depicted in Figure 3. The picture of high income, well-educated households with resident children can be confirmed by the survey. From this characteristic of "family" households, the survey also confirms that nearly all the SEC respondents are distributed in the age bracket when people normally have resident children (25–45 years). A high share of above average household grocery budget spending also follows high income. These characteristics are very much what could be expected from general e-commerce data on pioneering customers. More surprising is the higher share of females who are "The person[s] in the household who most often do the grocery shopping".[9] However, there is no straightforward explanation for this difference. Practically all of the respondents are car owners (99.6%)[10] and a slightly higher percentage of SEC respondents have 2–4 cars per household, probably caused by the registered income differences.

Concentrated resources from the customer's perspective   The marketing director from Specialty E-grocer X finds that the following valued resources may be concentrated from the perspective of their customers:

> There are a number of competing home delivery systems in the areas where we market our products, but the coverage rate of competitors is much lower than ours.

> We have an assortment that is comparable in size with some of the offline grocers and it is much larger than our direct Specialty E-grocer competitors that offer a much more narrow assortment.

> Our organization represents something unique signalling transparency and honesty. The staff is more professionalised than firms of comparable size and functions.

> The image and level of media attention is higher than other firms in the grocery sector and this may also add to the sense of belonging or being a member. The tighter personal contact to our customers is also rather unique.

Concentrated resources from the firm's perspective   In general, the marketing director does not think the customers or customer segments can be characterised as concentrated:

> In general it is naturally more problematic to us when a core/loyal customer stops transactions than when this happens to a more periodic or short enduring customer. The individual customer can always be replaced, but a loss of loyal customers over a longer period of time combined with an vicious circle of negative communication, may prove critical to the firm.

---

[9]This was the criteria for the selection/screening of respondent in the survey (Hansen, 2003).
[10]This figure shows a bias probably caused by the population ($n = 1222$) only being representative for people with Internet access.

We very much emphasize the development of the relation to all of our customers and work all the time to motivate them to remain customers, thus we do not want any of them to drop their relation with us. Still we have a significant in- and outflow of customers every month, so a loss of core customers can relatively easily be replaced.

Mapping Investments in Future Resource Stock

The marketing director: "Based on customer input and our own ideas, we work on different ways of improving our service and giving the customers larger degrees of freedom to select the elements in their own service package. There are significant differences concerning how large investments the different types of service improvements will incur and thereby the risk we take if the improvements should prove to fail and not generate necessary extra sales. Clearly, the risk for these investments is ours, not the customers. We may in the much longer-term see some possibilities in asking the customers to share with us some investments characterized by long investment pay back periods".

The strength and balance of the relation between Specialty E-grocer X and its customers

Existing resource stock In the third section, the existing resource stock is mapped. Based on this, Figure 4 presents an assessment of the total strength and balance (Emerson, 1962)[11] of the relation between Specialty E-grocer X and its customers. Here, the main elements of the resources possessed by Specialty E-grocer X is presented in the box in the right part of the figure.

These resources seem to be valued by their customers. In the box in the left part of the figure, this is opposed by the resources possessed by different customer segments. The Firm may perceive these resources valuable. Seen from the *perspective of the customers* Specialty E-grocer X represents a resource stock that is valuable in three areas: (a) the service delivery system, (b) a premium and specialised assortment and (c) a brand with unique characteristics. The presented evidence indicates that the resources under (a) and (b) are valued by the customers and that these resources are considered concentrated to some degree. The data concerning the brand of Specialty E-grocer X does not cover all elements of a brand building process. However, it consists of the combined effect of several

---

[11]Emerson uses the word "advantage" as a concept that corresponds to the "balance" of a relationship and "cohesion" that corresponds to the "strength "of a relationship.

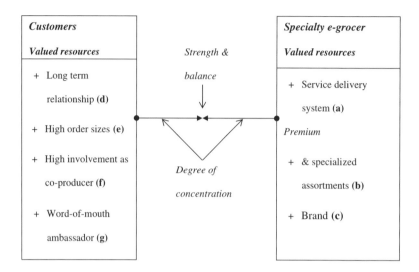

Figure 4: Assessment of strength and balance of the Specialty E-grocer X — customer relation.

elements: the customers trust the firm, they experience high customer satisfaction, they think it has a good image and they observe a positive (branding) effect of the delivery box. Together, these elements based on in-depth interview with customers support a perception of Specialty E-grocer X as representing a corporate brand with unique traces. The response from the marketing director indicates that elements like highly qualified staff and above average exposure in media, points in the same direction. However, these data cannot be confirmed by data based on customer interviews or surveys.

Each of the three areas (a, b and c) is a separate, potential valuable and concentrated resource, but if the three are combined, this clearly will add to the uniqueness of these resources. The assortment they offer is broader than their competitors and many of the individual products are not available in ordinary supermarkets. If this is combined with doorstep delivery, surely it will add to the uniqueness, because not only will it be difficult to find the assortment in ordinary shops, the customer also gets the broader assortment delivered on her/his doorstep free of charge. If we recombine with elements like high levels of trust and customer satisfaction, and add the image and sense of being a club member, then the level of concentration and uniqueness must be concluded to be relatively high. The products and services of Specialty E-grocer X will therefore be difficult for their customers to replace in the exact same configuration. Their customers may try to combine different offerings and products from other Specialty E-grocers, Specialty grocer shops and supermarkets. Still, the effort is much bigger, the quality may not be much higher and many customers may not even have the time to invest in this extra effort. However, Specialty E-grocer X does not offer the full assortment of groceries; therefore, the customers have to visit supermarkets anyway and this minimises the convenience advantage and may motivate some customers to drop Specialty E-grocer X and be satisfied with lower quality products and a narrower assortment.

If the perspective is reversed, then identification of the resource stock possessed by the customers valued by Specialty E-grocer X is in focus. This perspective is trickier, because BTC relations as compared to BTB relations represent many more customers with much smaller order sizes and annual sales per customer than in a BTB trade relation. It is therefore not very meaningful to focus on individual customers, but instead evaluate possible dependence on a customer segment level. As Specialty E-grocer X has not yet tried to segment their customers, the data on this issue is sparse, and the assessments regarding this perspective are thus tentative. Some indications of a pattern can, however, be proposed. A relatively large part of the customers must function as ambassadors, because most of the new customers are attracted via word-of-mouth communication with colleagues, friends, family, etc. Customers are above average willing, to act as co-producers free of charge in surveys, focus groups, visits, etc. The firm also underline that the relation to the customers is special with a closer personal contact. Altogether, this indicates that the pool of customers possess resources that are valued by Specialty E-grocer X and that dependence is closer than normally observed in BTC relations. Although not defined, the firm probably has customers that could be characterised as a core group. These customers can be identifiable as the combination of elements, e.g. long-term customer, large order/-scale customer, loyal, ambassador and co-producer. If, in the future, the firm identifies such a core group, the collaboration with this group may even get closer and if such customers are scarce in supply, then the firm is likely to be more dependent on this segment.

In *summary*, the strength of the relation based on the customers' perception of their relation to the firm is above medium, because the valued resources possessed by Specialty E-grocer X to some degree is concentrated. From the firm's perspective, the strength of dependence on customer segments is low to just below medium, depending on the segment in focus. The relation is clearly imbalanced, because Specialty E-grocer X is more difficult to replace for a customer than the customer or segments of customers are for the firm.

Investments in future resource stock   When mapping the existing resource stock in the previous section, the purpose was to make an assessment today of the strength and balance of valued/concentrated resource accumulated historically. The investments in future resource stock concerns investments that are implemented some time in the future. The specifity or uniqueness of these resources will depend on their perceived value/concentration.

The interview with the marketing director reveals that Specialty E-grocer X is working on different types of improvement projects that demand different levels of investments. They also have a clear attitude that only the firm is running the risk of sunk cost, not the customers. But in the long term, they do not exempt the possibility of involving the customers in special types of long-term investments. The data on this subject is general, but in future studies there is a need for a more detailed description of different possible investment projects and their impact.

Nevertheless an interesting feature appears when using the BTB theories on a BTC context. The study of the existing resource stock of Specialty E-grocer X and customer show similar results as studies of BTB relations. Here, the strongest part of an imbalanced relation decides the future development of a dyad (Kornum, 2003). However, the difference is that in a BTB relation, the strongest part will be able to secure that the risk of investments in specific resources is shared by the exchange partner, e.g. by co-financing the investment, by distributing the benefits from the investment unevenly or incorporating the benefits and costs of the investment in the relationship contract. The customers of Specialty E-grocer X, and other BTC customers, only, in specific context like a coop, have a tradition of sharing future relation-specific investments. In consumer goods sectors with infrequent buying patterns like furniture, the likelihood for the customer of obtaining any payback of the investment is not high and therefore such investments is not attractive. With more frequent buying patterns like groceries constructing a payback model including, e.g. lower prizes and/or better service seems to be a more feasible scenario due to the more frequent purchases. For the Specialty E-grocer who wants to expand the services this unilateral risk taking and possible models for involving the loyal customers, is an interesting feature that needs further investigation. Furthermore, based on the discussions in the third section, it is interesting to examine whether unilateral relation-specific investments will cause the firm to be more dependent on specific segments of customers.

Conclusions and Implications

The purpose of the previous chapter has been to examine to what extent resource dependence theory is applicable to a context consisting of the relation between an e-grocer and its customers. Confronting the initial theoretically derived proposals with the input from the case, points to a discussion on the theoretical applicability. To what extent is the theory applicable to a BTC e-grocery setting and to what extent does the case support the initial theoretically derived proposals?

The possible dimensions where dependence can occur between the e-grocer and its customers have been identified as (a) historically generated resource stock possessed by one or both parties and (b) future investments in resource stock. Furthermore, (a) and (b) can be examined from a firm and customer perspective, respectively. Thus, the conclusion will be based on these four perspectives in the next sections.

Existing resource stock — the customer's view on the value and concentration of resources possessed by the e-grocer The individual customer's view on the e-grocer with whom s/he trades is very similar to an individual firm's view on a BTB relation. The firm viewed from a customer perspective may in both instances possess valued resources that to some degree are concentrated, resulting in a situation where the customer is dependent on the providing firm. In the examined case, it became evident that not only each single resource of Specialty E-grocer X could be considered concentrated to some degree, but when the resources were viewed as a whole, this added to the uniqueness of the product-, service- and brand package that Specialty E-grocer X possesses. The customers mentioned three resource-bundles that they value and these bundles correspond with the one the firm expects its customers to value. Still, the customers' assessment of whether valued resources of Specialty E-grocer X is perceived as concentrated is not a part of the empirical data, on which this chapter is based. Consequently, it is not possible to confirm this and further investigations are needed to answer the question of customers' perception of concentrated resources. However, including such questions into future studies, e.g. in-depth interviews, seems to be straightforward. In summary, it can be concluded that viewing customer's potential dependence in relation to a specific provider is theoretically consistent, also in a BTC e-grocery context.

Existing resource stock — the firm's view on the value and concentration of resources possessed by the E-grocer's customers From this perspective, the firm can, of course, express its perception of the resources possessed by their customers. It can *value* its customers by underlining certain characteristics of the customers as a whole or as customer segments. In the case of Specialty E-grocer X, the marketing director was able to characterise the customers as a whole, although they had not yet segmented the customers, but planned to do so in the near future. The firm hereby indicates that some customers, representing, e.g.

larger order sizes or longer relationship duration, may be of higher value to the firm than other segments. So, the value dimension may be embedded in a segmentation analysis. Concerning the *concentration* of the valued resources, this is not relevant on the level of the individual customer, but may be relevant for specific segments, especially the core segment of long term, loyal, co-producing customers buying in large quantities. Still, the marketing director did not find that such segments could be concentrated because of the relatively high in- and outflow of customers each week. The analysis seems to point to two separate dimensions here. The first relates to the number in the total (national) market of consumers with similar characteristics as the core segment of E-grocer's customers. If Specialty E-grocer X attracts, e.g. 80% of the potential number of consumer with characteristics similar to the core segment of Specialty E-grocer X, then retaining the core segment becomes of high priority.[12] Then having estimated the potential occurrence of the core segment in the total market provides a measure to compare the in- and outflow from this core. Especially, the outflow is important because only time can show whether an (inflowing) customer becomes a long term and loyal customer. This clearly points to the fact that models and theories in this field need to include more dynamic elements, e.g. by identifying the relationship history of the individual customer and to compare/classify these histories into a new type of dynamic segmentation analysis. In *summary*, it can be concluded that resource dependence theory can be applied to the BTC e-grocery situation, albeit with the modification that because of the high numbers of customers, the dimension concentration is only applicable to segments of customers. Furthermore, especially the analysis of the dynamic aspect of outflow of core segment customers compared to the total market occurrence of the core segment should be of focal interest for theory development.

Future resource stock — the value and concentration of future investments in resources possessed by the E-grocer and customers   From the theoretically derived proposals, both the E-grocer and customers may be involved in future investments that are valuable and concentrated — relation-specific resources. However, the case does not include the customers' assessment of future investments of Specialty E-grocer X, but only includes the firm's evaluation of its own and its customers' future potential investments. The conclusion on applicability must then be considered as preliminary. Still, the firm confirms that it plans on

---

[12]This discussion parallels the Storbacka et al. (1994, p. 33) discussion on the patronage concentration as the RR/TIV ratio, where RR is relationship revenue and TIV is total industry volume.

investing in improvements of product and service offerings. An interesting difference between a BTB and BTC setting then becomes prevalent. In a BTB setting, investments in relation-specific assets is often mutual to some degree, or if
they are unilaterally held, then the investing party is often compensated by the
exchange partner via terms of trade, e.g. lower prizes or distribution costs. In a
BTC setting, the providing firm unilaterally holds investments in relation-specific
assets and it has the sole investment risk. The marketing director is well aware of
this investment risk. In *summary*, the resource dependence/transaction cost theory also seems applicable to the BTC E-grocery context, however further empirical studies is needed, especially of customer's perception of risk in connection to
grocery e-commerce (Hansen, 2002, 2003) and related to investment in relation-
specific assets.

Storbacka, Strandvik and Grönroos Revisited and Further Research

This chapter has taken, as its point of departure, the proposal by Storbacka et
al. (1994) in order to contribute to the understanding of what constitutes
relationship strength. Based on the conclusion, resource dependence theory in

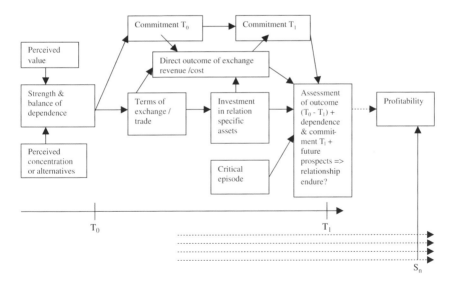

Figure 5: Relationship strength and profitability — static and dynamic dimensions.

general seems well suited to contribute to an understanding of what constitutes relationship strength between an E-grocer and its customers. Focusing on perceived value and concentration when assessing relationship strength, this only includes some of the constructs in the customer relationship profitability model. A further consequence of applying resource dependence theory is that it involves changes in the sequence of these constructs from the model (*ibid.*, p. 23). As suggested in Figure 5, the constructs in the model should be separated in static-relational and dynamic/intertemporal constructs. Thus, analysis of the strength and balance of resource dependence is static-relational and it maps the configuration of valued/concentrated resources generated historically and assessed today (T_0) (the day we monitor the phenomenon). In practice, the exchange partners assess the relationship strength again sometime in the future (T_1). What initiates the assessment in T_1 may be the "critical episode" Storbacka et al. (1994) propose, whether it is planned, e.g. negotiating terms of trade, recurrent, e.g. where errors in delivery is frequent or it is stochastic. As an outcome of the exchange episodes occurring between T_0 and T_1. "Customer commitment" (*ibid.*) is either neutral, rising or declining (Håkansson, 1982; Ring & Van den Veen, 1994; Hultmann, 1993). Also, "relationship revenue and cost" relate to the outcome of the exchange episodes between T_0 and T_1, but the performance is also affected by the terms of trade and the degree of investment in relation-specific resources.

The assessment in T_1 will include the total outcome of these (dynamic) phenomena and lead to "customer and/or firm satisfaction" or the reverse and to a decision of whether the relationship should endure ("longevity"). This includes an assessment of future prospects of the relationship and opportunity costs of staying in the relation instead of exiting (Ring, 1999). Thus, relationship profitability is an assessment of the outcome of a certain number of sequences S_n $((T_0 - T_1) + (T_0 - T_1) + (T_{n0} - T_{n1}))$, where the firm or the customer or both in cooperation decide the number of sequences, that have to be carried through, before assessment is activated (planned or stochastic).

As already indicated, the main difference between the Relationship Profitability Model and Figure 5 is that the latter explicitly identify static-relational and dynamic-intertemporal dimensions and that this in Figure 5 is combined with the causal chains leading to relationship profitability. Thus, several dimensions like dependence, the revenue/cost balance and commitment may have changed between T_0 and T_1. For example, in the Relationship Profitability Model customer commitment is influenced by customer satisfaction and customer commitment in the next turn influence relationship strength. In Figure 5, customer commitment, besides being influenced by customer satisfaction (direct outcome of exchange), also in T_0 is influenced by the strength and balance of the relationship, but in T_1

commitment also influences the assessment of the outcome from the period T_0 and T_1. Similarly, the level of customer commitment in T_0 influences the process that generates the outcome in T_1 and is also the basic level of commitment that the commitment in T_1 can be compared to. Consequently, commitment is embedded in a more complex and hopefully also more realistic causal chain than in the Relationship Profitability Model. In summary then inclusion of both static and dynamic elements in the model allocates the relationship strength constructs in their proper place, both in the causal chain and in the time continuum and shows that dependence perspectives can be combined with profitability perspectives of a relationship.

Still, until the constructs in Figure 5 in detail are discussed in relation to the underlying theories; the figure should be considered tentative. Such considerations should also be accompanied by empirical investigations in a set-up that allow for examining the proposed causal links in a dynamical context.

References

Arndt, J. (1983). The political economy paradigm: Foundations for theory building in marketing. *Journal of Marketing, 47(*Fall), 44–54.

Buvik, A., & Reve, T. (2002). Inter-firm governance and structural power in industrial relationships: The moderating effect of bargaining power on the contractual safeguarding of specific assets. *Scandinavian Journal of Management*, (18), 261–284.

Coviello, N. E., & Brodie, R.J. (1998). From transaction to relationship marketing: An investigation of managerial perceptions and practices. *Journal of Strategic Marketing*, 6, 171–186.

Dierickx, I., & Cool, K. (1989). Asset stock accumulation and sustainability of competitive advantage. *Management Science, 35* (12), 1504–1511.

Easton, G. (1992). Industrial networks: A review. In: B. Axelsson, & G. Easton (Eds), *Industrial networks — a new view of reality*. London: Routledge.

Emerson, R. M. (1962). Power-dependence relations. *American Sociological Review, 27*, 31–41.

Frazier, G. L., Sawhney, K., Shervani, T. (1990). Intensity, functions, and integration in channels of distribution. *Review of marketing 1990 Zeithaml VA*. Chicago: American Marketing Association.

Friese, S., Bjerre, M., Hansen, T., Kornum, N., & Sestoft, C. P. (2003). Barriers and motivators of online grocery shopping in Denmark. *Ebizz Øresund Report, Research Report January*.

Gaski, J. F. (1992). Some fundamental conceptual issues in intrachannel power research. *Advances in Distribution Channel Research, 1*, 115–133.

Grönroos, C. (1994). From marketing mix to relationship marketing: Towards a paradigm shift in marketing. *Management Decision, 32*(2), 4–20.

Grönroos, C. (1995). *The rebirth of modern marketing — six propositions about relationship marketing.* Meddelanden Working Papers, nr. 307.

Grönroos, C. (1997). Value driven relational marketing: From products to resources and competencies. *Journal of Marketing Management, 13*(5), 407–419.

Grönroos, C. (1998). *Service marketing theory — back to basics.* Working Papers, nr.1998-369 Helsingfors, 1998, 24 s.

Grönroos, C., Heinonen, F., Isoniemi, K., & Lindholm, M. (1999). *The netoffer model — developing Internet offerings for the virtual marketspace.* Meddelanden från Svenska Handelshögskolan, nr. 393 Helsingfors, 1999.

Gummesson, E. (1987). The new marketing — developing long-term interactive relationships. *Longe Range Planning, 20(4)*, 10–20.

Hägg, I., & Johanson, J. (Eds). (1982). *Företag I Nätverk.* Stockholm:SNS.

Håkansson, H. (Ed.). (1982). *International marketing and purchasing of industrial goods: An interaction approach.* Chichester: Wiley.

Håkansson, H., & Johanson, J. (1994). Network as a governance structure. Interfirm cooperation beyond markets and hierarchies. In: G. Grabner (Ed.), *The embedded firm. On the socioeconomics of industrial networks* (pp. 35–51). London: Routledge.

Håkansson, H., & Snehota, I. (1995). *Developing relationships in business networks.* London: Routledge.

Hansen, T. (2002). Forbrugerens valg imellem on-line og off-line indkøbskanaler — en litteraturgennemgang og forslag til yderligere forskning [*Consumer's choice between online and offline channels — a review and suggestions for further research.*] Working Paper, November, Institut for Afsætningsøkonomi, Handelshøjskolen i København.

Hansen, T. (2003). The online grocery consume. Results from two Scandinavian surveys. *Ebizz Øresund Report, Research Report January.*

Heide, J. B., & John, G. (1988). The role of dependency balancing in safeguarding transaction-specific assets in conventional channels. *Journal of Marketing, 52* (1), 20–35.

Hultman, C. (1993). *Managing marketing channels for industrial goods.* Linköping Studies in Management and Economics, Dissertation no. 25. Department of Management and Economics, Linköping.

Javidan, M. (1998). Core competence: What does it mean in practice? *Long Range Planning, 31*, 60–71.

Kornum, N. (2002). Characteristics and development of store based — and specialty e-grocer. Paper presented at the NOFOMA conference, Trondheim, 2002.

Kornum, Niels. (2003). Exploring the interconnectedness between relation-specific assets and resource importance: Identifying the combined dependence, bonding or lock-in effects influencing the ability to decide contractual arrangements. *Nordic workshop on transaction cost economics. Bergen.*

Pfeffer, J., & Salancik, G. R. (1978). External control of organizations. *A resource dependence perspective.* London.

Ravald, A., & Grönroos, C. (1996). The value concept and relationship marketing. *European Journal of Marketing, 30* (2), 19–30.

Ring, P.S. (1999). The cost of networked organizations. In: A. Grandori (Ed.), *Interfirm networks* (Chapter 9). London: Routledge.

Ring, P. S., & Van den Veen, A.H. (1994). Developmental process of cooperative interorganizational relationships. *Academy of Management Review, 19*(1), 90–118.

Stern, & Reve. (1980). Distribution channels as political economies: A framework for comparative analysis. *Journal of Marketing, 44* (Summer) 52–64.

Storbacka, K., Strandvik, T., & Grönroos, C. (1994). Managing customer relationships for profit: The dynamics of relationship quality. *International Journal of Service Industry Management, 5*(5), 21–38.

Weber, O. J. (2002). Resource dependency as barrier or driving force for grocery BTC e-commerce and subsequent changes in the supply chain. *Proceedings of the NOFOMA conference*, Trondheim, June 2002

Wilkinson, I. F. (1973). *Power in distribution channels* (pp. 1–34). England: Cranfield School of Management.

Wilkinson, I. F. (2000). *A history of network and channel thinking*. Working Paper.

Williamson, O. (1985). *Economic institutions of capitalism*. New York: Free Press.

Chapter 5

Knowledge Acquisition and Usage Behavior in Internet Banking

Daniel Nilsson

Introduction

Extensive research has found information to be crucial for consumers' understanding (Harrison, 2002). However, other research has found information to be not at all crucial, but rather that it is more important in terms of experiential learning, where people learn through their own action and reflection (Boyatzis & Kolb, 1995; Kolb, 1976, 1981; Meyer, 2003; Saunders, 1997; Sautter, 2000). Research has also determined that the consumers' knowledge influences the extent to which they search for information. Some research has shown that an increased level of knowledge results in a decreased search for information, which is explained by the fact that the consumers' need for information has decreased (Johnson & Russo, 1984; Mattila & Wirtz, 2002). Other research has found that an increased level of knowledge results in an increased search for information because the consumers then know what to search for (Brucks, 1985; Jacoby et al., 1978).

It is well known that some people learn most effectively by doing, whereas others learn by dealing with abstract conceptions and then relating them in practice (Evans, 1989). How do consumers acquire knowledge about Internet banking — through information or through usage and reflection? How does the consumers' knowledge influence their search for information? These questions will be studied within the Internet banking context. It is important to investigate these questions because the consumers' knowledge is an influential construct in understanding consumers' usage behavior (Brucks, 1985; Chiou, Droge, & Hanvanich, 2002; Park, Mothersbaugh, & Feick, 1994) and, therefore, may influence the consumers' use of the Internet channel to the bank (Davis, Bagozzi, & Warshaw, 1989). This chapter aims to increase the understanding of what influences the consumers' usage of a technological channel and what managerial implications are involved in how the distributor can influence the consumers' usage behavior. Banking services constitute a heterogeneous supply, and the Internet is a difficult channel to the bank for many consumers. Therefore, the consumers' knowledge assessment of Internet banking is an interesting area to study. Kolb's (1984) Experiential Learning Theory (ELT), on which this chapter is to a great extent based, has been used to explain learning and educational issues in several fields (Mainemelis, Boyatzis, & Kolb, 2002). A bibliography of research on ELT includes 1004 studies conducted in the fields of management (207), education (430), computer studies (104), psychology (101), medicine (72), as well as nursing, accounting, and law (Mainemelis et al., 2002). In spite of the extensive amount of research based on ELT, it does not seem as though any studies of ELT have been conducted in a context where the computer constitutes a channel to heterogeneous services.

Literature Review

Internet Banking and the Need for Knowledge

The financial sector is an example of where the relationship between buyer and seller is complicated because the services are heterogeneous (Eriksson & Mattson, 2002) and contain an extensive level of uncertainty (Eriksson & Sharma, 2003). Financial services, such as funds, placements, accounts, and mortgages, are often perceived as difficult for consumers to understand, thus complicating the consumers' decision-making process and attaching a high perceived risk to it (Harrison, 2002). If consumers have extensive knowledge of financial services, they are more likely to use Internet-based financial services than consumers with the same level of knowledge of the technology, but with less knowledge of financial services. The knowledge of a service influences the use of a technology; consumers who do not have knowledge of a certain service may be uncomfortable purchasing the service through the Internet. Consumers tend to prefer purchasing standardized products over the Internet, whereas complex services are more often bought in face-to-face interaction (Bobbit & Dabholkar, 2001). Products that are more often bought on the Internet, include the following: software, books, and music (Bobbitt & Dabholkar, 2001). These products involve little risk in terms of defects, fragility, style, fabric, and color differences; they are also products that consumers have higher levels of experience purchasing (Bobbitt & Dabholkar, 2001).

If consumers lack knowledge about financial services, they may not have the capacity to make favorable decisions based on their presumptions. The lack of financial knowledge may affect an individual's or family's capacity to make a long-term placement, which results in a position that is sensitive to descents in their economy. Research has shown that acquirement of additional information results in improved acting in financial matters (Braunstein & Welch, 2002). According to Mitchel (2003), a lack of financial knowledge may result in two possible scenarios. Individuals who do not understand a product or a service have a tendency to hesitate when they are buying. Consumers who intend to buy despite their lack of knowledge become vulnerable to salespeople who may try to sell them a product or a service that is inappropriate or that they do not need. Neither of these scenarios is good for the supplier of financial services. The first case results in an absent sale, and the second case may result in unsatisfied consumers and increased governance regulation. In the same way that the level of knowledge of financial services may influence the consumers' use of financial services, the level of knowledge of technology may influence the consumers' use of financial services in a technology-intensive context. If consumers learn about financial services, but not how to purchase them, the level of Internet banking usage will not increase. It is therefore important that consumers learn about financial services as well as Internet banking in order to become a regular Internet banking user (Mittal & Sawhney, 2001).

Adopting a new technology is complicated, and consumers have been found to retain conflicting perceptions about technology. Consumers' attitudes toward Internet technology have not been well investigated, and the research that has been conducted has produced conflicting results. Technology may simplify consumers' understanding of exchange, but, on the other, it may make it more difficult (Civin, 1999). Mick and Fournier (1998) have identified eight paradoxes associated with information technology. Some examples of these paradoxes are how consumers perceive that technology creates both freedom and enslavement, increases and decreases the feeling of competence, and fulfils and creates needs. These conflicting perceptions of technology make it difficult for consumers to gain a concrete perception of technology. The functions of a technology influence consumers' attitudes, which, in turn, influence how consumers interact in relation with the seller (Griffith, 1999). By gaining knowledge of a technology, consumers can learn to use a technology and, as a consequence, resolve these conflicting perceptions. Consumers with positive attitudes toward using the Internet for information searches are also more likely to use the Internet for purchasing services (Shim, Eastlick, Lotz, & Warrington, 2001). Research has also indicated that consumers who are strongly inclined to buy products or services electronically have other non-store shopping experiences as well as experience using personal computers (Shim, 2000). Therefore, bank consumers who are already experienced personal computer users are probably more willing to become repeat consumers of Internet banking than consumers who do not have computer use experience.

Consumers establish judgment about new situations, products, or services based on related past attitudes and experiences (Bobbit & Dabholkar, 2001). According to Bobbit and Dabholkar (2001), most people have been exposed to technological products, such as ATMs and personal computers. Consumers are much more likely to adopt a new technology if they have used similar technologies in the past and have formed favorable attitudes toward using these technologies (Bobbit & Dabholkar, 2001). Consumers' attitudes are often not based on their use of Internet banking, but rather on their observation of others using Internet banking or on their attitudes toward other technological products (Bobbit & Dabholkar, 2001). Consumers' attitudes toward using technological products in general may provide insight as to why consumers adopt a computer technology or not. If consumers have unfavorable attitudes toward using technological products, they will less likely have favorable attitudes toward Internet banking. Consumers instead will be more inclined to use bank branches as a channel to the bank (Thornton, 2001). Consumers' experience has a moderating effect in predicting their acceptance of Internet shopping. Consequently, experience with this technology leads to more use of this service (Carlson & Zmud, 1999). The importance of previous shopping experience on the Internet in terms of the consumers' future usage illustrates how important it is to turn existing Internet consumers into repeat consumers by providing them with satisfying Internet-shopping experiences (Shim, 2000).

How do Consumers Learn in a Technological Context?

Everybody learns. Some people learn quickly, whereas others learn slowly; some people learn about things that are easy to comprehend as valuable, whereas others learn things whose value is less obvious. Some people learn through formal education (e.g., in classrooms or organized discussions), whereas others learn from day-to-day experience (Evans, 1989). Experience results in learning and knowledge (Shih & Venkatesh, 2004). Knowledge has been found to be a strong influencing factor over individuals' behavior (Brucks, 1985; Chiou et al., 2002; Park et al., 1994), and, therefore, it will influence their use. As a consequence, the following question needs to be addressed: How can consumers' knowledge about Internet banking technology and financial services be developed? Some researchers have found that it is crucial that the consumer receives information

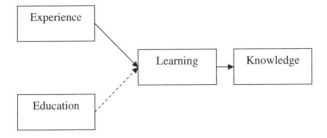

Figure 1: How knowledge can be acquired.

(Harrison, 2002), whereas other researchers have found information provided to the consumer not at all important, but rather the consumer should use and reflect (Boyatzis & Kolb, 1995; Kolb, 1976, 1981; Meyer, 2003; Saunders, 1997; Sautter, 2000).

The process of knowledge acquisition is continuous. Therefore, a change in experience or education results in a change in learning and knowledge, which influences the use of technology and, thereby, the experience and the information search behavior (see Figure 1).

Learning through Education

Information is what we share from our own knowledge and distribute to others. We obtain information through our senses, and, thereafter, we may transfer it to own knowledge (Van Beveren, 2002). Many researchers believe knowledge may be acquired through the information we receive from sources, such as suppliers, books, magazines or newspaper articles, advertising, classrooms, or our social network (Hoch & Deighton, 1989). Using these types of sources to increase consumers' knowledge often appeals to marketing managers because the message can often be controlled and repeated (Hoch & Deighton, 1989). The uses of financial services are often irregular, which results in that an increased knowledge acquired from previous experience tends to be limited (Harrison, 2002). Therefore, external sources have great significance to fill out knowledge and experience gaps. Because financial services are complex and convey a great uncertainty, it is important that banks offer suitable information that will help consumers use their financial services (Harrison, 2002). Information can be defined as data placed in a context, whereas data are facts that can be transformed to create information, which is presented through speech, pictures, or in written form (Van Beveren, 2002). Knowledge refers to an individual's beliefs, skills, experience, and information (Alexander, Schallert, & Hare, 1991), and knowledge can exist, be created, stored, or used only within an individual's brain (Van Beveren, 2002). For the purpose of this study, this definition of knowledge will be used.

Acquisition of Information

The quantity of searched information is affected by factors in the market surroundings, such as the importance of the product and the consumer's knowledge. However, contradictory research about these factors does exist. For example, some research has found that a great number of product options and a high level of product complexity result in limited information searches because the investment of thought rises. The other research has found that a high level of recognition and knowledge increases the information search behavior (Brucks, 1985), indicating that consumers are better equipped to collect and understand information if they already have knowledge. Assimilating information, therefore, demands some level of knowledge. Other research, however, has found that a high level of knowledge of the product decreases the information search behavior (Johnson & Russo, 1984; Mattila & Wirtz, 2002). This decreased information search behavior is often explained by the finding that consumers with extensive product knowledge have an advantage over consumers who lack product knowledge mainly because of their superior knowledge of alternatives (Johnson & Russo, 1984). Consumers with knowledge will be more likely to know specific facts about alternatives, as for example other banks' funds, rates, and fees, and, therefore, these consumers need less information about the product. However, another explanation is that consumers with extensive knowledge perform more efficient information searches because they know what is most useful for discriminating between brands and can determine more quickly which alternatives are inferior (Brucks, 1985).

The source of information goes not only through the supplier but also through the consumers' social network (Mattila & Wirtz, 2002). Consumers often confer with their social network for advice, and when they need help, the social network is available to provide them with information, which they, in turn, transform into knowledge. When consumers face problems with their Internet banking usage, help from someone with more experience in technology or financial services to solve the problems are usually needed (IT-kommissionens rapport, 1/2002). Consumers usually seek help from their surrounding social network, which includes their family, friends, colleagues, or neighbors (Axelrod, 1956; Bell & Boat, 1957). Several studies have shown that individuals prefer to turn to their social network for help rather than to strangers or formal agencies (Amato, 1990;

Burke & Weir, 1975; Croog, Lipson, & Levine, 1972). Because financial services and technology are complex and demand knowledge, consumers often need help when conducting their banking. Innovation creates uncertainty, and individuals in general are uncomfortable with uncertainty and tend to increase communication to interpret the innovation. Increased interactions with a social network affect behavioral decisions via informational and normative influences. Informational influence occurs when other relevant users inform the individual of their own personal experience and evaluation of the innovation or when the individual can observe someone in their social network using the innovation. In addition to informational influence, normative pressure from their social network to adopt or use the innovation reduces the uncertainty and the risk of adoption or usage because it provides strong evidence indicating that the behavioral decision to adopt or use is a good decision. Because the level of uncertainty declines as an individual becomes more and more knowledgeable about the innovation, more interactions with the other relevant users during the pre-adoption stages than during the post-adoption stages can be expected (Karahanna et al., 1999). Therefore, the consumers' use of social networks is likely to vary, depending on the consumers' level of knowledge of Internet banking.

Information acquisition involves expenses for the consumers, but knowledge based on previous experience is even more expensive because it demands that consumers buy and use the product. In theory, consumers are assumed to collect information from many sources before they make a decision to buy; in reality, information searches tend to be limited (Harrison, 2002).

Learning through Experience

Experience is the best teacher (Hoch & Deighton, 1989).

The role of experience is crucial because experience results in cumulative knowledge and learning (Shih & Venkatesh, 2004). According to Hoch and Deighton (1989), experience is more efficient than information in increasing the consumers' knowledge because the exposure is self-selected, and the motivation and involvement, therefore, tend to be higher. However, the drawback associated with relying on consumers' learning from experience is a lack of control over the learning content (Hoch & Deighton, 1989).

Lectures are not the most effective educational delivery mechanism available to increase learning; the most effective mechanism instead is "doing" (Helms, Mayo, & Baxter, 2003). However, what needs to be determined is which method is the most effective at increasing the consumers' knowledge of financial services and of the Internet as a channel to banking.

Experiential Learning Theory (ELT)

According to Goby and Lewis (2000), ELT is rooted in the theories of Carl Jung, who was one of the fathers of modern psychological thinking. In recent years, ELT has become widely used as a theoretical grounding for learning in several domains (Goby & Lewis, 2000). ELT defines learning as "the process whereby knowledge is created through the transformation of experience. Knowledge results from the combination of grasping and transforming experience" (Mainemelis et al., 2002). ELT focuses on learning through reflection on the personal experience, and the reflection links concrete experience to theoretical understanding (Goby & Lewis, 2000) through which learners make sense of their surroundings (Meyer, 2003). The core of this model is a description of the learning cycle — how experience is translated into concepts, which influences the choice of new experiences (Kolb, 1976; Saunders, 1997). ELT is based on a theory of learning that categorizes the process of learning from experience into four different phases, which are as follows: (1) concrete experience (CE) (sample word, feeling), (2) reflective observation (RO) (watching), (3) abstract conceptualization (AC) (thinking), and (4) active experimentation (AE) (doing) (Boyatzis & Kolb, 1995;). A person's learning style is defined by the person's reliance on these four learning modes.

The experiential learning cycle is a four-stage, ongoing cyclical process (Goby & Lewis, 2000). When the process starts, we have an existing experience. We then think about it, form opinions about it, consider the implications of these opinions on our understanding of our total experience, and approach the next similar experience in terms of our refined understanding (Goby & Lewis, 2000). For example, when Maria attends her first selection interview (CE), she finds herself recalling many details of the situation, such as the color of the furniture, the design of the room, the questions asked, how she responded, and how she felt at the time (RO). After the interview, Maria's friend, Joanne, asks her how the interview went. From Maria's experiences and observations, she draws general conclusions about how selection interviews are conducted, what to expect, and how to prepare (AC). Based on her conclusions, Maria imagines what the next interview will be like, thinking about what behavior she believes will be most appropriate (AE). With all the gained experience, Maria faces her next interview experience (CE) with an extended and deeper understanding of what to expect and how to behave (Goby & Lewis, 2000).

Method

In order to accomplish the goals of this study, I had to choose between conducting a statistical study with many respondents who use Internet banking and a more indepth study of a few consumers. Because my interests are focused mainly on concepts and procedures, I decided to conduct interviews with consumers who use the Internet as a channel to the bank. Four respondents between the ages 24 and 65, who use the same bank, were interviewed. Three of these respondents were interviewed on two different occasions, with 2 years between the interviews, thus making it possible to study any changes in the consumers' knowledge and their Internet banking usage. (Because the fourth respondent died before the second interview was conducted, only one interview with her was realized.) This method presents an opportunity to observe how changes in consumers' knowledge affect their Internet banking usage and how consumers acquire knowledge over time. To facilitate our study of how the consumers' knowledge, attitude, and usage have changed over a period of 2 years, the structure of the interviews was similar for both occasions. Seven interviews with four respondents, all of whom use Internet banking to some extent, were conducted. This chapter aims to increase the understanding of how the consumers' level of knowledge in financial services and Internet banking technology affects their usage behavior, which is possible to determine using the interview methodology.

All of the respondents, Bengt, Gunilla, Johan, and Ingegard, are users of Internet banking to some degree. They have used Internet banking for various lengths of time, ranging from 6 months to 7 years. The respondents have different backgrounds and different levels of knowledge concerning computers, the Internet, and financial services. These respondents were selected to represent the different groups of consumers in the market. For example, Bengt represents consumers with extensive knowledge of both technology and financial services, whereas Gunilla represents consumers who are not confident in these areas and have limited knowledge. Johan and Ingegard represent consumers who are in-between, namely consumers who have some sort of knowledge, either of technology or financial services. The aim of the interviews with these respondents was to portray consumers with different levels of knowledge but was not meant to result in any generalization of consumers' usage.

Bengt

Bengt, who was 55 years old at the time of the first interview, has been a customer at the same bank for the past 8 years. He is also a customer at another bank where he has some of his placements. He uses two different Internet banks, one for personal use and other for the company where he works. Bengt is a frequent user of computers, the Internet, and Internet banking. He has used Internet banking since it was introduced in 1996.

Gunilla

Gunilla, who was 54 years old at the time of the first interview, has been a customer at the same bank for the past 30 years, but she sometimes considers changing banks. She, however, believes that changing banks would be difficult and feels more comfortable staying with her current bank. Gunilla perceives banking to be complicated and difficult as a consequence of the many options she does not understand, such as the various accounts and credit cards available. She, therefore, lacks confidence when using financial services. Gunilla often encounters difficulties when using Internet banking and feels uncertain about the technology.

Johan

Johan, who was 24 years old at the time of the first interview, has been a customer at the same bank for as long as he can remember. Johan is faithful to his bank and has never even considered changing banks. As a student, Johan uses the Internet and computers frequently. He has used Internet banking for about 6 months, and when the first interview was conducted, he was using this channel once a month.

Ingegard

Ingegard is 65 years old and has been a customer at the same bank for 14 years; however, she has recently considered using an additional bank, a bank that she determined has more favorable conditions than her present bank. Ingegard, who has been an Internet banking customer for a year and a half, uses Internet banking mostly to check accounts and funds and to conduct transfers and payments.

Analysis

In this chapter, I will analyze the interviews with the respondents in order to find out the importance of knowledge, how knowledge can be acquired, and how knowledge influences information search behavior.

Perceived Usefulness and Perceived Ease of Use

The respondents perceive Internet banking to be useful because it results in a better overview of their banking business. However, they have different perceptions of the degree of difficulty associated with Internet banking. In contrast to Bengt, Johan, and Ingegard, who perceive Internet banking to be both useful and easy to use, Gunilla perceives Internet banking to be useful, but complex and difficult to use. The fact that Gunilla uses Internet banking despite having problems with it indicates that her perception of its usefulness is more influential than the difficulties associated with it on her usage behavior. For Gunilla to use Internet banking perceived usefulness is more important than ease of use; this result is equivalent to the Technology Acceptance Model (Davis, 1989). If a technology is useful, the consumer can usually overlook some complexity and difficulty using this channel. However, if the consumer perceives the technology not to be useful, it does not matter how easy the technology is to use (Davis et al., 1989). No level of ease of use can compensate for a technology that is perceived as useless (Davis et al., 1989). These findings suggest that the respondents are willing to disregard some difficulties associated with using this channel in exchange for what they perceive to be the advantages of Internet banking. The perception of Internet banking as a useful channel is the most important incentive for its usage. However, persuading consumers with positive attitudes toward Internet banking into using this service requires knowledge. This knowledge is obtained either from experiential knowledge, where the consumers' previous usage increases their knowledge, or from information mainly provided by the social networks.

Perceived usefulness and perceived ease of use have been shown to influence strongly consumers' attitudes toward a technology (Davis, 1989). However, for these attitudes to result in any actual usage, consumers must possess knowledge of both technology and financial services.

Consumers' Knowledge

Johan is knowledgeable about Internet banking technology, which has resulted in a positive attitude toward technology use. His knowledge of financial services, however, is limited. Johan's limited knowledge of financial services results in an uncertainty about these services and of how to use them. Bengt is the respondent who is most knowledgeable of both technology and financial services, which is clearly evident in his positive attitude toward Internet banking usage. Ingegard is knowledgeable of both technology and financial services; therefore, she is relatively confident in her usage abilities. Gunilla, who is unsure of what can happen in Internet banking, perceives Internet banking to be complicated and does not feel confident in this area.

> Gunilla: "I find the bank business to be difficult."
> Interviewer: "How do you mean?"
> Gunilla: "You have to consider so many different things; things that you do not understand."

Interviewer: "What kinds of things?"
Gunilla: "Different accounts and different credit cards and Visa®
cards and I feel so unsure" (Gunilla, interview and translation by
author, tape recording, Stockholm, Sweden, 2002)

Individuals have a tendency to hesitate when buying something they do not
understand (Mitchel, 2003). To make consumers use the services, it is, therefore,
important to increase their knowledge. If consumers intend to buy something
despite their lack of knowledge, they become vulnerable to salespeople who may
try to sell a product or a service to them that is inappropriate or that they do not
need. Neither of these scenarios is favorable to the supplier of financial services.
The level of knowledge of financial services may influence the consumers' use of
financial services, and the level of knowledge of the technology may influence
the consumers' use of financial services in a technology-intensive context.

Consumers' Experience

Johan sometimes faces difficulties with Internet banking. For example, when he
does his banking on the Internet and tries to go back a step, it does not work.
However, he has learned that he needs to log off and then log in again. Another
problem occurs when Johan's wife wants to do some Internet banking after he has
finished. They have discovered that if Johan logs off his Internet banking account
and then disconnects from the Internet, it is still not possible for his wife to log
in. They have to restart the computer in order to make it possible to log in. These
experiences have increased his knowledge, and, as a result, Johan has learned to
manage these problems.

Gunilla perceives that she is constantly learning more about Internet banking
and financial services as a result of the increased experience she gains when she
uses Internet banking. Gunilla feels that her knowledge of Internet banking usage
and financial services has increased and that she is now more confident in her
ability to use these services.

Consumers' Perception of Information

Kolb's (1976) model of experiential learning provides a good theoretical basis for
understanding the process of developing consumers' knowledge of their Internet
banking usage. The study indicates that experience gained from using technology
and financial services offers consumers a higher level of understanding and a richer

view of Internet banking than does traditional information provided by the banks. Thus, even information has a place in the learning cycle.

Ingegard perceives that her lack of information about both technology and financial services to be a huge problem. An information sheet is all the information she has received since she started to use Internet banking. When I asked her if she feels that she has received enough information about this technology, she answered:

> Absolutely not. I have had to learn [by] myself, and, fortunately, I have two sons [to help me] (*Ingegard, interview and translation by author, tape recording, Stockholm, Sweden, 2002*)

Consumers will buy the products they need if they understand which products they need and why they need them. I asked Ingegard what she would need more information about, and her reply was as follows:

> At [the] start, what services exist. After all, it is an assumption [that] I know what services exist for me to be able choose what to use (*Ingegard, interview and translation by author, tape recording, Stockholm, Sweden, 2002*)

During the first interview, Gunilla stated that she believes information is available, but she feels that the information would be difficult to understand because of her lack of knowledge of banking terms. Gunilla believes her Internet banking usage would be greater if she had received understandable information about the services and how to use them.

Bengt actively searches for more information on the Internet. During the first interview, Johan did express his desire for more information.

> The information has actually been really bad (*Johan, interview and translation by author, tape recording, Stockholm, Sweden, 2002*).

When the first interview with Johan was conducted, he had very limited knowledge of financial services. As a result, he believed that the information provided about financial services had been deficient. Therefore, he would like to receive more information about how to use the services. When he pays his bills, he often feels unsure of what he is supposed to do and finds it difficult to know what to write and where. He also has trouble knowing when to write Optical Character Recognition (OCR) numbers and if he is supposed to write messages or an invoice number.

> *"There exists a folder about the Internet bank, but there is not much more than that"* (*Johan, interview and translation by author, tape recording, Stockholm, Sweden, 2002*).

During the first set of interviews, all the respondents considered information to be crucial. With the exception of Bengt, all of the respondents considered information provided by the banks about technology and financial services to have been insufficient. Because Bengt actively searched for information on his own, he did not need the bank to provide him with information.

Two Years Later...

After 2 years of usage had passed, I asked the same questions during the second set of interviews with the respondents. However, the respondents now have different opinions about the need for information.

> I have not asked for information because I do not need any (*Johan, interview and translation by author, tape recording, Stockholm, Sweden, 2004*).

> If I desire any information, then it is just to click and read; it is not more difficult than that (*Johan, interview and translation by author, tape recording, Stockholm, Sweden, 2004*).

When the second set of interviews was conducted with the respondents, Johan stated that the information provided by the banks was sufficient and that he did not require any further information from the bank. Johan's change of opinion may be as a result of an increased knowledge of financial services. During the first set of interviews, Johan desired information that he felt should be offered to him from the bank, but at the time of the second interview, he no longer needed the bank to provide him with information. When the second set of interviews was conducted, he believed that he could search for information on his own if he needed it.

When the first set of interviews with the respondents was conducted, they all considered information to be crucial. With the exception of Bengt, who was the most knowledgeable respondent and was capable of searching for information on his own, all of the respondents considered the information from the banks to be insufficient. The respondents perceived that the banks did not offer any information about technology or financial services. After 2 years had passed, and the respondents had two more years of experience and an increased knowledge, they still had not received any information from the banks. In spite of the lack of information, the respondents had a different view of the importance of information and how it should be provided. During the second set of interviews with the respondents, it became evident that they all had become more confident in their Internet banking usage abilities as a result of their more extensive knowledge. Because the respondents had not received any information from the banks in the past 2 years, their increased knowledge is based on their usage, social networks, and support centers, and does not originate from information from the banks. During the second set of interviews, the respondents expressed less need for information provided by the banks. If they were in a situation where they needed information, the respondents felt that they could search for the information themselves. This change in the need for information provided directly from the bank indicates that consumers with limited knowledge of the product may desire that the bank actively provide information to them. Consumers with more knowledge feel that banks should not actively provide them with information, but should offer information that the consumers can search for themselves instead. This finding does not tell us whether consumers with more knowledge use more or less information, but it does tell us that consumers, depending on their level of knowledge, have different preferences regarding how information should be distributed.

Education Sources

Consumers receive information not only through the supplier but also through many other channels. One of the most often used information sources is the social network, which usually consists of family members and friends (Mattila & Wirtz, 2002). Consumers often confer with their social network when they face problems and need help, and the social network thereby provides information to these consumers, which can be transformed into knowledge.

Ingegard sometimes faces difficulties with Internet banking, and when I asked her about it, she said the following:

> But it does not have to be the bank's fault because I am not an expert at using computers. I am self-taught with my children's support *(Ingegard, interview and translation by author, tape recording, Stockholm, Sweden, 2002)*

When Bengt encounters problems with technology, he usually contacts a person in his family for assistance. If this person does not succeed in solving the difficulties, Bengt contacts a support center, which he has done several times in the past.

Ingegard does not feel confident about Internet banking because she is sometimes not aware of what is happening and does not know what to do. When I asked
her if she has used an Internet banking support center, she said the following:

> No, I usually call my son. He is [just] like them (*Ingegard, inter-
> view and translation by author, tape recording, Stockholm,
> Sweden, 2002*).

Occasionally, Johan encounters problems that he cannot successfully solve on
his own. In this situation, Johan contacts his brother for help. Johan also mentioned that if his brother could not solve his problem, he would not hesitate to
contact the Internet banking support center; however, this is something he has not
had to do as of yet. All of the respondents reported that they sometimes face problems and that the first person they contact for help is someone in their social network. If the person he contacted in his social network failed to solve his problem,
Bengt said that he has then turned to the Internet banking support center for help.
Johan said that he would contact the support center if someone in his social network could not solve his problems. Both Ingegard and Gunilla stated they would
not contact the support center. Only Bengt, the most knowledgeable respondent,
has contacted the support center as of yet, and Johan, who has extensive knowledge of the technology, said that he would not hesitate to contact the support center. These findings indicate a correlation between knowledge of technology and
use of support centers. This correlation may depend on several different factors,
but one factor may be that consumers who are more knowledgeable use Internet
banking for more complex services and, therefore, have a tendency to encounter
more complex problems. Because of the complexity of these problems, their
social network may not possess the knowledge required to help them. As a result,
these consumers would then need to contact Internet banking support centers for
assistance. Another explanation may be that consumers with limited knowledge
of technology are insecure about their ability to understand the help provided by
support centers.

Knowledge and Problems

Knowledge is of great significance. Respondents who are knowledgeable in both
technology and financial services have proved to be confident in their Internet
banking usage, whereas respondents with less knowledge have proved to be less
confident. The level of knowledge has been shown to influence the attitude of
respondents toward Internet banking usage and, therefore, indirectly the actual
usage.

One common aspect, which all respondents share, is that they, regardless of their prior knowledge, sometimes face problems with Internet banking. It is possible, however, to notice a difference in what kind of problem they face and the type of process they adopt to solve it. Respondents with less knowledge of financial services or technology more often face fundamental problems, such as not knowing what an OCR number or invoice number is or where to fill it in. In contrast, knowledgeable consumers face problems that are usually more complex; therefore, the person providing support must be more knowledgeable. When respondents with limited knowledge of Internet banking technology face problems, they contact someone only from their social network. Respondents with more knowledge, however, tend to contact someone from their social network first; they then seek assistance from an Internet banking support center if their social network cannot successfully solve the problem. Knowledge is an important factor that affects information search behavior. Our findings indicate that only those who already have extensive knowledge of technology or financial services contact Internet banking support centers.

Conclusion

The results from the analysis of the collected empirical material cannot be generalized, but they do indicate that knowledge is crucial. Consumers with limited knowledge about technology and financial services feel unsure of themselves when using these services, and, as a consequence, they tend to avoid using services they do not recognize. Furthermore, these consumers avoid actively searching for information. The respondents who have limited knowledge of technology and financial services increase their knowledge mainly through their limited usage and their social networks. The respondents who are more knowledgeable increase their knowledge through their usage, social networks, and support centers. Knowledgeable consumers are accustomed to using regular services and actively searching for more information. When these consumers face problems, they do not hesitate to contact their Internet banking support center.

The less knowledgeable consumers' use of Internet banking is often limited to occasional usage each month. As a consequence of their limited usage and limited search for information, these consumers' knowledge development will take a long time. Consumers who already have knowledge about Internet banking usage search for information more actively. In contrast, consumers who lack knowledge, and, therefore, should need information, do not search for information, thus making them more dependent on the information that the banks distribute to consumers. Increased information should help consumers become more confident in their Internet banking usage; they should also become more frequent visitors and use more services than they are aware of today. Consumers who already have knowledge about Internet banking use this channel more frequently than others do.

Consumers acquire knowledge through either information or experience. It does, however, seem as though the level of the consumers' present knowledge affects their information search behavior and usage, which, in turn, influence their potential to gain experience. Consumers with limited knowledge often desire information from banks, but they do not search for the information themselves, except from their own social networks. Therefore, their knowledge acquisition to a great extent relies on their limited usage and their social networks. Consumers with more knowledge have a different attitude toward information; they do not want information from the banks, but they do search for information to a greater extent. Their knowledge acquisition relies on experience gained through usage as well as on information they have obtained themselves from the supplier, their social network, or the Internet banking support center. This chapter supports the theory of technology acceptance. Perceived usefulness influences the consumers' usage behavior, but this chapter also found that knowledge was another factor influencing the consumers' usage behavior.

Managerial Implications

To help consumers make use of Internet banking to a greater extent, banks need to speed up the post-adoption process by improving the Internet banking system. If Internet banking web sites had a more pedagogic appearance and if the needed information was presented in an easy-to-use manner, consumers would be more likely to use Internet banking.

Consumers with limited knowledge of financial services and Internet banking technology do not search for information or contact a support center when they need help. Instead, they contact people in their social network, who may affect the consumers' behavior via their informational and normative influence. Because banks cannot influence the information that consumers receive from their social network, they should try harder to minimize the consumers' need for their social network in their Internet banking usage. The main reason that consumers with limited knowledge are not currently turning to their banks for assistance stems from the fact that they lack confidence in their ability to understand the help provided by support centers. To reach these consumers, banks should focus on providing their consumers with satisfying information and help. One suggestion would be for banks to use personal advisors with whom consumers could develop a relationship. This personal interaction would increase trust and build a stronger relationship between consumers and the bank, and consumers should be able to contact the personal advisor if they face problems in their banking business, regardless of which channel they are using.

References

Achrol, R.S., & Kotler, P. (1999). Marketing in the network economy. *Journal of Marketing, 63*, 146–163.

Alexander, P.A., Schallert, D.L., & Hare, V.C. (1991). Coming to terms: How researchers in learning and literacy talk about knowledge. *Review of Educational Research, 61*(3), 315–343.

Amato, P.R. (1990). Personality and social network involvement as predictors of helping behavior in everyday life. *Social Psychology Quarterly, 53*(1), 31–43.

Axelrod, M. (1956). Urban structure and social participation. *American Sociological Review, 21*(1), 13–18.

Bell, W., & Boat, M.D. (1957). Urban Neighborhoods and Informal Social Relations. *American Journal of Sociology, 62*(4), 391–398.

Ben-Porath, Y, (1980). The F-Connection:Families, friends, and firms and the organization of exchange. *Population and Development Review, 6*, 1–30.

Beveren, Van, John, (2002). A model of knowledge acquisition that refocuses knowledge management. *Journal of Knowledge Management, 6*(1), 18–22.

Bobbitt, L.M., & Dabholkar, P.A. (2001). Integrating attitudinal theories to understand and predict use of technology-based self-service: The Internet as an illustration. *International Journal of Service Industry Management,12*(5), 423–450.

Boyatzis, R.E., & Kolb, D.A. (1995). From learning styles to learning skills:The executive skills profile. *Journal of Managerial Psychology, 10*(5), 3–17.

Braunstein, S., & Welch, C (2002). Financial literacy: An overview of practice, research, and policy. *Federal Reserve Bulletin, 88*(11), 445.

Brucks, M. (1985). The effects of product class knowledge on information search behavior. *Journal of Consumer Research, 12*(1), 1–16.

Burke, R.J., & Weir, T. (1975). Receiving and giving help with work and non-work problems. *Journal of Business Administration, 6*, 59–78.

Carlson, J.R., & Zmud, R.W. (1999). Channel expansion theory and the experiential nature of media richness perceptions. *Academy of Management Journal, 42*(2), 153–170.

Chau, P.Y.K., & Tam, K.Y. (1997). Factors affecting the adoption of open systems: An exploratory study. *MIS Quarterly, 211*, 1–24.

Chiou, J.S., Droge, C., & Hanvanich, S. (2002). Does customer knowledge affect how loyalty is formed?, *Journal of Service Research, 5*(2), 113–124.

Civin, M.A. (1999). On the vicissitudes of cyberspace as potential-space. *Human Relations, 52*(4), 485–506.

Croog, S., Lipson, A., & Levine, S (1972). Help patterns in severe illnesses: The roles of Kin network, nonfamily resources and institutions. *Journal of Marriage and the Family,34*,32–41.

Davis, F.D. (1989). Perceived usefulness, perceived ease of use, and user acceptance of information technology. MIS Quarterly, September, 319–340.

Davis, F.D., Bagozzi, R.P., & Warshaw, P.R. (1989). User acceptance of computer technology: A comparison of two theoretical models. *Management Science, 35*(8), 982–1003.

Eisenhardt, K. (1989). Building theories from case study research. *Academy of Management Review,* 14(4), 532.

Eriksson, K., & Mattsson, J. (2002). Managers perception of relationship management in *heterogeneous markets, Industrial Marketing Management,* 31(6), 535.

Eriksson, K., & Sharma, D.D. (2003). *Modeling uncertainty in buyer seller cooperation. Journal of Business Research, 56, 961–970.*

Evans, N. (1989). Assessing prior experiential learning. *Industrial and Commercial Training, 21,* 3–5.

Gehrt, K., Ingram, T.N., & Howe, V. (1991). Nonstore versus store retailing: A situationally based market structure assessment. *Journal of Direct Marketing, 5,* 44–53.

Goby, V.P., & Lewis, J.H. (2000). Using experiential learning theory and the Myers–Briggs type indicator in teaching business communication. *Business Communication Quarterly, 63*(3), 39–48.

Granovetter, M.S. (1973). The strength of weak ties *American Journal of Sociology, 78,* 1360–1380.

Griffith, T.L. (1999). Technology features as triggers for sensemaking. *Academy of Management Review, 24*(3), 472–488.

Harrison, T. (2002). Consumer empowerment in financial services: Rhetoric or reality? *Journal of Financial Services Marketing, 7*(1)6–9.

Helms, M.M., Mayo, D.T., & Baxter, J.T. (2003). Experiential learning: The benefits of trade shows for marketing students and faculty. *Marketing Education Review, 13*(3), 17–25.

Hoch, S.J., & Deighton, J. (1989). Managing what consumers learn from experience. *Journal of Marketing, 53*(2), 1–20.

IT-kommissionens rapport 1/2002, Vem använder Internet och till vad? Spridningen av Internet bland befolkningen.

Jacoby, J, Chestnut, R.W., & Fisher, W.A. (1978). A behavioral process approach to information acquisition in nondurable purchasing. *Journal of Marketing Research,* 15(4), 532–544.

Johnson, E.J., & Russo, (1984). Product familiarity and learning new information. *Journal of Consumer Research, 11*(1), 542–550.

Kolb, D.A. (1976). Management and the learning process. *California Management Review, 18*(3), 21–31.

Kolb, D.A., (1981). Experiential learning theory and the learning style inventory: A reply to Freedman and Stumpf. *Academy of Management Review, 6*(2), 289–296.

Kolb, D.A. (1984). *Experiential learning: Experience as the source of learning and development.* Englewood Cliffs, NJ: Pretice-Hall.

Lee, J., & Allaway, A. (2002). Effects of personal control on adoption of self-service technology innovations. *Journal of Services Marketing, 16*(6), 553–572.

Mainemelis, C., Boyatzis, R.E., & Kolb, D.A. (2002). Learning styles and adaptive flexibility: Testing experiential learning theory. *Management Learning, 33*(1), 5–33.

Mattila, A.S., & Wirtz, J. (2002). The impact of knowledge types on the consumer search process: An investigation in the context of credence services. *International Journal of Service Industry Management, 13*(3), 214–230.

Meyer, J.P. (2003). Four territories of experience: A developmental action inquiry approach to outdoor-adventure experiential learning. *Academy of Management Learning and Education, 2*(4), 352–363.

Mick, D.G., & Fournier, S (1998). Paradoxes of technology: Consumer cognizance, emotions, and coping strategies *The Journal of Consumer Research, 25*(2), 123–143.

Mitchel, J.O. (2003). Should you improve consumers' financial literacy? *LIMRA's MarketFacts Quarterly, 22*(2), 37.

Mittal, V., & Sawhney, M.S. (2001). Learning and using electronic information products and services: A field study. *Journal of Interactive Marketing, 15*(1), 2–12.

Morgan, R.M., & Hunt, S.B. (1994). The commitment-trust theory of relationship marketing. *Journal of Marketing, 58*, 20–38.

Park, C.W., Mothersbaugh, D.L., & Feick, L. (1994). Consumer knowledge assessment. *Journal of Consumer Research, 21*(1), 71–82.

Saunders, P.M. (1997). Experiential learning, cases, and simulations in business communication. *Business Communication Quarterly, 60*(1), 97–114.

Sautter, E.T., Pratt, E.R. & Shanahan, K.J. (2000). The marketing WebQuest: An internet based experiential learning tool. *Marketing Education Review, 10*(1), 47–55.

Shih, C.F., & Venkatesh, A. (2004). Beyond adoption: Development and application of use-diffusion model, *Journal of Marketing, 68*(January), 59–72.

Shim, S., Eastlick, M.A., & Lotz, S. (2000). Assessing the impact of Internet shopping on store shopping among mall shoppers and Internet users. *Journal of Shopping Center Research, 7*(2), 7–43.

Shim, S., Eastlick, M.A., Lotz, S.L., & . Warrington, P. (2001). An online prepurchase intentions model: The role of intention to search. *Journal of Retailing, 77*, 397–416.

The Swedish Competition Commission, (Konkurrensverket 2001) Konsumentrörligheten på de finansiella marknaderna" Konkurrensverkets rapportserie: 2001:5

Thornton, J., & White L. (2001). Customer orientations and usage of financial distribution channels. *Journal of Services Marketing, 15*(3), 168–185.

Chapter 6

Intentions as Indicators of the Future of Customer Relationships: An Internet Marketing Application

Magnus Söderlund

Introduction

A significant amount of research on customer relationships is inspired by a paradigm with the following causal variables: (1) the customer's perception of attribute-level performance (e.g., reliability and courteous employee behavior) affects (2) the customer's global evaluation of the supplier (e.g., in terms of customer satisfaction, perceived service quality, or perceived value). This evaluation, in turn, is assumed to affect (3) the customer's behavioral intentions – and these intentions affect (4) overt customer behavior. Finally, it is assumed that customer behavior has an impact on (5) the firm's profitability. This reasoning is sometimes referred to as the satisfaction-profit chain.

A closer look at how contemporary research in this tradition is carried out, however, results in a highly unbalanced picture: substantial attention is devoted to the *determinants* of a selected evaluation construct (e.g., customer satisfaction). The relationship between evaluation constructs (e.g., satisfaction versus perceived service quality) has also attracted many researchers. But relatively little attention has been allocated to the *consequences* of this or that global evaluation. For example, only about 5 percent of all correlations between customer satisfaction and other variables included in Szymanski and Henard's (2001) meta-analysis pertain to consequences. In addition, studies that deal with consequences

Managing Customer Relationships on the Internet
Copyright © 2006 by Elsevier Ltd.
All rights of reproduction in any form reserved
ISBN: 0-08-044124-6

usually focus on intentions rather than on overt behavior. An intention-behavior association, then, is often assumed rather that demonstrated in empirical terms. It can be noted that this assumption is sometimes obscured – particularly when researchers refer to their intention variables as "behavior" in titles and abstracts. In other words, the customer's intentions serve as main dependent variables in much research on supplier–customer relationships. This research appears to be based on premises such as this: "If I, the researcher, am able to show that my model of the antecedents of my favorite evaluation construct is characterized by a significant correlation between the evaluation measure and an intention measure, well, then my model is supposed to be good". Similar assumptions are made in research on advertising effectiveness, particularly when the intention constitutes the final variable in a hierarchy-of-effects model.

This type of reasoning is not necessarily flawed; a large body of research carried out by attitude theorists indicates that intentions mediate the relationship between an evaluation construct, such as an attitude, and behavior (cf. Notani, 1998). In fact, attitude theories, with the objective of explaining and predicting behavior, provide the main rationale behind the use of intention measures for many researchers interested in the satisfaction-profit chain and advertising effectiveness. The assumption of an intention–behavior link is one main rationale behind the present paper, too. In addition, however, we believe that intention is a legitimate topic *per se* for academic research, regardless of the impact of intention on behavior. The reason is that intention serves as a unique human construct, in the sense that it allows us to make contact with a future that is yet to materialize. Indeed, the capability of forming intentions is an activity that distinguishes humans from, say, squirrels and snakes. Yet this capability, we believe, is overshadowed by the sometimes often very pragmatic concerns with behavior in attitude theory. Indeed, we find it somewhat strange that academic papers and textbooks never contain the words "intention theory". This paper, therefore, is an attempt to address this lacuna, and the paper deals mainly with intention per se rather than attitudes and behavior.

Given the importance attached to intention as a mediating variable among both attitude theorists and marketing scholars, it is somewhat surprising that intention is seldom the subject of careful conceptualization. That is to say, researchers whose studies deal with intention do not usually define the construct, and they often unknowingly lump different types of intentions together under the same heading (Sheppard, Hartwick, & Warshaw, 1988; Warshaw & Davis, 1985). However, different types of intention variables – reflecting different theoretical constructs – are not always strongly correlated (Fishbein & Stasson, 1990; Sheppard et al., 1988; Warshaw & Davis, 1985). In addition, and with specific reference to satisfaction–profit chain research, several studies, such as Söderlund

(2002, 2003), Söderlund and Öhman (2003, 2004), show that satisfaction is not equally correlated with different intention constructs. Results from studies of this type have yet to see wider diffusion, but they clearly suggest that marketers should select their intention variables with care; the selection of one particular intention variable over another produces different results with regard to the view of how intentions mediate the global evaluation-behavior relationship. Given that associations are generally interpreted in terms of causality, the mere selection of one specific intention indicator may also affect conclusions about causal relationships – and, in turn, in the case of marketing practitioners, affect marketers' decisions about what to do in their relationship marketing efforts.

This paper examines another potential difference between intention constructs – the absolute levels (in terms of the mean response level) they reach when captured in marketing research surveys. This issue has received less attention than the potential for different strength in associations with other variables. Some previous results, however, indicate in passing that different intention measures reach different levels (cf. Söderlund, 2002; Söderlund & Öhman, 2003). That is to say, when measured with the same response format (say, a 10-point scale where 1 = weak and 10 = strong), the mean response level is not the same for intention variables that are designed to capture different intention constructs. The main rationale behind pursuing the issue in this paper is that it serves to further highlight the importance of how intentions are conceptualized and operationalized in research on supplier–customer relationships. It can also be noted that some firms formulate explicit relationship goals in terms of intention levels. This practice is also encouraged by some authors. In a recent article, for example, Reichheld (2003) claims that firms should substitute a single question for all satisfaction and retention-related questions they use in their marketing research – a question about word-of-mouth intentions ("How likely is it that you would recommend Company X to a friend or a colleague?"). Moreover, according to Reichheld, the levels reached by the responses to this question should serve as the main basis for managerial action. However, if different intention measures reach different levels, and when the level of *one* single and incautiously selected intention is monitored (which is typically the case), the value of this practice, in terms of its potential for decision support, can be questioned.

The purpose of this paper, then, is to explore if measures of different intention constructs reach different levels when captured in marketing research. The empirical context is the use of intention measures to assess the effectiveness of marketing communications on the Internet. This type of marketing is becoming more prevalent; its growth is fueled by increases in the on-line population, time spent on-line, and the number of people adopting Internet commerce. And intentions have become a common means to assess the effectiveness of Internet-related marketing (cf. Huizingh & Hoekstra, 2003; Kimelfeld & Watt, 2001; Li, Daugherty, & Biocca, 2002). Banner advertising is perhaps the most well-researched type of marketing communications on the Internet, but here we focus on the use of websites as means of communication by organizations whose main activities take place outside the Internet. In this case, the website provides additional information about the core offer; in contrast to banner communication, the purpose of the site is not to produce a flow of visitors to other sites, but to support the organization's main activity. Indeed, a website used in this way can be seen as a relationship-building activity – it offers more depth in the relationship between the customer and the supplier.

Theoretical Framework

Overview of the Framework

We begin by examining a traditional intention construct: intentions-as-plans. It is labeled "traditional" because it is often used in theories in which intention is conceptualized as a mediator between attitudes and behavior. The theory of reasoned action (Ajzen & Fishbein, 1977) and the theory of planned behavior (Ajzen & Madden, 1986; Ajzen, 1991) are typical examples. Given that an intention construct of this type is a proposition that the individual makes about himself/herself in relation to a future act in which he or she is the acting subject (e.g., "I plan to buy a new car during the next year"), however, we argue that intentions-as-plans is *one* among several propositions that the individual makes about himself in relation to a future act. In the following step, therefore, we introduce additional propositions of this type that have been referred to as intentions in the literature (or has been used a variables assumed to mediate the attitude–behavior relationship). Next, we offer an attempt to distinguish between intention constructs in terms of self-determination – a dimension that we believe will aid our understanding of why different intention constructs may reach different levels when they are used in marketing research.

Intentions-as-plans

In existing literature, particularly in attitude theories, an intention often refers to the individual's *planned choice* to carry out a particular behavior in the future. An intention in this sense involves choosing or deciding to carry out the act. It has been argued that such intentions capture motivational factors that influence behavior; "they are indicators of how hard people are willing to try, of how much effort they are planning to exert, in order to perform the behavior" (Ajzen, 1991, p. 181). Similarly, Bandura (1986) views intentions as "the determination to perform certain activities or to bring about a certain future state of affairs," and Howard (1989, p. 35) stresses "plan" in his intention definition. In empirical studies, typical measurement items are "I am planning to...," "I intend to...," "I will choose...," "I am going to choose...", and "I will select...." Here, we refer to intention of this type as intentions-as-plans (IP). It can be noted that IP represent a potentially heterogeneous group of intentions, in the sense that an individual may not view his/her propositions about intending, choosing, selecting and planning as identical. However, given that a clear typology in this area is yet to be developed, we will subsume them under the same general label (i.e., IP) in the present paper.

Intentions in Terms of other Propositions about the Future

Given that intentions-as-plans are propositions that the individual makes about himself/herself in relation to a future act, it becomes clear that an individual can connect himself or herself with his/her own future behavior in many other ways than those that have an explicit content of planned choice. In fact, we believe that the individual continuously make many different propositions about the future and with regard to many different acts; they represent a window of the future. We are thus assuming that most people are concerned with their future. After all, we have to spend the rest of our lives there. Propositions about the future made in the present, then, serve to make life manageable. Generally, a proposition of this type has the form "I – connection – future act", and it is a basic unit in a network of propositions that emerge when individuals engage in future-oriented cognitive activities such as mental simulation, planning, imagination, goal setting and ruminations. The conceptual boundaries between these cognitive activities are far from clear, because a comprehensive typology of various propositions about the future is yet to be developed. In an attempt to offer building blocks for a more complete framework than the traditional view of intention-as-plans, we now turn to two additional ways of framing the individual's propositions of about his/her future acts. We use the term intention as the overall label for these propositions in order to make contact with previous research.

Intentions-as-expectations   One frequently used intention construct is behavioral expectations. It refers to the individual's assessment of the subjective probability that he or she will perform a particular behavior in the future. Typically, this is measured with questionnaire items such as "The likelihood that I would do A is...," "The probability that I will do B is...," "Rate the probability that you will do C," and "How likely are you to do D?"; the respondent is thus asked to estimate the probability that he or she will perform the act. This is perhaps the reason why behavioral expectations are sometimes labeled self-predictions (cf. Fishbein & Stasson, 1990). We refer to intention of this type as intentions-as-expectations (IE). Such intentions appears to be relatively more popular than the other intention constructs discussed in this study. Incidentally, and as noted in the introduction, it is an intention-as-expectation question that Reichheld (2003) suggests could replace all other questions used in marketing research with the objective of predicting the firm's growth.

Intentions-as-wants   An additional intention construct is a conceptualization in terms of wants. It has been used by Fishbein and Stasson (1990) and Norman and Smith (1995). This construct is found in several formal models of intentionality and in the "folk concept" of intentionality (Malle & Knobe, 1997). Wants also appear in Heider (1958), who stresses that intention is often taken as the equivalent of wish or wanting. Given that wants serve to connect the individual with his/her future acts, we refer to them as an intention construct in this paper.

Self-Determination as a Classifying Dimension for the Intention Constructs

In this section, we use the level of self-determination as a means to distinguish between the three intentions constructs (IE, IP, and IW). Self-determination is defined as the individual's perception of the extent to which he or she needs to pay attention to factors beyond herself/himself in order to form his/her proposition about his/her future acts. Self-determination, then, is an individual-level variable that can take on values from low (the proposition is perceived to be completely determined by various factors outside the individual) to high (the cause of one particular proposition is held to be the individual who makes the proposition). In relation to authors who have dealt with (a) the extent to which the individual *is* free in terms of behavior and (b) the individual's *subjective experience* of acting voluntarily, we are concerned with the individual's subjective experience of freedom in *cognitive* activities (here: forming propositions about future acts). Given self-determination as a classification basis for intention constructs, we also assume that the three intention constructs in focus here are located at different points on the self-determination continuum.

Consider, first, the case of IE: we assume that the individual who is forming behavioral expectations (e.g., "To what extent am I *likely* to come back to Conrad Hotel in Dublin for another holiday?") needs to take into account a variety of factors beyond himself/herself. For example, in a holiday context, and if the individual is considering spending his/her holiday with the family, she/he needs to assess the likelihood that family members want to go back to the same hotel. This individual must also estimate the chances of obtaining a room at the hotel given that many other people, who she/he does not know, and whose plans are even less known, want to stay at the same hotel. The behavioral expectation assessment, then, implies that careful thoughts are devoted to *other* people's expectations, plans, and wants – and to several other restrictions and facilitators in the environment. Therefore, and when the IE proposition does materialize, we assume that it is characterized by a relatively low sense of self-determination.

With regard to IP, the judgment task becomes slightly different. In forming such judgments (e.g., "To what extent do I *plan* to come back to Conrad Hotel in Dublin for another holiday?"), focus is transferred to factors that affect the individual's conscious choice. Some of the factors from the IE task, including external factors, such as other persons' intentions, are likely to remain in the assessment. But we expect that several external factors are eliminated – and that more room is allowed for self-related factors. For example, when I assess the extent to which I plan to do X, I am likely to look relatively less closely at my noncognitive habits and the uncontrollable parts of my environment – and more at "myself". This view is consistent with, for example, Azjen's (1991, p. 181) notion of intentions-as-plans; they are "indicators of how hard people are willing to try, of how much effort they are planning to exert, in order to perform the behavior." Moreover, it is not difficult to change one's plans. In fact, planning can easily – at will – take different routes without much effort. Therefore, we expect a relatively closer connection with the individual's volition and thus a higher level of self-determination in the IP case compared to the IE case.

Moving further on to IW, the cognitive task (e.g., "To what extent do I *want* to come back to Conrad Hotel in Dublin for another holiday?") changes again. Compared to IE and IP, the number of external factors to consider is likely to decrease, because to "merely" want something is subject to few external restrictions. Thus, we are assuming that a relatively high level of self-determination is involved in wanting things to happen in the future. A similar view is at hand in Csikszentmihalyi and Graef (1980, p. 404) who assume that wanting to do something is an expression of "being free".

In sum, we have assumed that IE, IP, and IW are located at different points on a self-determination dimension; individuals "zoom in" on themselves to a larger extent when they assess their future in terms of high self-determination propositions. An attempt to explicitly examine this potential difference in empirical terms, but only for IE and IW, is provided by Söderlund and Öhman (2004), and it shows that respondents perceive that they need to take significantly more account for other persons' opinions when they are forming IE rather than IW propositions about future acts. This difference, we argue in the next section, is one reason why a marketing researcher is likely to obtain different levels of intention given the use of different intention measures.

Why are Different Intentions Expected to reach Different Levels?

Hardly any studies have examined the potential for different intention measures to reach different levels. In passing, however, some studies, such as Söderlund (2002), and Söderlund and Öhman (2003), report differences in levels for different intention measures. The main pattern that emerges is as follows: the level of the variable (i.e., its value in terms of its mean) is increasing as we move from IW to IP and further on to IE.

Why, then, do such differences exist? The main reason, we believe, is that the cognitive process of assessing propositions about the future is affected by the level of self-determination. We have already suggested, in the previous section, that when the level of self-determination is low rather than high, more external variables are taken into account, which thus increases the total number of variables that affects the assessment. And the larger the number of variables that needs to be taken into account, the higher the level of activation of associations in memory. In other words, a high level of activation increases the salience of the act.

Salience, in turn, has been shown to increase the individual's perception of how likely the act is to take place. For example, it has been shown that individuals who are explicitly asked to analyze reasons about why or why not they would perform an act (thus increasing the salience of the act) are more likely to predict that they will perform the act (Wilson & LaFleur, 1995). Previous studies also suggest that salience increases the likelihood that the act is indeed performed; several studies show that asking people to predict whether they will undertake a target behavior increases the probability of performing that behavior compared to people who have not made such predictions (cf. Morwitz, Johnson, & Schmittlein, 1993). One explanation for this "mere-measurement effect" (sometimes referred to as the self-prophecy effect) is that the activity of measuring intentions (i.e., a request made by the researcher) makes intentions and related attitudes more accessible for the respondent, and this heightened level of accessibility fuels consistency mechanisms that serve to make the respondent's behavior consistent with cognitions (Spangenberg, Sprott, Grohmann, & Smith, 2003). Moreover, when behavior takes place in social settings, the individual is influenced by his/her beliefs about what other people believe to be correct or appropriate (i.e., normative beliefs), and such beliefs are assumed to become activated when faced with the task of predicting behavior (Sprott, Spangenberg, & Fisher, 2003). Existing theories are basically silent with regard to the effects of the behavioral effects of *different* ways of making the act salient (e.g., in terms of researchers who formulate their intention measures in terms of IE, IP, or IW), but if we assume that high self-determination propositions are less likely than low self-determination propositions to incorporate beliefs about what other people think is appropriate, and also assuming that much behavior takes place in a social environment, it seems as if behavioral expectations are likely to make acts particularly salient and thus that behavioral expectations have a comparatively larger effect on behavior than other intentions. Indeed, previous research shows that intentions-as-expectations outperform intentions-as-plans as behavioral predictors (cf. Sheppard et al., 1988; Warshaw & Davis, 1985).

Thus, given the capacity for increased salience of low self-determination propositions about future acts, and assuming that salience pushes response score upwards when an individual is faced by the task of formulating propositions about his/her future acts, we expect that response scores will take on increasingly high values as we move from IW to IE. In the following, we turn to an empirical attempt to assess the level of such response scores.

Research Method

Research Design

We selected one specific consumption act, watching one particular Swedish TV news program, as the point of departure for the data collection. The program is called Aktuellt, and it has been broadcasted on a daily basis since 1958. Similar to many other contemporary organizations whose main activities take place outside the Internet, it has a webpage. This webpage (accessible at www.svt.se) provides information about the program (a presentation of the staff, the program's history, and schedules), and the opportunity to watch (and re-watch) the most recent programs on-line. Nothing can be bought on this page, and there are no ads for other products; the web site provides television viewers with extra information. Indeed, its main function appears to be a relationship-building *vis-à-vis* existing viewers.

The data on intention levels were collected with a questionnaire designed in a way that is typical for much advertising effectiveness research. The first part measured the participant's frequency of watching Aktuellt and his/her satisfaction with the program. Next, the participant was instructed to study a color reproduction of Aktuellt's webpage. It contained a picture of the news anchors and a message from the editor-in-chief about the main characteristics of the Aktuellt program. After examining this information, the participant was asked to respond to some items related to his/her attitude towards the website, attitude towards the program – and his/her intentions to watch Aktuellt during the coming month.

The participants took part in marketing seminars within undergraduate and MBA programs. Groups from four different education programs were included in the study (n = 95). For each group, we distributed the questionnaires to the participants at the beginning of the seminar, we supervised the completion task, and we controlled the environment in the sense that no talking amongst participants was permitted. Moreover, responses to all questionnaire items were explicitly encouraged. This reduced nonresponse behavior to a minimum. Thus, a convenience sample was used, and the main rationale is that this study has theory application as a goal; the theoretical propositions we are assessing are general, and thus any respondent group can provide a test of the propositions. With this view, the representativeness of the sample is not a major issue, because if a theory is supposed to apply to consumers in general, it can be rejected if its predictions are falsified for any subgroup. Given the importance of falsification as a means to scientific progress, a relatively homogenous group of respondents is indeed desirable, because sample heterogeneity inflates error terms of statistical tests and reduces the chance of detecting systematic violations of a theory when it is false (Calder, Phillips, & Tybout, 1981).

Measures

With regard to the specific future act that an intention references, marketing scholars have examined several different acts (under the broad labels "intention" or "behavioral intention"), for example, searching for product information, purchasing a product for the first time, repurchases, word-of-mouth, and complaints. Here, however, we decided to focus on the individual's intentions to watch the Aktuellt program. This particular program was expected to be familiar to all respondents (indeed, this was the case, as revealed by the frequency-of-watching item in the questionnaire), so what we deal with here is akin to *repatronizing* intentions in existing literature. Moreover, a decision had to be made with regards to multiple-item or single-item operationalizations. On the one hand, a single-item approach means that reliability in terms of internal consistency cannot be computed, and in the typical case no other reliability assessment is made. This approach, then, means that a measure with unknown reliability may have a low level of reliability. On the other hand, however, many assessments of the attitude–intention link have been made with single-item intention scales (Sutton, 1998), and, Rossiter (2002) has strongly argued that intentions should not be captured with multi-item scales.

Given this, *intentions-as-expectations* were assessed using the following statement: "I will watch Aktuellt during the coming month" (1 = very unlikely,

10 = very likely). Similar items, with an emphasis on probability/likelihood, have been used in satisfaction-profit chain-related research by Boulding, Kalra, Staelin, and Zeithamll (1993) and Brady and Robertson (2001). Similar items also appear frequently in studies of web advertising effectiveness (cf. Kimfield & Watt, 2001; Li et al., 2002). *Intentions-as-plans* (IP) were assessed with the response to this statement: "I will choose to watch Aktuellt during the coming month" (1 = Do not agree at all, 10 = Agree completely). Intention items of this type, explicitly stressing "choose", appear in Taylor and Baker (1994). As indicated in the theoretical section on intentions-as-plans, however, other authors prefer items in terms of "will try to" (Ajzen & Madden, 1986), "plan to" (Morwitz et al., 1993), and "intend to" (Ajzen & Madden, 1986). Huizingh and Hoekstra (2003) is an example of authors who use IP when assessing web advertising effectiveness with an explicit "intend to" phrasing. Yet to date there is little empirical evidence about the potential for differences in the meaning of such items (except that some authors, who use multi-item scales in which several of these aspects are included, show that they are internally consistent in terms of high alphas). *Intentions-as-wants* were measured with this item: "I want to watch Aktuellt during the coming month" (1 = Do not agree at all, 10 = agree completely). Intention items with a specific "want-content" have been used by Fishbein and Stasson (1990) and Norman and Smith (1995).

It can be observed that the three intention items may appear similar to a respondent. Indeed, they may appear to be part of the same multi-item measure. Such measures are often advocated in literature on marketing research, and they are used so frequently that many respondents are likely to be familiar with them. However, they may foster a mindless response behavior in the sense that each item receives the same score. Given this, we believe that our intention measures provide us with inputs to a fairly strong test of theory; given the easiness with which the respondent may use the same response position for each item, actual differences in scores will signal, we believe, that there are indeed differences between the theoretical constructs represented by the individual items.

In addition, in order to assess the (nomological) validity of the intention measures, a measure of customer satisfaction was used (as a pretest measure, i.e., before the participants were exposed to the reproduction of the Aktuellt website). Because numerous studies have shown that satisfaction is positively associated with intentions, particularly intentions-as-expectations and intentions-as-plans, it was assumed that a reasonable level of validity would be at hand if the intentions measures in this study were positively and significantly correlated with the satisfaction measure. In order to measure satisfaction, then, the following question was asked: "Think about your accumulated experience during the past month of Aktuellt. How would you summarize your impressions of the program?" It was followed by three satisfaction items used in several national satisfaction barometers. Examples of specific studies in which the satisfaction scale consists of the three items are Fornell (1992) and Fornell, Johnson, Anderson, Cha, and Bryant (1996). These were the items: "How satisfied or dissatisfied are you with Aktuellt?" (1 = very dissatisfied, 10 = very satisfied), "To what extent does it meet your expectations?" (1 = not at all, 10 = totally), and "Imagine a television news program that is perfect in every respect. How near or far from this ideal do you find Aktuellt?" (1 = very far from, 10 = can not get any closer). Alpha for this scale was 0.82. And the satisfaction measure was indeed positively and significantly correlated with each of the three intention measures; the zero-order correlations ranged from 0.264 to 0.432 ($p < 0.01$ in each case).

Analysis and Results

The mean level reached by each of the three intention measures was computed, and the outcome is presented in Table 1.

In the following step, paired samples t tests were used to assess if the level of intention-as-plan (IP) measure (in our view, the traditional measure of intention in existing literature) differed significantly from the other two intention measures. This was indeed the case for each comparison, that is for IP versus IE ($p = 0.027$) and for IP versus IW ($p < 0.01$). This pattern of decreasing means is consistent with what Söderlund (2002) found in a study of airline passengers and also consistent with the Söderlund and Öhman (2003) results regarding restaurant visits. Obviously, and as predicted, it is easier for the marketer to obtain a high intention level when IE measures are used. It can be noted that each intention measure in the present study was positively and significantly associated with all other intention measures; the correlations ranged from 0.57 to 0.87 ($p < 0.01$ in each case). Yet at the same time they do reach different levels (and the main reason, we argue, is that they are located at different points on a self-determination continuum).

Table 1: The mean level of the intention measures.

Intentions-as-expectations (IE)	8.34
Intentions-as-plans (IP)	7.92
Intentions-as-wants (IW)	7.16

Discussion

Given that the frequent use – but also an incautious use – of intentions in assessing the future of customer relationships, the results obtained in this study imply that the investigator should make the selection of intention measures more explicitly than what has characterized measuring (and theorizing) attempts to date. From a practitioner's point of view, a careful selection is particularly important when goals (typically in terms of loyalty) are formulated in terms of intentions, and when goal outcomes are assessed by market research and monitored over time. In this case, then, the mere selection of one intention measure may provide a different picture of the customers' view of the future compared to the selection of another measure. And different pictures may imply different activities – and different levels of selected activities. For example, a measurement approach resulting in a high level of intention-as-expectations may signal that not much is needed in relationship marketing efforts ("We are approaching the ceiling of the scale, so we must be really good!"), but a low level of intention-as-wants may signal that much remains to be done in order to create viable relationships with customers ("Something must be wrong; there is only a modest level of willingness to come back to us again"). A provocative argument by Reichheld (2003) has been mentioned previously (i.e., an intention-as-expectation question may replace all other marketing research questions), and our three types of intention measures, and their implications, can be seen in light of what Reichheld suggests that the analyst should do with the responses to intention questions. Basically, he suggests that customers should be segmented with regards to their scores, and he also suggests that customers who score 9 or 10 on his 11-point scale, the "promoters", are particularly valuable. Furthermore, Reichheld claims that a main task for managers is to increase the number of promoters and to reduce the number of other customers. In our case, given this "top-box-approach" to scores and managerial action, the proportion of customers who score at least 9 or 10 varies considerably between the measures: 63 percent for IE, 49 percent for IP, and 41 percent for IW. Given Reichheld's approach and our data, then, it seems as if the need for action is heavily predicated on the specific intention measure one is using.

It should be noted that our study does not imply that one specific intention measure is "better" than any other; the main implication is that they are *different* in the sense that they appear to capture different aspects of the customer's assessment of his/her own future. Yet the finding that different measures reach different levels has some normative implications when it comes to management efforts involving intention measures – particularly goal setting in terms of explicit, quantitative levels (e.g., "Our goal is that 90 percent of our customers should claim that they want to use our services again"). It is often claimed that marketing-related goals should have motivational properties, in the sense that levels that are too easily reached may provide little motivation among employees. This implies that target levels formulated in terms of measures with relatively low self-determination content, such as intentions-as-expectations, may be associated with too little of a challenge.

In fact, one may ask what a firm should do – in terms of marketing efforts – if its goal is that customers should perceive that they are more or less forced to come back to the firm due to (from the customer's point of view) uncontrollable factors in the environment. Measures that take account of uncontrollable factors in the customer's environment may in fact shift the firm's attentions to factors that the firm may have little influence on, and given that control is related to motivation, the result may be a relatively low level of motivation among those whose task it is to deal with customers. Consider, instead, measures related to intention constructs located at the high end of the self-determination dimension, such as intention-as-wants: an employee who successfully enhances customer wants is likely to feel that he or she has really accomplished something.

References

Ajzen, I., & Fishbein, M. (1977). Attitude-behavior relations: A theoretical analysis and review of empirical research. *Psychological Bulletin, 84*(5), 888–918.

Ajzen, I., & Madden, T J. (1986). Prediction of goal-directed behavior: Attitudes, intentions, and perceived behavioral control. *Journal of Experimental Social Psychology. 22*, 453–474.

Ajzen, I. (1991). The theory of planned behavior, *Organizational behavior and human decision processes. 50*, 179–211.

Bandura, A. (1986). *Social foundations of thought and action: A social cognitive theory.* Englewood Cliffs, NJ: Prentice-Hall.

Boulding, W., Kalra, A., Staelin, R., & Zeithaml, VA. (1993). A dynamic process model of service quality: From expectations to behavioral intentions. *Journal of Marketing Research, XXX* (February), 7–23.

Brady, M. K., & Robertson, C. J. (2001). Searching for a consensus on the antecedent role of service quality and satisfaction: An exploratory cross-national study, *Journal of Business Research. 51*, 53–60.

Calder, B J., Phillips, L W., & Tybout, A M. (1981). Designing research for application. *Journal of Consumer Research, 8*, September, 197–207.

Csikszentmihalyi, M., & Graef, R. (1980). The experience of freedom in daily life. *American Journal of Community Psychology, 8*,(4), 401–414.

Fishbein, M., & Stasson, M. 1990. The role of desires, self-predictions, and perceived control in the prediction of training session attendance. *Journal of Applied Social Psychology, 20, (3)*, 173–198.

Fornell, C. (1992). A national satisfaction barometer: The Swedish experience, *Journal of Marketing*, *56*, January, 6–21.

Fornell, C., Johnson, M. D., Anderson, E. W., Cha, J., & Bryant, B. E. (1996). The American customer satisfaction index: Nature, purpose, and findings. *Journal of Marketing*, *60*, October, 7–18.

Heider, F. (1958). *The psychology of interpersonal relations*. New York: Wiley.

Howard, J.A. (1989). *Consumer behavior in marketing strategy*. Englewood Cliffs, New Jersey: Prentice-Hall.

Huizingh, E., & Hoekstra, J. C. (2003). Why do consumers like websites? *Journal of Targeting, Measurement and Analysis for Marketing*, *11*(4), 350–361.

Kimelfeld, Y. M., & Watt, J. H. (2001). The pragmatic value of on-line transactional advertising: A predictor of purchase intention. *Journal of Marketing Communications*, *7*, 137–157.

Li, H., Daugherty, T., & Biocca, F. (2002). Impact of 3-D advertising on product knowledge, brand attitude, and purchase intention: The mediating role of presence. *Journal of Advertising*, *XXXI*(3, Fall), 43–57.

Malle, B. F., & Knobe, J. (1997). The folk concept of intentionality. *Journal of Experimental Social Psychology*, *33*, 101–121.

Morwitz, V. G., Johnson, E., & Schmittlein, D. (1993). Does measuring intent change behavior? *Journal of Consumer Research*, *20*, June, 46–61.

Norman, P., & Smith, L. (1995). The theory of planned behaviour and exercise: An investigation into the role of prior behaviour, behavioural intentions and attitude variability. *European Journal of Social Psychology*, *25*, 403–415.

Notani, A. S. (1998). Moderators of perceived behavioral control's predictiveness in the theory of planned behavior: A meta-analysis. *Journal of Consumer Psychology*, *7*(3), 247–271.

Reichheld, F. F. (2003). The one number you need. *Harvard Business Review*, December, 46–54.

Rossiter, J. R. (2002). The C-OAR-SE procedure for scale development in marketing. *International Journal of Research in Marketing*, *19*(4), December, 305–417.

Sheppard, B. H., Hartwick, J., & Warshaw, P. R. (1988). The theory of reasoned action: A Meta-Analysis of past research with recommendations for modifications and future research. *Journal of Consumer Research*, *15*, December, 325–343.

Spangenberg, E. R., Sprott, D. E., Grohmann, B., & Smith, R. J. (2003). Mass-communicated prediction request: Practical application and a cognitive dissonance explanation for self-prophecy. *Journal of Marketing*, *67*, July, 47–62.

Sprott, D. E., Spangenberg, E. R., & Fisher, R. (2003). The importance of normative beliefs on the self-prophecy effect. *Journal of Applied Psychology*, *88*(3), 423–431.

Sutton, S. (1998). Predicting and explaining intentions and behavior: How well are we doing? *Journal of Applied Social Psychology*, *28*, 1317–1338.

Szymanski, D. M., & Henard, D. H. (2001). Customer satisfaction: A Meta-Analysis of the empirical evidence. *Journal of the Academy of Marketing Science*, *29*(1), 16–35.

Söderlund, M. (2002). Customer satisfaction and its effects on different behavioural intention constructs. *Journal of Customer Behaviour*, *1*, 145–166.

Söderlund, M. (2003). The retrospective and the prospective mind and the temporal framing of satisfaction. *European Journal of Marketing, 37*(10), 1375–1390.

Söderlund, M., & Öhman, N. (2003). Behavioral intentions in satisfaction research revisited. *Journal of Consumer Satisfaction, Dissatisfaction and Complaining Behavior, 16,* 53–66.

Söderlund, M., & Öhman, N. (2004). Caution in the use of different intention measures in service research. In: B. Edvardsson, A. Gustafsson, S.W. Brown, & R. Johnston (Eds), *Service Excellence in Management: Interdisciplinary contributions,* Proceedings from QUIS 9, Karlstad University, June 15–18, pp. 299–308.

Taylor, S. A., & Baker, T. L. (1994). An assessment of the relationship between service quality and customer satisfaction in the formations of consumers' purchase intentions. *Journal of Retailing, 70*(2), 163–178.

Warshaw, P. R., & Davis, F. D. (1985). Disentangling behavioral intention and behavioral expectation. *Journal of Experimental Social Psychology, 21,* 213–228.

Wilson, T. D., & LaFleur, S. J. (1995). Knowing what you'll do: Effects of analyzing reasons on self-prediction. *Journal of Personality and Social Psychology, 68*(1), 21–35.

Chapter 7

Business Networks: The Context for Firm Learning about Internet Use

Angelika Lindstrand and Kent Eriksson

Introduction

The internet is often considered a channel in isolation from other channels and also isolated from the context of firms that use the internet (Afuah, 2003; Sultan & Rohm, 2004). Most of the literature on how internet technology is used is based on theories of technology acceptance (Davis, 1989) or innovation adoption (Rogers 1995). These theories focus on the properties of the technology, and how these properties become accepted and used by those who are intended to use the technology. The innovation adoption model identifies the relative advantage of the technology, its complexity, compatibility, and trialability. The technology acceptance model (TAM), for instance focuses how behavioural use result from perceived usefulness and ease of use. The usefulness and ease of use, as perceived by the user depends on background factors, such as past experience, education, etc. Numerous empirical studies have verified that these models work in both (Venkatesh & Davis, 2000). However, recent developments have identified a gap in the previous studies, since they do not explicitly tie together perception and usage behaviour (Shih & Venkatesh, 2004). Findings of an exploratory study suggest that internet usage is tied together with the firm's value chain configuration, cost structure, customer relationships, and channels (Sultan & Rohm, 2004). Internet usage is thus tied in with the configuration of the firm's resources. Another study found that the initial use of services depends on the buyers' experience with a new distribution channel, but that the importance of such channel experience decreases over time (Carlson & Zmud, 1999). The same study found that experience with the communicating partner became increasingly an important determinant of use over time. It has also been found that internet makes product experience a more important factor when purchasing on the internet (Biswas & Biswas, 2004), and a replication of the TAM concluded that there is a need to focus product and service attributes in future research (Henderson & Divett, 2003). Taken together, it seems that use of the internet to do business is determined by the firm's resource configuration and experiences. This may provide a stronger explanation for the connection between perception and the use of internet, since perceptions are formed through experience by use of resources (Penrose, 1959). The purpose of this paper is thus to provide a better explanation of how perception led to the use of internet, and to do so by focusing on how experiences influence and how firms learn to use firm resources in a broader sense than just internet resources.

Surprisingly, and to the best of our knowledge, no studies have so far focused how internet technology is part of the firm learning from experiences. Theories of learning and experience have the potential to bridge the gap between perception and behaviour because they explicitly analyse how business practice routines are formed and changed (Walsh & Ungson, 1991; Hargadon & Sutton, 1997). This chapter analyses how firm learning can explain how firms make decisions concerning their use of the internet in exchange within their business network. In doing so, the chapter takes a different focus of analysis than most other studies do (Hoffman & Novak, 1996). This paper analyses firm learning in general, and states that internet technology is a part of this learning, albeit one of many parts. Most other studies state that learning about the technology is the important part. However, for firms that engage in exchange with customers, learning about the technology is only one part of the exchange. This is further emphasized by Prahalad and Ramaswamy (2004), who argue that a trend in the internet market is that value is co-created by buyers and sellers when they match the resources of their respective networks and that this is a highly experience-based process.

The chapter first discusses the TAM, then learning from routines in networks, and concludes by suggesting a new model for the study of internet use.

The Technology Acceptance Model

TAM explains why people use new technologies. It is specifically designed for the adoption of information-technology-related products. The model is depicted in Figure 1, and it identifies that the behavioural intention to use a system leads

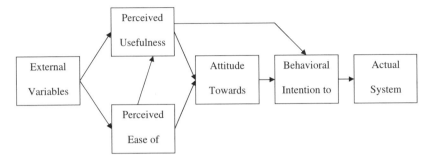

Figure 1: Technology acceptance model (from Davis, 1989).

to actual system use. Behavioural intention is an attitude where the user is committed to engage in use of the technology. Behavioural intention to use is caused by a positive attitude towards use and a perceived usefulness. The key components of TAM are perceived usefulness and perceived ease of use. The perceived usefulness is defined as "the extent to which a person finds that using the system will enhance his or her job performance" (Doll, Hendrickson, & Deng, 1998). The usefulness of knowledge is the ability of the knowledge to provide decision-makers with a rationale upon which to make their decisions, and thereby to promote action. The usefulness of knowledge is related to using particular knowledge in a particular decision-making situation.

The perceived ease of use is defined as "the extent to which a person believes that using the system will be free of effort" (Doll et al., 1998). External variables refer to background variables, such as education, age, and context of technology use.

Numerous empirical studies have found that TAM consistently explains a substantial proportion of the variance (typically about 40%) in behaviour and intention to use IT (Venkatesh & Davis, 2000). Davis (1989) pointed out the prominence of perceived usefulness: users are driven to adopt an application primarily because of the functions it performs for them and secondarily by how easy or hard it is to get the system to perform those functions. It means that a high score on ease of use can never compensate for a system that users perceive useless.

Learning and Knowledge in Firms

In a world of ever-changing markets, a crucial objective for firms is to identify and exploit business opportunities in their external environments (Shane & Venkatraman, 2000; Hitt, Ireland, Camp, & Sexton, 2001). The usefulness of the internet is connected to the opportunities that come with it. External factors, such as the environment and the business network surrounding the firm determine the opportunities associated with the internet. Firms must focus on how to adapt to environmental change and to exploit opportunities that will create value and growth for the organization, whether in local or foreign markets (McDougall & Oviatt, 2000). In a firm's quest to exploit opportunities, knowledge becomes one of the most critical competitive factors (Grant, 1996; Kogut & Zander, 1992; Spender, 1996).

In her *Theory of the Growth of the Firm*, Penrose (1959) considered knowledge gained from experience, or experiential knowledge, as an important determinant of the firm's growth and exploitation of entrepreneurial opportunities. Subsequent studies have elaborated the role of experiential knowledge (Johanson & Vahlne, 1977, 1990) and have provided empirical support for its importance in firm learning (Delios & Beamish, 1999), firm learning on how to use technology in general (Tyre & von Hippel, 1997), and firm learning of how to use the internet (Eriksson, Nilsson, & Kerem, 2005).

The accumulation of learning and knowledge for firms has been an interest for researchers and practitioners for many years. The general assumption that "learning will improve performance" has guided most theorists of organizational learning (Fiol & Lyles, 1985). Duncan and Weiss (1979) define knowledge accumulation or learning as "the process within the organization by which knowledge about action-outcome relationships and the effect of the environment on these relationships is developed" (p. 84). This implies that for learning to occur the firm must find the knowledge potentially useful (Huber, 1991). This ability to find knowledge useful is largely a result of how the firm is able to relate prior experiences to its present business activities (Cohen & Levinthal, 1990).

Firms learn by engaging in business activities; and as a consequence, they gain knowledge from their experiences (Zahra, Ireland, & Hitt, 2000). Experience of the internet is an ambiguous concept because it refers both to experience of the exchange content and of the delivery channel. For instance, experiences determine how partners assess exchange, through one or multiple channels, and how they perceive channel richness (Carlson & Zmud, 1999). Exchange is often done in a channel, making determination of which experience, is the important one, that of content or that of delivering, is especially difficult. Experience has, *per se*, been operationalized as relationship duration and interaction frequency (Levinthal & Fichman, 1988). Similarly, theories of social practice also hold that more use leads to more automatic and taken-for-granted behaviour (Brown & Duguid, 2001). A study showed that buyers' experience with the internet is important when they start to use a service, but that the importance of such channel experience decrease over time (Carlson & Zmud, 1999). This result indicates that experiences with the internet are important at first, but that they decreases in importance relative to the benefits of other factors as the buyer continues learning to exchange in the new way. The same study found that experience with the seller's business offering became increasingly important over time. Even though experience with the channel decreases in importance, the understanding and exchange with the seller becomes more important. Perhaps the consumer feels more confident about the medium for exchange, and starts to focus on the content and the potential for value addition in the relationship as a whole. The process of learning (for firms) is dynamic, involving a number of steps, including knowledge acquisition (what knowledge is obtained), information distribution (what information is shared with others), information interpretation (what meaning is given to the shared information), and information storing (in organizational memory) for future use (Huber, 1991).

The experiences a firm undergoes are later stored in the firm's organizational memory (Argyris & Schön, 1978; Walsh & Ungson, 1991). The storage of knowledge is important for the firm. Without it the firm must undergo similar experiences (knowledge acquisitions) over and over again. The storage of knowledge thus becomes cost effective and helps the firm in future decision-making, but in being the firm's knowledge base, the stored knowledge is also important for the firm's specific capabilities in that it affects its competitiveness. These effects of stored knowledge will not come about without retrieval of knowledge from the firm's organizational memory (Huber, 1991; Walsh & Ungson, 1991). Afuah (2003) argues that the internet expands organizational boundaries, which implies that the organizational memory becomes increasingly dispersed by use of the internet.

Theory-in-use, Routines, and Levels of Learning

Organizations store knowledge in their procedures, norms, rules, and forms (March, 1991), and these routines are frequently an inseparable combination of internet technology, organizational structure, and social interaction (Orlikowski et al., 1995). In that way learning is constrained by existing ways of perceiving, interpreting, and doing things, which Argyris and Schön (1978) have labeled the firm's theory-in-use. This theory-in-use (shared interpretation) is embedded in the technical and non-technical operating procedures, internal routines, norms, values, strategies, and behaviours of an organization as well as its external organizational actions such as products, promotion, and distribution (Argyris & Schön, 1978; Fiol & Lyles, 1985; March & Simon, 1958). Theory-in-use, inferred from observations of how people actually behave, implies an understanding of how things are done, and therefore it affects knowledge acquisition, interpretation, storage, and retrieval (Argyris & Schön, 1978; Corsini, 1996; Cyert & March, 1963; Huber, 1991; Shrivastava & Schneider, 1984; Walsh & Ungson, 1991). Learning occurs for an organization when it responds to changes in its environment, detects errors, and takes actions to correct them. A firm's theory-in-use determines what knowledge it perceives as being useful in the process of responding to environmental changes. Theories-in-use thus represent deeply embedded routines for both applied knowledge and learning practices (Argyris & Schön, 1978). A firm's theory-in-use helps it interpret and understand cause and effect relationships, and thus guides it behaviour. The reasoning behind stored knowledge and theory-in-use serving as the fundamental guides of future behaviour is closely connected to the organizational routines of the firm, in that much of a firm's stored knowledge is deposited in routines (Cyert & March, 1963; Cohen, 1991; Levitt & March, 1988; March & Simon, 1958; Nelson & Winter, 1982). Because a firm typically applies its knowledge in the process of doing business (Kogut & Zander, 1993), this applied knowledge can be described as the firm's routine for doing business.

Routines provide a way for the firm to retrieve knowledge from its organizational memory. By storing organizational experience, routines allow organizations to quickly transfer that experience to new situations. Routines are vital, because a large share of an organization's activities is carried out through routines (Cyert & March, 1963; March & Simon, 1958), which gives structure to the organization and to its behaviour.

Even though routines make up much of the structure for business activities, this does not mean that routines are static and cannot change. Feldman (2000) suggests that routines are not static but instead works in progress. Feldman writes that, from her observations, "organizational routines involve people doing things, reflecting in what they are doing, and doing different things (or doing the same things differently) as a result of the reflection" (p. 625). Thus, routines store knowledge and at the same time provide a basis for new learning. This type of learning, which maintains the central features of an organization's theory-in-use and restricts itself to detecting and correcting errors within that theory-in-use, has been referred to as single-loop learning (Argyris & Schön, 1978) or exploitation of existing knowledge (March, 1991). Single-loop learning, which concerns refinement, selection, implementation, and execution, relies heavily on routines.

A higher order type of learning, referred to as double-loop learning or exploration, involves a modification of an organization's underlying norms, policies, and objectives (Argyris & Schön, 1978; March, 1991). The result from double-loop learning has long-term effects and impacts on the organizations as a whole. This type of learning occurs when error is detected and corrected in ways that aim at adjusting the firm's theory-in-use, rather than specific activities or behaviours, and thus double-loop learning is the exploration of new possibilities.

Networks

The internet promotes the network form of organizing in three ways: first it expands organizational boundaries since it makes it possible to outsource some production that has traditionally been done in-house, and to internalize certain production that has been done externally (Afuah, 2003). Second, it moves production towards the interface of the buyer and seller, where they co-create value by matching the resources of their respective networks (Prahalad & Ramaswamy, 2004). Third, the internet promotes the growth of firms that perform a mediating function by supporting network infrastructure, i.e., telecom, banks, online retailers, etc., (Stabell & Fjeldstad, 1998; Sarkar, Butler, & Steinfeld, 1998). Internet-related business accentuates the role of interactivity and networks, which means that the performance of a firm is not solely a result of the firm itself (Essler & Whitaker, 2001). Firms must also rely on resources coming from outside the firm. The external resources that help the firm develop its performance are often supplied by other firms. Access to external resources is contingent upon firm participation in business relationships, where firms exchange resources with one another. Because of the multitude of relationships that firms are engaged in, they become embedded in business networks (Achrol & Kotler, 1999; Ahuja, 2000; Anderson Håkansson, & Johanson, 1994; Hallén, Johanson & Seyed-Mohamed, 1991; Granovetter, 1985; Larson, 1992). Network embeddedness makes it essential, for understanding a firm's behaviour, to include as a critical element the network within which a firm acts. A study of European and US e-business found that the successful ones enable their buyers to exchange more in their own network (Amit & Zott, 2001).

A firm's business network consists of a limited number of links to a variety of actors, such as suppliers, subsuppliers, customers, customers' customers, and competitors. Each firm is thus engaged in a set of business relationships in which it coordinates its activities and resources with counterparts, based on their activities and resources (Blankenburg-Holm & Johanson, 1992). The connectedness of firm activities and the resources those activities employ makes the firm's network relationships interdependent (Anderson et al., 1994). Interdependent activities and resources, such as production, administrative activities, social relations, technology, and knowledge need to be adapted and coordinated to bring about a better match between the firms within a network (Hallén et al., 1991). Studies of internet-based research point to the importance of integrating the network of connected actors and the content that these actors actually desire (Stabell & Fjeldstad, 1998).

Because of adaptation, cooperation, and coordination in a business network, network relationships between firms will influence strategic decisions, performances, and business developments of the firms (Dyer & Singh, 1998; Håkansson & Snehota, 1995). A prerequisite for this influence is the existence of trust and commitment between the relationships in the network, and these factors becomes even more important in internet business (Brynjolfsson & Smith, 2000). Adaptation and coordination between a business relationship and the network will not come about without some commitment by the relationship and its embedded network (Ahuja, 2000). The internet blurs the boundaries between the organization and the network, which makes it more important to consider the network and the organization together when it comes to firm learning (Holland & Lockett, 1997).

Network Knowledge

In a firm's quest for exploitation of business opportunities, knowledge to attain this is needed. Coordination of activities and use of resources require knowledge as well. When interacting with the environment, firms collect knowledge concerning counterparts, competitors, cooperation with other firms, product development, strategies, marketing channels, organizing practices, international ventures, etc. Much of the knowledge utilized in a firm is available through its relationships with other firms in a network (Burt, 1997; Granovetter, 1985; Gulati, 1998, 1999; Kraatz, 1998; Rowley, Behrens, & Krackhardt , 2000; Stuart, 1998). This idea is supported by Powell, Koput, and Smith-Doerr (1996), who found that a complex network of interconnections is required for innovations to occur in the biotechnology industry, and that no single relationship is more instrumental than another in this knowledge-creating process. Dyer and Nobeoka (2000) conclude, in a study of Toyota and its knowledge-sharing network, that the network is not only an important unit of analysis for explaining a firm's competitive advantage, but also "can be more effective than a firm at the generation, transfer, recombination of knowledge" (p. 364). The main reason for this superiority is the greater diversity of knowledge within a network compared to a firm (Dyer & Nobeoka, 2000). By means of business networks, viewed as information reservoirs, firms learn over time through social exchange processes, to cooperate and thereby coordinate their activities. This capacity to interact increases a firm's access to knowledge, to transfer of knowledge, and to integration of knowledge residing both inside and outside of the firm (Lorenzoni & Lipparini, 1999). The internet accentuates the use of networks, both in terms of number of connected actors and the intensity of relevant information exchange between them (Afuah & Tucci, 2001), and consequently, internet-based network knowledge becomes both more dispersed and more accessible.

In studies concerning firms' business developments, emphasis has been placed on business network relationships as the primary vehicle for resource commitment and experiential knowledge generation (Chen & Chen, 1998; Blankenburg-Holm, Eriksson, & Johanson, 1996; Johanson & Vahlne, 1990). Market knowledge is assumed to be based on experience from current business network activities, or on current business interactions with firms in the network. A firm's relationships within business networks are shown to be very important assets. Learning through experience in interactions seems to concern the components of the network, in terms of basic questions such as who are the actors and who is doing business with whom? (Axelsson & Johanson, 1992). The experience gained within a network contains information about how to handle and coordinate business with counterparts: what services and products are included, how to produce these, which channels are useful, how to adapt to customer and supplier needs, which costs and benefits are associated with the counterpart, where knowledge resides in the network, and how all of this will affect the performance of the firm. Hargadon and Sutton (1999) describe a firm, specialized in product development, as a broker of knowledge between different parts of a network. In relation to some counterparts, the firm exploits solutions made and knowledge acquired through business relationships with other counterparts. A prerequisite for such use of business networks is the storage of knowledge in the firm's organizational memory. What has been learned in one or more network relationships is stored and then retrieved through routines for later use in other network relationships for the development of new products geared to other customers (Hargadon & Sutton, 1997). In this manner the knowledge gained in the network affects the future performance of the firm through its organizational routines. By being an efficient mode of network, the internet can mitigate underinvestment (Nault, 1997), increase efficiency in value-chain links, business relationships, and reduce costs (Sultan & Rohm, 2004). Internet-based network connections benefit from that the network may be easily accessed in terms of whom to connect with, but there is still a need for routines of exchange to exist before the content of the exchange adds value to the actors. Routines for exchange that include the context of the internet are thus instrumental to network development and configuration (Orlikowski Yates, Okamura, & Fujimoto, 1995).

Network Knowledge and Performance

Given that a large part of a firm's knowledge accumulation takes place within its network relationships, these relationships and the knowledge within them are the primary vehicles for the firm's development and performance (Dyer & Singh, 1998; Rowley et al., 2000). The effects of network experience on firm performance have been discussed in terms of innovation (Ahuja, 2000; Hargadon & Sutton, 1997; Powell et al., 1996), alliance formation (Gulati, 1998, 1999; Stuart, 1998), systems competition (Katz & Shapiro, 1994), and acquisitions (Beckman & Haunschild, 2002).

Uzzi (1997) states that the knowledge developed in embedded relationships and in joint problem solving between firms improves for a participating firm its economy of time, allocative efficiency, adaptation, and investment. Accordingly, products reach the market faster by matching consumer demand to production (Uzzi, 1997). Often the experience from interaction and the capability to interact accelerates the focal firm's knowledge access and transfer, yielding significant effects on company growth and innovation (Lorenzoni & Lipparini, 1999). The creation and sharing of knowledge in a network can also affect efficiency, as in relative productivity advantages for all participating parties (Dyer & Nobeoka, 2000). Blankenburg-Holm et al. (1996) and Blankenburg-Holm, Eriksson, and Johanson (1999) show that the embeddedness of relationships in networks increases commitment in relationships, and indirectly increases profitability and value creation for the firms in the relationship.

Perceived Usefulness of Network Knowledge

"Usefulness of knowledge" implies "the perceived potential the information has for usage" (Menon & Varadarajan, 1992, p. 66). Usefulness is related to the use of knowledge in the firm's business activities. The accumulated knowledge of a firm represents past experiences, which are then related and used to solve problems in current business activities (Cohen & Levinthal, 1990). The perceived usefulness of a firm's knowledge, which is closely connected to the firm's learning process, depends therefore on its ability to solve today's business problems and to exploit business opportunities.

The usefulness of knowledge is recognized through interaction with other actors in the network. This interaction generates experiences that increase the knowledge of how to use the information (i.e., future usefulness) (Venkatesh & Davis, 2000). The usefulness of knowledge is related to using particular knowledge in a particular decision-making situation. The perceived usefulness of knowledge in a decision-making situation is contingent upon (1) the perceived meaningfulness of particular knowledge (does it make sense to the user), (2) the perceived goal relevance (how is the knowledge related to the task at hand), (3) the perceived operational validity (can anything be done with the knowledge), and (4) the innovativeness (how new or non-obvious is the knowledge)

(Shrivastava, 1987). The perceived usefulness of particular knowledge by decision-makers implies that the knowledge stored in firms can be retrieved from where it is stored.

Connected to the retrieval of particular knowledge is a firm's theory-in-use and routines, which clarify underlying cause-and-effect relationships and which also guide firm behaviour, including how information will be interpreted and what information will be perceived as useful. The perception of what knowledge, within a firm's store of acquired knowledge is useful, is important for analysing and resolving problems, since particular knowledge used by decision-makers is likely to influence the final outcome or performance of the firm. A firm's theory-in-use determines what the firm perceives as being useful knowledge, as it seeks solutions to its problems in the context of what it has done in the past (Cyert & March, 1963). A firm's perceived usefulness of knowledge thus represents deeply embedded routines for applied knowledge about and from business networks, and for learning practices, which come into play as the firm searches for means of learning about specific relationships or networks.

Suggesting that a certain piece of knowledge is perceived as useful does not, however, mean that the perception is necessarily correct. Menon and Varadarajan (1992, p. 66) propose that one conclusion to be drawn is that credibility of knowledge is important, and thus they state that "its usefulness is a necessary and, in many cases perhaps even a sufficient, condition for use." The perceived usefulness of knowledge is particularly important because it has been found to be a good predictor of user behaviour (Davis, Bagozzi, & Warshaw, 1989; Venkatesh & Davis, 2000).

A Framework for the Role of the Internet in Networks

The expectations for future events and for the possible opportunities that lie within those expected events guide firm behaviour. Business opportunities that involve the internet are likely to concern intermediary business models, where buyers and sellers co-create value by matching their respective networks (Stabell & Fjeldstad, 1998; Prahalad & Ramaswamy, 2004). When firms encounter a business opportunity, they need knowledge to exploit it. To exploit opportunities that involve the internet, knowledge is needed both about the number of connections that can be reached *via* the internet, and the content that is exchanged in those connections (Afuah & Tucci, 2001). In seeking the opportunity, a firm will consider how useful its existing capabilities and knowledge are. These capabilities include the firm's current internet competency (Tippins & Sohi, 2003). Thus, opportunities will guide selection of knowledge that a firm perceives as useful in its business activities. According to Cyert and March (1963), useful knowledge can be found in the vicinity of the current alternative, that is, in the firm's already successfully applied options. For instance, small and medium-sized export firms that expand internationally with much involvement of the internet, are young, aggressive, and expansive (Moen, 2002). These firms follow the mode of expansion that they have found successful. This means that particular knowledge, perceived as useful, can be found in a firm's accumulated knowledge and routines (i.e., in its theory-in-use). The firm's evaluation of whether knowledge in the form of routines is useful or not is based on anticipated profit (Nelson & Winter, 1982). In the internet case, profits can be anticipated from very new ways of conceptualizing business (Sharma & Sheth, 2002), which are all based on intermediation in networks. Thus, business opportunities guide the perceived usefulness of routines, given that the concept of business opportunity includes the notion of anticipated profit.

We argued earlier that much of a firm's useful knowledge is derived from its experiences of activities within the network. For instance, a study of bed and breakfast (B&B) owners suggested that they use the internet only for advertisements to foreign guests (Lituchy & Rail, 2000). It seems logical then that a firm wanting to exploit an opportunity will find network experiential knowledge useful. The B&B firms would find experience of audio and video internet customer contact, feedback solicitation, foreign language application, and local supplier referal useful to determine which of these are best apt to expand customer business (Lituchy & Rail, 2000). What the firm has learned in the past becomes incorporated into routines for determining how to handle the network.

Because of the effect that network knowledge has on a firm's performance, we suggest that there exist routines that are specific for handling the network, which we define as network routines. The internet promotes formation of network routines both by standardization, such as through Microsoft products, and through unique configurations for each interactive user through co-creation (Kiang, Raghu, & Shang, 2000). These network routines may concern cooperation and adaptation (within the network), which will facilitate coordination of activities and resources between involved parties. For instance, the internet brings new ways to coordinate activities since some functions previously made within the firm can be outsourced to a market, whereas others that were previously made by other firms can be internalized within the firm (Holland & Lockett, 1997). Network routines are developed through experience gained by interaction within networks, whereby firms learn which network configuration give them the most benefit in the form of knowledge and performance. The internet provides opportunity for the intermediary network configuration to become particularly more important (Sarkar et al., 1998).

We propose that the business opportunities a firm encounters will affect the perceived usefulness of network routines (Figure 2). A firm that encounters a business opportunity will perceive a certain degree of usefulness in its network routines and network configurations because they are its capability for developing business. The usefulness of network routines determines how routines for doing business *via* the internet and other channels is done. Through performance evaluation, a firm can come to realize that new learning through interaction in the network is needed instead. This can be a complex evaluation where the internet may be an important factor in different ways, such as in negotiation, purchase, and post-purchase support. For instance, customer preference for banking *via* the internet depends both on the channel and the content, and in both aspects, both the customer and the bank have their own network routines. This is a complex situation, where exchange is best achieved by a match between customer and bank (Morrison & Roberts, 1998).

This chapter has put the internet into the perspective of the firms learning about how to do business. The key concepts used in models, such as the TAM are valid also in this model, only they are incorporated into the wider context of how firms pursue growth through perceived business opportunities. We argue that the internet should be understood in the context of business, since it determines how the internet is integrated into the routines of doing business. In doing so, we clarify the effect that the perception of the internet has on actual firm behaviour on the internet.

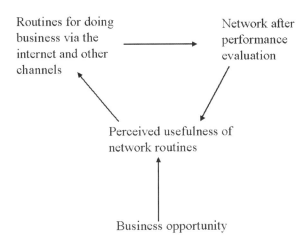

Figure 2: Framework for firm learning through the formation of network routines.

References

Achrol, R., & Kotler, P. (1999). Marketing in the network economy. *Journal of Marketing*, *63*, 146–163.

Afuah, A. (2003). Redefining firm boundaries in the face of the internet: Are firms really shrinking? *Academy of Management Review*, *26*(1), 34–53.

Afuah, A., & Tucci, C. (2001). *Internet business models and strategies: Text and cases.* New York, NY: McGraw-Hill Irwin.

Ahuja, G. (2000). Collaboration networks, structural holes, and innovation: A longitudinal study. *Administrative Science Quarterly*, *45*, 425–455.

Amit, R. & Zott, C. (2001). Value creation in e-business. *Strategic Management Journal*, *22*, 493–520.

Anderson, J.C., James, C., Håkansson, H., & Johanson, J. (1994). Dyadic business relationships within a business network context. *Journal of Marketing*, *58*, 1–15.

Argyris, C., & Schön, D.A. (1978). *Organizational learning: A theory of action perspective.* Reading, MA:Addison-Wesley.

Artman, H., & Zall, S. (2005) Finding a way to usability. *Cognition, Technology and Work*, *7*, 6.

Autio, E., Sapienza, H.J., & Almeida, J.G. (2000). Effects of age at entry, knowledge intensity, and imitability on international growth. *Academy of Management Journal*, *41*(5), 909–924.

Axelsson, B., & Johanson, J. (1992). Foreign market entry — The textbook vs. the network view. In: B. Axelsson, & G. Easton (Eds), *Industrial networks. A new view of reality.* London: Routledge.

Barkema, G.H., & Vermeulen, F. (1998). International expansion through start-up or acquisition: A learning perspective. *Academy of Management Journal*, *41*(1), 7–26.

Beckman C.M., & Haunschild, P.R. (2002). Network learning: The effects of partners' heterogeneity of experience on corporate acquisitions. *Administrative Science Quarterly*, *47*, 92–124.

Biswas, D., & Biswas, A. (2004). The diagnostic role of signals in the context of perceived risks in online shopping: Do signals matter more on the web. *Journal of Interactive Marketing*, *18*(3), 30–45.

Blankenburg-Holm, D., Eriksson, K., & Johanson, J. (1996). Business networks and cooperation in international business relationships. *Journal of International Business Studies*, *27*(5), 1033–1053.

Blankenburg-Holm, D., Eriksson, K., & Johanson, J. (1999). Creating value through mutual commitment to business network relationships. *Strategic Management Journal*, *20*, 467–486.

Blankenburg-Holm, D., & Johanson, J. (1992). Managing network connections in international business. *Scandinavian International Business Review*, *1*(1), 5–19.

Brown, J.S., & Duguid, P. (1991). Organizational learning and communities of practice: Toward a unified view of working, learning and innovation. *Oraganization Science*, *2*(1), 40–57.

Brynjolfsson E., & Smith, M. (2000). Frictionless commerce? A comparison of internet and conventional retailers. *Management Science, 46*(4), 563–585.

Burt, R.S. (1992). *Structural holes. The social structure of competition.* Cambridge, MA: Harvard University Press.

Burt, R.S. (1997). The contingent value of social capital. *Administrative Science Quarterly, 42,* 339–365.

Carlson, J.R., & Zmud, R.W. (1999). Channel expansion theory and the experiential nature of media richness perceptions. *Academy of Management Journal, 42*(2), 153–170.

Chen, H., & Chen, T.-J. (1998). Network linkages and location choice in foreign direct investment. *Journal of International Business Studies, 29*(3), 445–467.

Cohen, M. (1991). Individual learning and organizational routine: Emerging directions. *Organization Science, 2*(1), 135–139.

Cohen, M.D., & Bacdayan, P. (1994), Organizational routines are stored as procedural memory: Evidence from a laboratory study. *Organization Science, 5*(4), 554–568.

Cohen, W.M., & Levinthal, D.A. (1990). Absorptive capacity: A new perspective on learning and innovation. *Administrative Science Quarterly, 35*(1), 128–152.

Cook, K.S., & Emerson, R.M. (1984). Exchange networks and the analysis of complex organizations. *Research in the sociology of organizations* (Vol. 3, pp. 1–30). Greenwich: JAI Press.

Corsini, R. (1996). *Concise encyclopedia of psychology.* New York: Wiley.

Cyert, R.M., & March, J.G. (1963). *A behavioural theory of the firm.* New York: Prentice-Hall.

Daft, R.L., & Weick, K.E. (1994). Toward a model of organizations as interpretation systems. *Academy of Management Review, 9*(April), 284–295.

Davis, F.D. (1989). Perceived usefulness, perceived ease of use, and user acceptance of information technology. *MIS Quarterly, 13*(September), 319–340.

Davis, F.D., Bagozzi, R.P., & Warshaw, P.R. (1989). User acceptance of computer technology: A comparison of two theoretical models. *Management Science, 35*(8), 982–1003.

Delios, A., & Beamish, P. (1999). Ownership strategy of Japanese firms, transactional, institutional and experience influences. *Strategic Management Journal, 20,* 915–933.

Deshpande, R., & Zaltman, G. (1982). Factors affecting the use of market research information: A path analysis. *Journal of Marketing Research, 19*(February), 14–31.

Deshpande, R., & Zaltman, G. (1987). A comparison of factors affecting use of marketing information in consumer and industrial firms. *Journal of Marketing Research, 24*(February), 114–118.

Doll, W.J., Hendrickson, A., & Deng, X. (1998). Using Davis's perceived usefulness and ease-of-use instruments for decision making: A confirmatory and multigroup invariance analysis. *Decision Sciences Journal, 29*(4), 839–869.

Duncan, R., & Weiss, A. (1979). Organizational learning: Implications for organizational design. In: B. Staw, & L.L. Cummings (Eds), *Research in organizational behavior* (Vol. 1, pp. 75–132), Greenwich, CT: JAI.

Dyer, J., & Nobeoka, K. (2000). Creating and maintaining a high-performance knowledge-sharing network: The Toyota case. *Strategic Management Journal, 21*(3), 345–367.

Dyer, J., & Singh, H. (1998). The relational view: Cooperative strategy and sources of interorganizational competitive advantage. *The Academy of Management Review, 23*(2), 660–679.

Emerson, R.M. (1981). Social exchange theory. In: M. Rosenberg, & R. Turner (Eds), *Social psychology: Sociological perspectives*. New York: Basic Books.

Eriksson, K., Hohenthal, J., & Johanson, J. (1998). A model of learning in international business networks. In: *Yearbook 1998: Learning*. Wissenshaftszentrum Berlin.

Eriksson, K., Kerem, K., & Nilsson, D. (2005). Customer acceptance of internet banking in estonia. *International Journal of Bank Marketing, 23*(2), 200–216.

Erramilli, M.K. (1991). The experience factor in foreign market entry behavior of service firms. *Journal of International Business Studies, 22*(3), 479–501.

Essler, U., & Whitaker, R. (2001). Re-thinking e-commerce business modelling in terms of interactivity. *Electronic Markets, 11*(1), 10–16.

Feldman, M.S. (2000). Organizational routines as a source of continuous change. *Organization Science, 11*(6), 611–629.

Fiol, C.M., & Lyles, M.A. (1985). Organizational learning. *Academy of Management Review, 10*(4), 803–813.

Granovetter, M. (1973). The strength of weak ties. *American Journal of Sociology, 78*(6), 1360–1380.

Granovetter, M. (1985). Economic action and social structure: The problem of embeddedness, *American Journal of Sociology, 91*, 481–510.

Grant, R.M. (1996). Toward a knowledge-based theory of the firm. *Strategic Management Journal, 17*(Winter special issue), *109–122.*

Gulati, R. (1998). The architecture of cooperation: Managing coordination costs and appropriation concerns in strategic alliances. *Administrative Science Quarterly, 43*(4), 781–814.

Gulati, R. (1999). Alliances and networks. *Strategic Management Journal, 19*(4), 293–317.

Håkansson, H., & Snehota, I. (1995). Developing relationships in business networks. London: Routledge.

Hallén, L., Johanson, J., & Seyed-Mohamed, N. (1991). Interfirm adaptation in business relationships. *Journal of Marketing, 55*(April), 23–37.

Hargadon, A., & Sutton, R.I. (1997). Technology brokering and innovation in a product development firm. *Administrative Science Quarterly, 42*(4), 716–749.

Henderson, R.M., & Clark, K.B. (1990). Architectural innovation: The reconfiguration of existing product technologies and the failure of established firms. *Administrative Science Quarterly, 35*, 9–30.

Henderson, R., & Divett, M.J. (2003). Perceived usefulness, ease of use and electronic supermarket use. *International Journal of Human-Computer Studies, 59*, 383–395.

Hitt, M.A., Ireland, R.D., Camp, S.M., & Sexton, D.L. (2001). Guest editors introduction to the special issue strategic entrepreneurship: Entrepreneurial strategies for wealth creation. *Strategic Management Journal, 22,* 479–491.

Hoffman, D.L., & Novak, T.P. (1996) Marketing in hypermedia computer-mediated environments: Conceptual foundations. *Journal of Marketing, 60,* 50–68.

Holland, C.P., & Lockett, A.G. (1997). Mixed mode network structures: The strategic use of electronic communication by organizations. *Organization Science, 8*(5), 475–488.

Huber, G.P. (1991) Organizational learning: The contributing processes and the literatures. *Organization Science, 2*(February), 88–115.

Johanson, J., & Mattsson, L.-G. (1988). Internationalization in industrial systems: A network approach. In: N. Hood, & J.-E. Vahlne (Eds), *Strategies in global competition.* New York: Croom Helm.

Johanson, J., & Vahlne, J.-E. (1977). The internationalization process of the firm: A model of knowledge development and increasing foreign market commitments. *Journal of International Business Studies, 8*(1), 23–32.

Johanson, J., & Vahlne, J.-E. (1990). The mechanism of internationalization. *International Marketing Review, 7*(4), 1–24.

Katz, M.L., & Shapiro, C. (1994). Systems competition and network effects. *The Journal of Economic Perspectives, 8*(2), 93–115.

Kiang, M., Raghu, T., & Shang, K. (2000). Marketing on the internet — Who can benefit from an online marketing approach. *Decision Support Systems, 27,* 383–393.

Kogut, B., & Zander, U. (1992). Knowledge of the firm, combinative capabilities, and the replication of technology. *Organization Science, 3*(3), 383–397.

Kraatz, M.S. (1998). Learning by association? Interorganizational networks and adaptation to environmental change. *Academy of Management Journal, 41*(6), 621–643.

Larson, A. (1992). Network dyads in entrepreneurial settings: A study of the governance of exchange relationships. *Administrative Science Quarterly, 37,* 76–104.

Lea, M., O'Shea, T., & Fung, P. (1995). Constructing the networked organization: Content and context in the development of electronic communications. *Organization Science, 6*(4), 462–478.

Levinthal, D.A., & Fichman, M. (1988). Dynamics of interorganizational attachments: Auditor–client relationships. *Administrative Science Quarterly 33,* 345–369.

Levitt, B., & March, J.G. (1988). Organizational learning. In: W.R. Scott, & J. Blake (Eds), *Annual review of sociology* (pp. 31–40). Palo Alto, CA: Annual Reviews Inc.

Lindstrand, A. (2003). How to use network experience in ongoing international business. In: A. Blomstermo, & D.D. Sharma (Eds), *Learning in the internationalization process of firms.* UK: Edward Elgar.

Lituchy, T., & Rail, A. (2000). Bed and breakfasts, small inns, and the internet: The impact of technology on the globalization of small businesses. *Journal of International Marketing, 8*(2), 86–97.

Lorenzoni, G., & Lipparini, A. (1999). The leveraging of interfirm relationships as a distinctive organizational capability: A longitudinal study. *Strategic Management Journal, 20,* 317–338.

Luo, Y., & Peng, M.W. (1999). Learning to compete in a transition economy: Experience, environment and performance, *Journal of International Business Studies*, *30*(2), 269–296.

Madhok, A. (1997). Cost, value and foreign market entry mode: The transaction and the firm. *Strategic Management Journal*, *18*(1), 39–61.

March, J.G. (1991). Exploration and exploitation in organizational learning. *Organization Science*, *2*(1), 71–87.

March, J.G., & Simon, H.A. (1958). *Organizations*. New York: Wiley.

McDougall, P.P., & Oviatt, B.M. (2000). International entrepreneurship: The intersection of two research paths. *Academy of Management Journal*, *43*(5), 902–906.

Menon, A., & Varadarajan, P.R. (1992). A model of marketing knowledge use within firms. *Journal of Marketing*, *56*, 53–71.

Moen, O. (2002).The internet and international marketing: An empirical analysis of small and medium sized Norwegian firms. *Quarterly Journal of Electronic Commerce*, *3*(1), 31–41.

Morrison, P., & Roberts, J. (1998). Matching electronic distribution channels to product characteristics: The role of congruence in consideration set formation. *Journal of Business Research*, *41*, 223–229.

Nault, B. (1997). Mitigating underinvestment through and IT-enabled organization form. *Organization Science*, *8*(3), 223–234.

Nelson, R., & Winter, S. (1982). *An evolutionary theory of Economic change*. Cambridge, MA: Belknapp Press.

Orlikowski, W.J., Yates, J., Okamura, K., & Fujimoto, M. (1995) Shaping electronic communication: The metastructuring of technology in the context of use. *Organization Science*, *6*(4), 423–444.

Penrose, E.T. (1959). *The theory of the growth of the firm*. Oxford: Basil Blackwell.

Pentland, B.T., & Reuter, H.H. (1994). Organizational routines as grammars of action. *Administrative Science Quarterly*, *39*(3), 484–510.

Powell, W.W., Koput, K.W., & Smith-Doerr, L. (1996). Interorganizational collaboration and the locus of innovation: Networks of learning in Biotechnology. *Administrative Science Quarterly*, *41*, 116–145.

Prahalad C.K., & Ramaswamy, V. (2004). Co-creation experiences: The next practice in value creation. *Journal of Interactive Marketing*, *18*(3), 5–14.

Rindfleisch, A., & Moorman, C. (2001). The acquisition and utilization of information in new product alliances: A strength-of-ties perspective. *Journal of Marketing*, *65*, 1–18.

Rogers, E.M. (1995). *Diffusion of innovations*. (4th ed.) New York: The Free Press.

Rowley, T., Behrens, D., & Krackhardt, D. (2000). Redundant governance structures: An analysis of structural and relational embeddedness in the steel semiconductor industries. *Strategic Management Journal*, *21*(3), 369–386.

Sarkar, M., Butler, B., & Steinfeld, C. (1998). Cybermediaries in electronic marketspace: Toward theory building. *Journal of Business Research*, *41*, 215–221.

Shane, S., & Venkataraman, S. (2000). The promise of entrepreneurship as a field of research. *Academy of Management Review*, *25*(1), 217–226.

Sharma, A., & Sheth, J. (2002). Web-based marketing — The coming revolution in marketing thought and strategy. *Journal of Business Research, 22*, 1–23.

Sharma, D.D., & Johanson, J. (1987). Technical consultancy in internationalisation', *International Marketing Review, 4*(Winter), 20–29.

Shih, C.-F., S.C., & Venkatesh, A. (2004). Beyond adoption: Development and appliation of a use-diffusion model. *Journal of Marketing, 68*, 59–72.

Shrivastava, P. (1987). Rigor and practical usefulness of research in strategic management. *Strategic Management Journal, 8*(1), 77–92.

Shrivastava, P., & Schneider, S. (1984). Organizational frames of references. *Human Relations, 37*(10), 795–809.

Spender, J.-C. (1996) Making knowledge the basis of a dynamic theory of the firm. *Strategic Management Journal, 17*(1), 45–62.

Stabell, C.B., & Fjeldstad. Ø.D. (1998). Configuring value for competitive advantage: On chains, shops, and networks. *Strategic Management Journal, 19*(5) 413–437.

Stuart, T.E. (1998). Network positions and propensities to collaborate: An investigation of strategic alliance formation in a high-technology industry. *Administrative Science Quarterly, 43*, 668–698.

Sultan, F., & Rohm, A. (2004). The evolving role of the internet in marketing strategy: An exploratory study. *Journal of Interactive Marketing, 18*(2), 6–19.

Tippins, M., & Sohi, R. (2003). IT competency and firm performance: Is organizational learning a missing link? *Strategic Management Journal, 24*, 745–761.

Tyre, M.J., & von Hippel, E. (1997). The situated nature of adaptive learning in organizations. *Organization Science, 8*(1), 71–83.

Uzzi, B. (1997). Social structure and competition: The paradox of embeddedness. *Administrative Science Quarterly, 42*, 35–67.

Venkatesh, V., & Davis, F.D. (2000). A theoretical extension of the technology acceptance model: Four longitudinal field studies. *Management Science, 46*(2), 186–205.

Walsh, J.P., & Ungson, G.R. (1991) Organizational memory. *Academy of Management Review, 16*, 57–91.

Zahra, S.A., Ireland, D.R., & Hitt, M.A. (2000). International expansion by new venture firms: International diversity, mode of market entry, technological learning and performance. *Academy of Management Journal, 43*, 925–950.

Chapter 8

Airlines' Internet Marketing Channels: Antecedents to Customer Relationships

Daniel L. Grenblad

The Airline Ticket

This chapter examines the problem area of managing customer relationships in Internet-based marketing channels. Marketing channels can be defined as "...sets of interdependent organizations involved in the process of making a product or service available for consumption or use" (Sterns, El-Ansary, & Coughlan, 1996, p. 1).

Companies have several formats of marketing channels they can use and need to manage (Stern, et al., 1996). The Internet is now established as a commercial media and investments are often said to be made in "the online channel." But, is the Internet one monolithic marketing channel? This is the first research question that this chapter will address by analyzing an airline industry case. The chapter also uses the case to give a partial answer to the second research question: What are the antecedents to customer relationships when Internet-based marketing channels are used?

The case is primarily based on interviews with a total of 25 airline and travel agent representatives in the USA and Sweden conducted in 1999, 2003, and 2004. Most of the interviewed representatives are from traditional airlines. Low-cost airlines are fewer, but still represented. The results are applicable on both airline categories. Secondary sources have supplemented the interviews.

Three reasons make airlines interesting to study regarding Internet-based marketing channels: First, the airline industry is information intense (Porter & Millar, 1985), making valuable commercial use of the Internet highly feasible with its information-handling capacities. Second, as the Internet was beginning to be used

Managing Customer Relationships on the Internet
Copyright © 2006 by Elsevier Ltd.
All rights of reproduction in any form reserved
ISBN: 0-08-044124-6

commercially in the mid-1999s, airlines were among those early pioneers and have since then gained relatively long experience. Thirdly, the airline industry has gained success in using Internet commercially, measured as the ratio of sales from online to offline.

Furthermore, the situation in the airline industry makes customer relationships interesting for actors in that industry as well. Price has become an important factor, if not the most important, when buying airline tickets — second only to safety. Several factors have led to this situation. The deregulation of the industry that started in 1978 in the USA and 1992 in Europe continues and puts prices under competitive pressure and market forces, resulting in price decreases. Differentiation (Levitt, 1980) was low between the traditional airlines, which has led to the commoditization of the product offering and an increased price sensitivity among the ticket buyers. New low-cost airlines entered the market, further increasing the pressure for the incumbent airlines operating according to the "traditional" business model. Both the traditional airlines and low-cost airlines face buyers who perceive price as a primary decision variable during purchase. For airline practitioners, Internet and customer relationship management is a possible marketing strategy to become less price dependent and offer an alternative basis to compete. Academic research can benefit from increased knowledge of customer relationships, especially over the Internet where the power in the marketing channel might be shifted toward the customer (Bauer, Grether, & Leach, 2002). It has been proposed to enlarge the scope of the quality factors of the customer relationship by considering more antecedents to relationships (Wiertz, Ruyter, Keen, & Streukens, 2004).

Several delimitations are made in this presentation. The relationship between an airline and its end-customers are in focus; other relationships are only briefly discussed as a part of the analysis of the focal relationship. The airlines in this chapter refer to scheduled airlines. Charter, freight, and taxi airlines are excluded. Other actors that sell tickets, such as airline's ticket offices, call centers, consolidators, and tour operators are outside the scope of this chapter. It is only relationships for commercial purposes that are analyzed. The stages before the customer's awareness (Dwyer, Schurr, & Oh, 1987) of the airline are not considered in the chapter. Instead, the analysis assumes that there is at least an evaluation of alternative airlines taking place, based on a need for flying.

Airlines' Different Internet Marketing Channels

There are different organizations involved in the airlines' ticket sales on the Internet, some of these are presented below as types of actor roles. Each of these actor roles represents groups of actors, who are connected in a network of relationships (see Figure 1). Are these actors forming one marketing channel? In other words, is the Internet one monolithic marketing channel for airlines?

Airlines are here referring specifically to the scheduled airlines, as mentioned earlier. Global Distribution Systems (*GDS*) are the aggregators that gather the Airlines' and other travel producers' offerings in one place and make them available to travel retail sellers equipped with a suitable computer system. In essence, the GDS sell ticket information distribution to the Airlines and information access to the travel agents. Airlines began to develop GDS jointly in groups of Airlines. It resulted in four major GDS companies: Amadeus, Galileo, Sabre, and Worldspan. For a long time, the dominant way of selling Airline tickets was through the GDS to Traditional Travel Agents, like Airline of type "A." *Traditional Travel Agents* refers to the brick-and-mortar travel agents that have a broad range of products in categories such as airlines, hotels, car rental, and so on.

Four types of Internet seller actors have been identified. *Agent Web* is a travel agent with Internet as a customer interface that sells different Airlines' tickets, makes hotel and car reservations etc. Three sub-categories of Agent Web actors are: (a) the web-only agent, (b) the traditional physical travel agent that has added

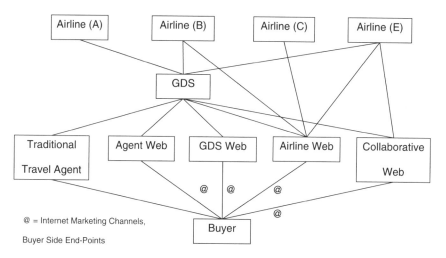

Figure 1: Airlines' internet marketing channels. *Source*: Adapted from Dembrower and Grenblad (2003) and Grenblad and Rosén (1999)
Note: A marketing channel's graph illustrating alternatives that Airlines can use to sell and distribute tickets. Airlines (A) through (D) depict typical ways of using the Traditional Travel Agents and Internet sellers.

an additional customer interface on the web, and (c) the *GDS Web* which is owned by a GDS, the wholesaler, and makes the GDS information and tickets available directly to the buyer. The GDS Web is drawn separately in Figure 2 due to the ownership link, even though it functions like an Agent Web. *Airline Web* is a web interface owned and operated within an airline's organization. The Airline Web often only offers its own tickets. Some of the Airline Webs also have other airlines' tickets to offer, in which case tickets on airlines in the same alliance are more commonly offered. The tickets are either taken directly from the airline's own inventory, or taken indirectly through the GDS. In the mid-1990s, Airlines started to use web sites operated by themselves to sell tickets in addition to the GDS channel, as depicted by "Airline B." One of the pioneers was British Midland, which started to sell tickets online in January 1995. Some low-cost carriers chose to only sell through their own Airline Web to cut transaction costs associated with ticket sales. The lowest cost occurs when the retail web site is directly linked to the Airline's inventory, like "Airline C." Some Airlines still use a GDS, even for their Airline Web (Dembrower & Grenblad, 2003; Grenblad & Rosén, 1999).

The Internet opportunities also gave birth to a new form of collaboration between Airlines, where they created a joint-venture web site, *Cooperative Web*. In this case, there is a mix of directly connected Airlines and airlines indirectly connected through a GDS. Several Airlines' tickets are aggregated to one web site and then sold on the web site directly to the end-customer. Airlines involved as an owner of a Cooperative web is shown as "Airline D." Today, the traditional Airlines use several marketing channels simultaneously, and buyers alternate their choice of channels for purchases (Dembrower & Grenblad, 2003).

It is important to make the distinction that the Internet is an infrastructure/media and is not in itself alone a marketing channel. Equally important to note is that the Internet is not always hosting only one of the seller's marketing channels, but several, which becomes evident after investigating the airline industry case. As shown above, selling airline tickets through the Internet involves several different types of actors interconnected differently, in other words there are several marketing channel types or formats on the Internet. Each actor type in turn consists of different actors/companies, this means that there are several marketing channels in each format. An implication is that when managing marketing investments, it is not enough to decide to allocate investments to "the Internet"; it needs to be more specific. In addition, it is also relatively easy to switch between Internet-based marketing channels, since an alternative channel and/or competing offer is "just one click away" for the buyer. Understanding the different formats of Internet-based marketing channels is therefore crucial. Cost cutting was initially a key driver for using the Internet as a means to sell

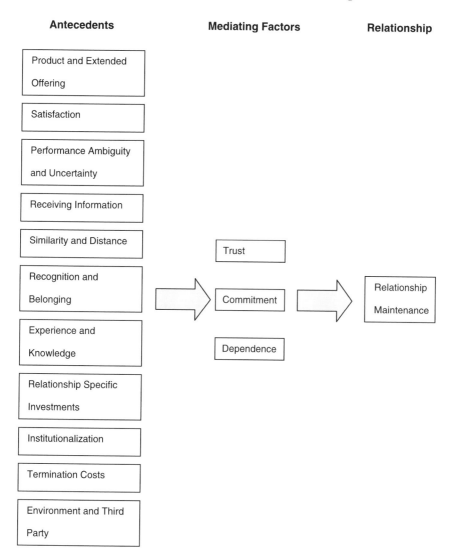

Figure 2: A model for relationship maintenance.
Note: Selected antecedents leading to relationship maintenance, from a combination of relationship marketing and market-as-network theories.

airline tickets. Today, the relationship aspect and customer equity is likely to increase in importance due to a new competitive situation, as mentioned in the introduction. The airlines' customer relationships will be analyzed next by closer examination of the antecedents to relationship maintenance in the Internet-based marketing channels described above.

Marketing and Relationships

In marketing strategy, a major challenge lies in allocating financial and other resources for marketing purposes, for instance between marketing channels. When marketing expenditures result in assets rather than costs, they become an investment. Relationships are a type of asset that makes marketing an investment, rather than a cost (Grönroos, 2003; Mattsson, 1997). One element of customer equity is Customer relationships, which are suggested to be prioritized among the customer equity elements (Blattberg & Deighton, 1996; Rust, Lemon, & Zeithaml, 2004). Customer relationships can exist independent of the two other customer equity elements: the offering's value and the brand (Lemon, Rust, & Zeithaml, 2001). When a company wants to invest in customer relationships, it can in practice be done through one or more marketing channels such as those on the Internet. Through effectiveness and efficiency, high returns on the marketing investments are aimed for.

Marketing theory can assist in these efforts; especially two theory schools are promising in the context of managing relationships. Exchange (Bagozzi, 1975), rather than discrete transaction, is the foundation for both the markets-as-networks approach (Hammarkvist, Håkansson, & Mattsson, 1982; IMP Group, 1982) and the relationship marketing approach (Berry, 1983; Grönroos, 1994; Gummesson, 1987, 1995), or more stringently, relationship marketing management (El-Ansary, 2005). In this chapter, these research siblings are treated as one theoretical school, whereby relationship marketing theory is enriched by contributions from markets-as-networks theory, despite that they have some inconsistent assumptions. Commercial relationships are fundamental in both research approaches and therefore deemed suitable for the purpose of this chapter. Moreover, it has been proposed that an increased research interaction between relationship marketing and the market-as-networks approach would offer much to gain (Mattsson, 1997).

In its limited form, exchange-based marketing theory only treats customer–supplier relationships, while more extensive forms also treat relationship between other entities (Egan, 2003; Mattsson, 1997). For example, in relationship marketing with an extensive scope, the relationships can be described as belonging to one of at least 10 different types (Morgan & Hunt, 1994), or even 30 (Gummesson, 1995), when classified according to the entities involved. The relationship in focus here is the one between the focal firm (the airline) and the end-customer. As described by Bonoma (1982), the buying roles performed by individuals in companies may include both a buyer and an user. For business trips, the individual who buys the ticket could be a travel manager, and the user of the ticket could be a sales executive traveling to meet a prospect. In many instances, other people in companies have also played a role in purchasing. There could be already existing purchasing agreements with resellers and suppliers of the travel service that combined with company travel policy guide the purchasing decision. For leisure trips, a similar situation might be at hand. Purchasing decisions for vacations are often made jointly by spouses in a household (Davis & Rigaux, 1974). This means that several individuals can be involved on the buying side in the case of airline ticket purchasing. Here the main attention is on the buyer, that is, the one who books and pays for the ticket.

A purpose of the airline's investments in marketing channels is to maintain a relationship with the end-customer, the buyer. Customer relationships have been defined somewhat differently, I make the following interpretation and definition of the term:

> *A customer relationship is a commercially-based interaction between a buyer and a seller with ongoing exchanges of resources and/or cross-entity activity processes.*

The actors directly involved in a customer relationship are the customer and the seller. They interact over time by communicating in different ways. Typically, several episodes of exchanges leading to commercial transactions occur during the period of interaction. Here, there is a transfer of title and possession of airline tickets. Other relationships affect the customer relationship indirectly.

One definition of relationship marketing is "…all activities directed toward establishing, developing, and maintaining successful relational exchanges" (Morgan & Hunt, 1994, p. 22). These three general sub-objectives are in large directly comparable with those of customer equity management, which simplified is described as customer acquisition, relationships expansion, and customer retention (Blattberg, Getz, & Pelofsky, 2001). Relationship marketing uses relationship maintenance as a term for keeping a relationship, which is the desirable causal outcome — if it is or will be profitable. Positive or increased relationship maintenance effects make the relationship last. Trust and commitment are suggested as mediating factors resulting in different levels of relationship maintenance (Morgan & Hunt, 1994). Dependence is a possible third mediating factor to relationship maintenance (Bendapudi & Berry, 1997). A question that immediately arises is: What "sources" lead to trust, commitment, and dependence? There are a number of such suggested anteceding factors. These antecedents are more concrete areas where marketing investments can be allocated to and are subsequently this chapter's focus. The mediating factors are not discussed further.

A successful marketing investment is one that increases profitable relationship maintenance and thus customer equity. Some antecedents that can increase relationship maintenance and are applicable to Internet-based marketing channels are selected for analysis of the case. These antecedents are grouped in 11 themes (see Figure 2) and are further described below in the context of the empirical data. Some of the antecedent themes come from relationship-marketing literature, including: product value, satisfaction, performance ambiguity, receiving information, similarity, relationship-specific investments, recognition and bonding, and termination costs. The market-as-networks literature enriches these themes with overlapping antecedents in the same or corresponding themes: extended offering (resources and process), satisfaction, uncertainty, distance, and transaction-specific investments. Some additional themes treated by the market-as-networks literature include: experience, institutionalization, and environment and third party. Identifying antecedents to relationships are difficult because many of these factors are also described as outcomes of interaction, they are "dependent" (IMP Group, 1982). Disregarding this possible tautological challenge, the selected antecedents can be compared across each marketing channel on two levels of relationship maintenance effects:

- A first-level relationship maintenance effect occurs when the absolute level of each relationship antecedent positively influences a relationship by making a transaction episode more likely. That is, does it make a single purchase transaction in the marketing channel more likely than in other channels?
- Second-level relationship maintenance effect occurs when the relationship antecedent is making increasingly favorable contributions to the relationship maintenance as the relationship exists for a longer period. That is, if it is more favorable with a relationship compared with a single transaction episode. Or put differently, is it worth it to enter a relationship, or is it better to "shop around" for each purchase? After a long enough time or when extensive resources are invested, second-level maintenance effects can cause a lock-in to the relationship.

Customer Relationship Antecedents in the Airline Case

What are the antecedents to customer relationships when Internet-based marketing channels are used? More specifically, what effects do the antecedents have on the maintenance of a customer relationship in the respective marketing channel? Each antecedent is analyzed in isolation; the combined effects of several antecedents in interplay might be different. Also note, it is the respective marketing channel format that is analyzed, not each actor or actor role as an isolated entity in a marketing channel.

Product and extended offering When the customer believes that the company's products match well with her/his needs, relationship maintenance is positively affected (Rust et al., 2004). The Agent Web allows the Traditional Travel Agent to achieve cost advantages by using the Internet and thereby avoiding costs associated with physical retail offices and staff. However, this is compared with the physical store. When an Airline Web bypasses the GDS and connects directly to their own inventory, it can lower costs even further than the Agent Web. The Airline Web can increase the value of the product offering through cost savings of up to between 10 and 15% of the ticket price, compared with the Traditional Travel Agent channel offline (Grenblad & Rosén, 1999). The Collaborative Web can achieve the same level of transaction costs. Owing to the higher efficiency in this marketing channel and the resulting lower prices, some buyers will prefer to buy from the Airline Web or Collaborative Web. This higher product value would suggest repeat purchases and relationship maintenance. Still, this advantage in the channel does not differentiate between buyers who perform single transaction episodes and continuous exchange episodes in a relationship; it only results in the first-level relationship maintenance effects. As noted earlier, the product offering is outside the scope of this chapter. For example, issues like changing destinations or aircraft seats are not considered here. However, the marketing channels are still affecting the product in its extended sense. As a result, the effect of the marketing channels are worth considering, since relationship maintenance can increase if the supplier provides resources that are superior compared with competing alternatives (Morgan & Hunt, 1994). With a direct channel to the buyer, the airline can provide resources and services in a more controlled way that increase value further. This in turn, can augment (Levitt, 1980) the product offering with purchase and/or consumption process support and contribute to increased competitiveness through product differentiation, such as advance seat selection and Internet check-in. Some of these services can be "learned" by the Airline Web as it is used over time and pre-selected when a repeat purchase happens. In this way, the, airline creates second-level relationship maintenance effects. In addition to making a value judgment as a fit between the buyer needs and the focal supplier offering, the value judgment can also be made on a comparative basis. Relationship maintenance increases if the value of the product is superior compared with competing alternatives (Anderson & Narus, 1990; Morgan & Hunt,

1994). For the Agent Web, this represents a possible advantage, since it often has a broader assortment of alternative suppliers to compare and choose from than the Airline Web. Some Airline Webs do allow for this as well, but providing a broader supplier assortment in the default search option is seldom the case in the booking process for Airline Webs. The Agent Web does this as normal procedure and can therefore appear more neutral. While the Airline Web offers depth of information, the Agent Web offers breadth of information. In parallel to the offering, the processes around the purchase can influence the relationship positively if they fit the buyer's processes (Ford, 1980). The activity of travel includes much more than the air travel alone. Obviously, there are often ground transportations and lodging requirements too. Less obvious perhaps is that companies have an average travel administration cost of 6–8% of the air ticket price (American Express, 1999, 2003). One interviewed intermediary presented an example of a large Swedish company with an estimated travel administration cost as high as 30% on top of direct costs of the various tickets, lodging, and car rental fees, and so on. Direct and indirect travel costs are substantial enough to receive attention in a company. These rank third in importance among the controllable costs and before advertising (American Express, 1999). The Traditional Travel Agent, and to an increasing degree the Agent Web, offer processes that improve the buying organization's travel administration and management — for example, by enforcement of travel policies and reporting expenses.

Satisfaction   Satisfaction aspects influence relationship maintenance both before and after usage of the offering. If the customer's rating of the overall quality of the supplier is high, it leads to increased relationship maintenance (Rust et al., 2004). The right expectation level can be better set by controlling the information given prior to the usage of the airline's services, so that the perceived delivered service is on par with or exceeds expectations and results in positive satisfaction. This speaks in favor of the Airline Web as a tool for the airline to achieve satisfaction among buyers. On the other hand, third-party marketing channels can be perceived as neutral and giving unbiased advice on the different airline's offerings, which suggest that Agent Web or GDS Web channels would in this sense be more suitable for managing satisfaction from the buyers' perspective. In cases where the Traditional Travel Agent, Agent Web, or GDS Web suggest or recommend the use of an airline that later leads to dissatisfaction, it is thereby hurting their own brands. Also, if the customer's past experience(s) of the product and/or interaction is positive it increases relationship maintenance (Bendapudi & Berry, 1997). As noted above on product value, the airline can better influence the delivered offering in broad terms in the Airline Web channel. Putting the offering aside and only evaluating the purchasing interaction, which might have taken place in any of the marketing channels; it is a possible source for second-level relationship maintenance effects as well. If a buyer is satisfied with a past purchase from one marketing channel, there is an increasing likelihood that it will be reused. If a buyer is unsatisfied, but perceives that she/he will be satisfied in future exchange episodes, it strengthens relationship maintenance (Ford, 1980; Turnbull, Ford, & Cunningham, 1996). An unsatisfied buyer can more easily register a complaint and get reassurance of improvements and/or compensation, if a direct marketing channel is used such as Airline Web.

Performance ambiguity and uncertainty   When the customer perceives that the performance of the product and/or interaction is difficult to evaluate prior to the consumption, the ambiguity favors continuous exchange episodes with the same supplier (Bendapudi & Berry, 1997). This aspect suggests that the buyer tends to stay in a relationship once it is entered into and knowledge of the product has been acquired through experience. Since services are produced and consumed simultaneously (Rathmell, 1966), it is difficult to evaluate them prior to consumption. Direct contact with the buyer can make it easier for the airline to offer peripheral cues (Shostack, 1977) to the quality of their service. With the Airline Web, the airline can better handle the performance ambiguity that exists. The uncertainty on the offer's value diminishes over time in a relationship (Ford, 1980), which means that a second-level relationship maintenance effect can occur.

Receiving information   If the customer is frequently confronted with the supplier's advertising and direct mailing, which she/he gives attention to, it is positive for relationship maintenance (Rust et al., 2004). Relationships are strengthened when the supplier provides information on changes and the supplier communicates its expectations on the customer's actions to her/him (Morgan & Hunt, 1994). The buyer can receive timelier and more complete information from the producer of the service regarding relevant changes, such as departure time and allocated aircraft, when a direct channel is used such as Airline Web. In this way, the supplier can also better provide information directly on its expectations on the customer, such as arriving at check-in 40 min prior to departure.

Similarity and distance   The relationship maintenance increases when there is similarity between buyer and supplier. For example, the customer believes that the image of the supplier fits her/his personality, or the customer believes that the supplier has high ethical values regarding customers and employees (Rust et al., 2004). Similarly, relationship maintenance increases if the customer's stated values are similar to the customer's belief of the supplier's values regarding corresponding issues (Morgan & Hunt, 1994). The airline can better influence its image and present its ethical values when communicating directly to the buyer over the Airline Web. There can be spillover effects from a third-party's brand affecting the image of the airline indirectly, suggesting that Agent Web or Traditional Travel Agent channels would also influence this mechanism. Hence, it is important for some airlines to be on an approved list of partners among certain travel agents. In spite of this, the Agent Web typically does not provide information related to similarity, such as the airline's image versus the buyer's personality or match of ethical values. The focus is instead on safety, ticket price, schedule, and route network aspects of each respective airline instead. However, there is a limit for how similar the parties can be since the basis for the exchange is a need complementarity (Johanson & Mattsson, 1985; Turnbull et al., 1996), in other words being different. Mutual goals (Wilson, 1995) can balance the similarity versus difference in other traits of the buyer and seller in a cooperative customer relationship, which is easier to achieve solutions for in a direct channel such as the Agent Web.

Recognition and belonging   Two types of affiliation increase the relationship maintenance: first, customer–supplier affiliation, in which the customer perceives that she/he is recognized as unique and special by the supplier, not just one of many, and second, customer–customer affiliation, in which the customer feels that she/he has affiliations with other customers common to the supplier by being in the same community (Rust et al., 2004). The Airline Web seems to be superior in making the buyer feel more recognized as unique and special for at least two reasons: first, the airline can better tailor the offering and communication to the individual buyer with a direct and unfiltered channel, and second, agents have shifted away from selling airline's tickets (seller's side advocacy) and moved towards giving advice to the customers on purchasing (buyer's side advocacy). This partially explains why the agents are not interested in supporting recognition between a single airline and the buyer. The recognition and feeling of belonging is more likely to occur with the agent instead of the airline when the Traditional Travel Agent or Agent Web is used. None of the airlines' marketing channel formats have yet been found to use the latter mechanism of offering buyer-to-buyer interaction over the Internet, even though some actors have considered it. Travel Agents limit themselves to perform airline customer surveys that are made available to their customers as written reports.

Experience and knowledge   Relationship maintenance is positively influenced by knowledge held by each of the parties about the other party and/or the interaction, for example: through experience or otherwise, the customer perceives that she/he posses knowledge about the procedures of using the supplier's products. Likewise if, the customer perceives that the supplier has a lot of information about her/him. (Rust et al., 2004) Experience from the focal relationship with the counterpart will affect the relationship evaluation, along with experiences from third parties in other relationships (Ford, 1980). Traditional Travel Agents are the older of the marketing channels and represent accumulated knowledge of how airline tickets are bought. Those who are experienced travelers and have used the airline services several times might perceive a lower total uncertainty and could therefore be willing to accept a higher risk when purchasing tickets by trying out a new marketing channel. Inertia, however, works against this.

Relationship specific investments   Termination of the relationship is less likely if it means a loss of relationship-specific investments (RSI) that have been made (Bendapudi & Berry, 1997), which also have been labeled (durable) transaction-specific investments (Ford, 1980). Relationship maintenance increases when the investing partner is seen as more committed by the other party for whom the adaptations are made. Furthermore, it can be expected that the investing partner becomes more dependent on the relationship, since the rationale of making the investment is to receive future returns. Adaptations are made both deliberately and undeliberately (IMP Group, 1982). The relationship is less likely to be terminated if the customer has investments in a loyalty program accrued from purchasing from the supplier repeatedly, such as mileage points that can be converted into a ticket, and terminating the relationship will result in a loss of that asset. The customer receives higher service level/preferential treatment due to a loyalty program. When there is some effort associated with the process of information acquisition or transfer to the other party, there can be a RSI effect. The experience and knowledge section above treated the absolute level at a certain time and the consequences on assessing the offer and partner. On the other hand, the RSI aspect includes, among other things, the process of reaching of a certain level of knowledge and the asset it represents. A buyer might invest time and effort on a web site to enter personal and company data, preferences for a ticket search engine, or creating profiles for reoccurring configurations of purchased products. Over time, the airline will have a lot of information, entered by the buyer and collected through usage, on the customer that can be reused through the Airline Web. Compare this with the augmented offering and the related value increase above. The airline can also make RSI on their side; the information system the airline has invested in for the Airline Web can favorably demonstrate the airline's commitment to the customer as perceived by the buyer. This is especially true for larger buyers for whom the adaptations of the IT-system for information exchange between the parties can be implemented. But, already the standardized interface can contribute to this effect when it is perceived that the design investments are made with the specific buyer in mind. A third-party's investment in their web sites cannot be expected to increase the airline–customer relationship maintenance due to RSI, while the Airline Web is better positioned to add positive effects. RSI can, as exemplified, result in second-level maintenance effects. They can even cause a lock-in to the relationship, for example, when the RSI are extensive adaptations for a specific buyer that are useless to other potential buyers.

Institutionalization The norms and procedures that guide the episodes can influence the relationship maintenance both positively and negatively (Ford, 1980). Over time, companies could adopt a taken-for-granted view on which marketing channel to use. Routines emerge over time to guide actions and decisions in organizations as a response to recurring situations (Simon, 1945). A travel agent could have a travel office set up on the buyer's location that is perceived as a part of the buyer's own organization. If this physical travel agent also has an Agent Web, it could routinely be used due to institutionalization originating from the physical presence at the buyer's location. For a leisure traveler, personal routines could also develop. One family might perceive that the traditional Christmas trip not only includes going to the family cottage in the Alps. Other routines associated with the preparing for the trip, such as high tea at the Grand Hotel next to the travel agent where the tickets are picked up, would also be a necessary part of the whole meaning of "the Christmas trip." An Agent Web is more likely to develop an institutionalized agent–buyer relationship, since the episodes of interaction are potentially more frequent, resulting from other purchases being made there, such as rail tickets. Third-party suppliers influence the airline–buyer relationships in other ways too, as described below.

Termination costs Here, termination costs are switching costs that do not increase with continued usage of the company's products and maintenance of the relationship, as is the case with RSI. Termination costs include searching for and qualifying a new supplier. The Agent Web, with its broader selection of offerings, is typically better positioned in the case of a customer switching airlines. In effect, the Airline Web can retain its relationship with the customer. The focal airline, on the other hand, loses the interaction both in the purchasing and usage process. As noted earlier, some of the Airline Web actors do offer tickets on other airlines than their own. In this case, the focal airline can maintain a relationship with the buyer, even though a competing offering is bought, and the airline can later benefit as the customer returns as for subsequent travel.

Environment and third party The availability of alternative partners and other traits of the market influence the relationship. Indirect relationships to other actors are influential on the focal relationship (Ford, 1980). The GDSs were designed in the 1960s and 1970s and built using mainframe computer technology. Not only are they large and highly complex systems, but people with the required programming skills are also rare to find today on the labor market. As a result, the legacy IT systems of the GDS are difficult to change and to adapt to new market situations. They were originally designed with the business traveler in mind, who was less price sensitive and more interested in schedule as buying criteria. In addition, the price levels at the time were government regulated and instead of market-driven. Today, the price is a primary buying criteria on the demand side and competitive force on the supply side. A technological change for information management allowed for a new solution in the Collaborative Web channel, which better corresponds to the needs of today. Past or predicted actions of third parties are thus also affecting the focal dyad (Ford, 1980). The industry's structure consists of several airlines that are competing fiercely for the buyers and a subsequent relationship with them. In light of this, it might seem surprising to find them simultaneously cooperating to create a Collaborative Web marketing channel. A partial explanation lays in the changes in the environment described above that have had several impacts on the airline marketing channels. Airlines created a new marketing channel through the Collaborative Web, while also creating new kinds of relationships with competitors. The actions of third-party technology development companies enabled this development and introduced pressure in the airline industry to get involved in the joint venture. This connectedness of the actors in a network allows for bridging, where a relationship to one actor is used to connect to a third-party actor (Smith & Laage-Hellman, 1992). The Travel Agents, Agent Web, and GDS Web have relationships with buyers, which the airline can reach by bridging through the intermediaries. In this way, the value of one relationship depends on other relationships. Another specific structural factor is the position in the marketing channel network. The position considered is even broader still; it is the position in the larger network that could include actors outside the focal firm's own industry (IMP Group, 1982). The GDS holds a unique position centrally in the marketing channel network, which partly could explain why they have higher profits than the Airlines (Dembrower & Grenblad, 2003). The parties' actions are affected by the trends on their market, such as internationalization and market dynamics (IMP Group, 1982).

Implications for Practitioners and Theory

Marketing practitioners who seek effectiveness and efficiency in their marketing investments should consider that the Internet does not always host only one marketing channel for a selling company, but several with distinct traits and consisting of different actors, as shown in this chapter. When investments are made on the marketing channel level, these differences result in changes to different aspects of relationship maintenance. Furthermore, each of the antecedents of relationship maintenance offer different means to affect the customer relationship and should also be considered to improve investment allocation decisions, once a channel is chosen for investments. It is reasonable to believe that depending on the circumstances, the return on these marketing investments varies between investments in the antecedents in a specific marketing channel and between the marketing channels. Finally, customer relationships with different categories of customers are likely to require different Internet-based marketing channels in a multichannel approach. The chapter offers airlines, including low-cost airlines, sources of improved customer relationships and in the long-term possible lower price dependence. Other industry practitioners can benefit from insights on how airlines, forerunners of e-business, have managed their Internet-based marketing channels.

Customer relationship equity is one element of customer equity building that overlaps two other elements: product equity and brand equity. As seen in this chapter, product value is considered an antecedent to relationship maintenance. Image is considered in the similarity and distance antecedent group, and is not only related to the brand equity element. The inter-concept differences between these three customer equity elements would be fruitful to develop further. This chapter offers a model for relationship maintenance that would benefit from empirical testing, for example to compare it with other suggested models such as Wilson (1995). The empirical material presented here also have limitations, since the buyers were not interviewed or surveyed. Future testing of the model should consider both the buyer and the seller.

Several antecedent themes are included in the model presented in this chapter; those from relationship marketing literature are enriched by market-as-network literature's interpretation of antecedents in the same theme. New antecedents, typically not considered in relationship marketing literature, are added from market-as-network literature. Both the relationship marketing and network approach literature contributes with sometimes overlapping and several times complementing explanations for relationships. Further idea exchange between the two research approaches has been proposed (Mattsson, 1997), after the limited attempt in this chapter, such theory convergence or research interaction is encouraged since it enriched the analysis of the airline industry case.

Acknowledgments

Portions of the empirical material have been collected together with Maria Dembrower and Pernilla Rosén, respectively. Comments on the text have gratefully been received from the anonymous reviewers, the editors, Adel El-Ansary,

Björn Axelsson, Christopher Hobbs, Claes-Robert Julander, Cristina Machado, Eveline Bernasconi, Mats Vilgon, Monica Sharp, and Sara Melén. This chapter has been made possible by highly appreciated financing from Torsten Söderberg and Ragnar Söderberg Trusts.

References

American Express. (1999). *Global T & E expense management survey* (Survey). American Express.

American Express. (2003). *European expense management study – Executive summary* (Survey). American Express.

Anderson, J. C., & Narus, J. A. (1990). A model of distributor firm and manufacturer firm working partnerships. *Journal of Marketing, 54*(1), 42–58.

Bagozzi, R. P. (1975). Marketing as exchange. *Journal of Marketing, 39*(4), 32–40.

Bauer, H. H., Grether, M., & Leach, M. (2002). Building customer relationships over the internet. *Industrial Marketing Management, 31*, 155–163.

Bendapudi, N., & Berry, L. L. (1997). Customers' motivations for maintaining relationships with service providers. *Journal of Retailing, 73*(1), 15–37.

Berry, L. L. (1983). Relationship marketing. In: L. L. Berry, G. L. Shostack, & G. D. Upah (Eds), *Emerging perspectives on services marketing* (pp. 25–28). Chicago, IL: American Marketing Association.

Blattberg, R. C., & Deighton, J. (1996). Manage marketing by the customer equity test. *Harvard Business Review, 74*(4), 136–145.

Blattberg, R. C., Getz, G., & Pelofsky, M. (2001). Want to build your business? Grow your customer equity. *Harvard Management Update, 6*(8), 4–6.

Bonoma, T. V. (1982). Major sales: Who really does the buying? *Harvard Business Review, 60*(3), 107–119.

Davis, H. L., & Rigaux, B. P. (1974). Perception of marital roles in decision processes. *Journal of Consumer Research, 1*(1), 51–63.

Dembrower, M., & Grenblad, D. L. (2003). Sales channels – A barrier to entry in the airline industry. Paper presented at the 7th Airtransport Research Society Conference – ATRS, July 10–12, Toulouse, France.

Dwyer, F. R., Schurr, P. H., & Oh, S. (1987). Developing buyer–seller relationships. *Journal of Marketing, 51*(2), 11–27.

Egan, J. (2003). Back to the future: Divergence in relationship marketing research. *Marketing Theory, 3*(1), 145–157.

El-Ansary, A. I. (2005). Relationship marketing management: A school in the history of marketing thought. *Journal of Relationship Marketing, 4*(1), 1–24.

Ford, D. (1980). The development of buyer-seller relationships in industrial markets. *European Journal of Marketing, 14*(5/6), 339–354.

Grenblad, D. L., & Rosén, P. (1999). *Internet – A sales channel in the Airline Industry* (Vol. 99:EP:D/40). Linköping: Linköping University Electronic Press.

Grönroos, C. (1994). From marketing mix to relationship marketing: Towards a paradigm shift in marketing. *Management Decision, 32*(2), 4–21.

Grönroos, C. (2003). Taking a customer focus back into the boardroom: Can relationship marketing do it? *Marketing Theory, 3*(1), 171–173.

Gummesson, E. (1987). *Marketing – A long term interactive relationship: contributions to a new marketing theory.* Stockholm: Marknadstekniskt Centrum.

Gummesson, E. (1995). *Relationsmarknadsföring : Från 4 P till 30 R* (1st ed.). Malmö: Liber-Hermod.

Hammarkvist, K.-O., Håkansson, H., & Mattsson, L.-G. (1982). *Marknadsföring för Konkurrenskraft (Marketing for competitiveness).* Malmö: Liber.

IMP Group. (1982). An interaction approach. In: H. Håkansson (Ed.), *International marketing and purchasing of industrial goods* (pp. 10–27). Chichester: Wiley.

Johanson, J., & Mattsson, L.-G. (1985). Marketing investments and market investments in industrial networks. *International Journal of Research in Marketing, 2*(3), 185–195.

Lemon, K. N., Rust, R. T., & Zeithaml, V. A. (2001). What drives customer equity. *Marketing Management, 10*(1), 20–26.

Levitt, T. (1980). Marketing success through differentiation – of anything. *Harvard Business Review, 58*(1), 83–92.

Mattsson, L.-G. (1997). Relationship marketing and the markets-as-networks approach – A comparative analysis of two evolving streams of research. *Journal of Marketing Management, 13*(5), 447–461.

Morgan, R. M., & Hunt, S. D. (1994). The commitment-trust theory of relationship management. *Journal of Marketing, 58*, 20–38.

Porter, M. E., & Millar, V. E. (1985). How information gives you competitive advantage. *Harvard Business Review, 63*(4), 149–161.

Rathmell, J. M. (1966). What is meant by services? *Journal of Marketing, 30*(4), 32–36.

Rust, R. T., Lemon, K. N., & Zeithaml, V. A. (2004). Return on marketing: Using customer equity to focus marketing strategy. *Journal of Marketing, 68*(1), 109–118.

Shostack, G. L. (1977). Breaking free from product marketing. *Journal of Marketing, 41*(2), 73–80.

Simon, H. A. (1945). *Administrative behavior.* New York, NY: Free Press.

Smith, P., & Laage-Hellman, J. (1992). Small group analysis in industrial networks. In: B. Axelsson, & G. Easton (Eds), *Industrial networks: A new view of reality* (pp. 37–61). London: Routledge.

Stern, L. W., El-Ansary, A. I., & Coughlan, A. T. (1996). *Marketing channels* (5th ed.). Upper Saddle River, NJ: Prentice-Hall.

Turnbull, P. W., Ford, D., & Cunningham, M. T. (1996). Interaction, relationships and networks in business markets: An evolving perspective. *Journal of Business and Industrial Marketing, 11*(3/4), 44–62.

Wiertz, C., Ruyter, K. D., Keen, C., & Streukens, S. (2004). Cooperating for service excellence in multichannel service systems – an empirical assessment. *Journal of Business Research, 57*(4), 424–436.

Wilson, D. T. (1995). An integrated model of buyer–seller relationships. *Academy of Marketing Science, 23*(4), 335–346.

PART II

Chapter 9

Internet, Internationalisation and Customer Value Creation — The Case of Medical Information on the Internet

Mats Vilgon and Per Andersson

Introduction

During the late 1990s, when the Internet became widely used and accessible, it was something like a Klondike period for web-based business. There was an entrepreneurial spirit to question much of the established business and industry logic made possible by the technology and a rich supply of venture capital. Many new business ventures were launched aimed at selling and supporting software, hardware, infrastructure and service providing for the operation and utilisation of the Internet itself. New companies, initially and later also the established and traditional companies, were experimenting with the electronic business, as attempts to use the Internet as a channel for distribution of products, as a new channel for market communication and reaching out to new markets. Since the digital economy was about to develop there was an idea that there was only room for one industry-leader in each industry. The concepts of positive feedback and the winner takes it all (see e.g. Shapiro & Varian, 1999) pushed many of the ventures to aim at several national markets, and even the world market, already from the beginning. Hence, the business concepts at the time favoured an international launch. We also witnessed a type of business that combined several offers and value propositions into a package made accessible on the Internet, at times the businesses also sought revenues from a variety of sources.

Managing Customer Relationships on the Internet
Copyright © 2006 by Elsevier Ltd.
All rights of reproduction in any form reserved
ISBN: 0-08-044124-6

These businesses were mushrooming in almost any sector and they all signalled a revolutionary spirit to the established industry and way of doing business. One of the more successful examples of a consumer-oriented electronic marketplace is E-bay, serving as an online auction for almost any product. A striking example of a failure was Boo.com that aimed at being a shopping mall for fashion garments made available worldwide. Amazon.com, the virtual bookstore that has become the somewhat virtual shopping mall, is an example of a Internet-based venture that has been searching a long time for its core business. On the industrial market side, Endorsia.com is an example of a forward-supporting venture linking several industrial goods providers with a large number of distributors worldwide. The big three US automakers formed Covicint to combine efforts and form a single global business-to-business supplier exchange for coordination of the automation industry supply side. These ventures may be called e-portals, e-commerce exchanges or e-marketplaces (cf.European Commission, 2004).

During the early days of these new Internet ventures, we saw both new entrepreneurial attempts and existing industry members that experimented with developing Internet-based ventures. There were apparently various situations where Internet-based coordination between companies was present and affecting both the coordination of each venture as well as industries at large. Three important dimensions of industrial and market development were at hand. First, the creation of new Internet ventures emerged in an international context. Second, they were linked to new forms of value-creation processes for the users and customers. Lastly, they often required new forms of cooperation between established and new companies. This chapter focuses on these three inter-related dimensions of new Internet ventures.

Prior Research and Theoretical Emphasis

Early research on new Internet ventures had a tendency to focus the empirical interest on physical goods and the infrastructure industry supporting the Internet and less attention to informational contents industries and service outputs as exchange objects of the business ventures. There also seemed to be a lot of research emphasis on the structuring of internal organisation, the company prerequisites for success, contractual channel arrangements and a market optimising perspective. Less attention was put on the core market exchange and its value constellation setting. There also seemed to be less attention directed to the organisational and inter-organisational processes underlying the new Internet-based ventures and the formational processes of the ventures.

The early theoretical explanations of these IT-supported developments were, at the time, typically focusing on a set of theoretical issues. One line of thinking was the Porterian competitive strategy explanation, stating that existing companies could strengthen their competitive advantage with IT (Porter & Millar, 1985). Another field of theory was based on the transaction cost theory explanations to the business use of IT (see e.g. Malone, Yates, & Benjamin, 1987; Brynjolfsson & Smith, 2000). The technology-supported ventures could bypass middlemen and other costly activities in the transaction between the production and demand. Hence, the explaining factor was the reduced economics in coordination, implicit in the ventures, striving for a cost-efficient market (see e.g. Wigand, 1997). General, conceptual thinking about the creation of electronic marketplaces was found in research on marketing and value creation processes with a specific focus on IT, Internet and electronic business contexts (e.g. Bakos, 1991; Sarkar, Butler, & Steinfield, 1998; Bakos & Brynjolfsson, 1999).

Another stream of research focused on the concept of business models, a popular concept for companies to use when developing business over the Internet. These contributions of classifications of new business ventures by Timmers (1998, 1999), who set the initial framework, have been further elaborated upon (e.g. Mahadevan, 2000; Essler & Whitaker, 2001). The ambition in those has been to classify the mechanics of the venture, in terms of what is produced and by which means, and what the costs and revenues of the business are. That is, the classic production function perspective of a company is being challenged. These studies imply that there seems to be more dimensions into these kinds of ventures than the suggested optimisation of a market by the cutting of distribution and communication costs.

Problem Area: Three Inter-Related Issues

New Forms of Cooperation

This article draws attention to three important, interrelated dimensions connected to the emergence of new Internet-based companies, some of which were not given priority in the early attempts to study and analyse these new ventures. First, at times, we can see specialised actors appear on the market for new Internet ventures. In some situations, we encounter new integrators instituting a new role around the Internet-based market solutions. These actors may generally be labelled integrators. A group of such integrators has been mirroring the physical realm and therefore been labelled electronic: "shopping malls", "markets" or "department stores". These Internet-run coordinators may come from one or several formerly connected or unconnected industries. Like in so many e-marketplace cases, Internet applications are integrated and integrating new constellations of companies and activities of the new value system that is to be transferred to customers.

The degree to which they engage and involve customers in the development of these new solutions vary as they define their role at the market differently. Hence, in order to develop, transfer and combine new offerings to customers, companies increasingly engage in new types of alliances and cooperations, establishing "unexpected" constellations that connect companies. At times, these connections are in formerly unrelated business areas or company constellations. When establishing a new business logic, either within radically new or within an existing actor constellations, the process of introducing new forms of cooperation is often associated with tensions and shifts of power between actors. This is apparent in converging and dissolving industries where the consolidation of roles in between companies is questioned and challenged. Companies in these sectors often experience problems and significant inertia in the processes of introducing radical changes in business logic, on both the supplier and the buyer side. Often the initial change and guidance for the restructuring of the sector comes from emergent and new actors to the industry. In some cases, Internet-based solutions are at the heart of such power struggles and tensions.

Changes in the development and transfer of new value systems to customers may naturally also take place within an existing actor constellation, for example, as a result of the current trend of gaining scale economies by focusing at "core business", and massive outsourcing of auxiliary or non-core activities. Hence, a number of previous in-house coordination becomes market-coordinated, thereby existing relationships with suppliers and industrial manufacturers have taken radical steps into outsourcing of production, product design, purchasing, procurement, service functions, etc., moving towards , in the extreme case, the creation of a virtual organisation with the brand as the "core capability". At the same time, these suppliers may turn into powerful integrators, with the role of tying together the systems of outsourced activities. The value provided to these customers is not only connected to the physical offer but also the coordinative activities performed by these suppliers. In the midst of these changes, the Internet often function as a facilitating resource in the reconfiguration process. As the activities are moved from one actor to another, they also become re-organised and questioned. The Internet-based management becomes an option to drive both efficiency and effectiveness. Creating these underlying inter-organisational networks or "value constellations", is the first important issue and problem area. (This issue is mainly covered as empirical descriptions in our case on the emergence of medical information services on the Internet.)

Internationalisation

New Internet ventures are often described in terms of new distribution ventures reshaping global market structures, and also the shape of internationalisation processes. Internet companies represent one type of new "intermediary", for which the market has been global from the very beginning, i.e. they are what have been named "Born Globals". Such Born Globals, it has been argued, possess international market knowledge before their first foreign market entry, and their selection of foreign market entry mode is based on their existing knowledge and the knowledge supplied by their network ties (for a general discussion see e.g. Sharma & Blomstermo, 2003). It can be assumed that such network ties are important also for the types of Internet companies focused on here. General marketing channel researchers like Stern, El-Ansary, and Coughlan (1996) state that many of today's intermediaries are likely to evolve into international super distributors, representing a number of manufacturers across many product lines. In some cases, global manufacturers are "pulling out" intermediaries into the international arena, as a consequence of, for example, the implementation of new sourcing strategies. The exploration of international markets is believed to be one of the major paths of renewal in distribution. The factors that drive an Internet-based intermediary and enterprise out into the international arena are part of the issue. For example, what happens when they are pulled out or have to defend their position in their home region by establishing positions in new markets, sometimes also redefining what constitutes their "home regions" is part of the internationalisation issues facing new Internet companies. This is our second issue and problem area.

Creating Customer Value Propositions

Constellations of companies cooperate in the new Internet ventures to handle the value creation processes when sometimes radically new business models and new customer values are created. In addition these new value creation processes and new Internet ventures, we have argued, represent to a varying degree ambitions and realisations of the internationalisation of the business at hand, as well as the driving forces of internationalisation. Internet-based marketplaces play an important role in the creation of sometimes new customer value systems. Internet-based ventures and marketplaces operated over the Internet providing information services supporting the medical and health care sector, which is in focus of this chapter, sometimes change established ways of providing customer value in this area. These and similar Internet ventures introduce to varying degrees changes in the business logic and "new" value propositions to their customers. Using Ramirez' (1999) terms, new value co-production in value constellations of business units can be assumed to involve important managerial problems and issues when new Internet ventures are created. A co-productive view of value creation in value constellations focuses on the interactive aspects of value production, connecting to the problem of coordination described above. Values are co-invented, combined and reconciled, i.e. established interactively between new and established actors in the network. This interactive, co-production view of value creation when studying the processes whereby new Internet-based ventures are created, embraces the third problem area in this chapter.

Research Questions

To sum up, the purpose of this study is to further the understanding of the market-side driving forces underlying the development of new Internet business ventures. The chapter probes into the value propositions developed in such ventures and the addressed markets, including the international ambitions of the ventures. Hence, we aim at increasing the understanding of customer value and its development in these businesses and as explanations for the development of these ventures. These processes need also to take into account that the value creation processes require coordination of new value constellations of companies and take place in an internationalisation context. To guide us we have set up three broad questions to cover the three inter-related issues: What new value constellations of companies and patterns of coordination are created when a new Internet-based venture is established? What problems and issues are connected to the fact that these new Internet ventures often establish positions in new international markets? What new value propositions are presented and introduced to customer when a new Internet business venture is established?

We will focus on a specific form of ventures in that we study the launching of what is called electronic marketplaces run over the Internet. We will use a broad definition of it since we assume an evolutionary perspective to business development at hand. Hence, some of the ventures may become more or less of a strict electronic marketplace over some time span. As mentioned earlier, Internet ventures for medical information services are in focus. The study builds on an earlier study (Andersson & Vilgon, 2000), which analysed the patterns by which, mostly new, company constellations were mobilised to create new customer value propositions over the Internet. At that time the so-called: "dot.com" hype was at its peak (see e.g. Nevaer, 2002) and most of the ventures that were launched, and also in our focus, were from outside the current industry. They tended to be entrepreneurial and often funded by venture capital. The core of both that and this empirical study consists of in-depth, longitudinal case studies focusing on the changes in business logic. The sources for the empirical work are: archival data, company's internal written notes and reports as well as other official records and interviews with managers and sector officials.

This chapter is structured as follows. First, we present a brief analytical framework based on key notions of value, customers and internationalisation. Hence, the market side of the new ventures is put in focus. Second, we describe a number of projects and ventures using the Internet for providing medical information to their customers in the Swedish context. Third, we analyse these ventures in terms of which customers and (international) markets that are put in focus and what values do they develop over time. And finally, we discuss the development process or path the ventures and some intrinsic key characteristics of the patterns found in the study.

General Analytical Framework

In order to build a framework for understanding the formation of Internet-based business, the study draws on various fields connected to the issues in focus. In this section we summarise briefly the main areas and references. Further references can be introduced in the analysis part following the empirical section. First, we draw on texts on customer value aspects connected to various schools of marketing; what it might be and how it is formed. This includes ideas of value constellations, which provide us with a link to the second area on which the analytical framework of the study is built, inter-organisational network thinking. Lastly, the study builds on theories for internationalisation as an explanation for the Internet-based business.

First, in the area of customer value, value creation, and value constellations and relationships, Ramirez's (1999) idea of value co-production in value constellations of business units is built on. His co-productive view of value creation in value constellations focuses on the interactive aspects of value production, connecting his perspective to the industrial relationship and network schools, below. Values are co-invented, combined and reconciled, i.e. established interactively between the new and established actors in the network. We adopt this interactive, co-production view of value creation when studying the processes whereby new Internet-based ventures are created. Furthermore, Wind (1990) introduces the notion of "value-in-use" focusing on the actual value the offer represents. Anderson and Narus (1999) discuss how to define value in the market offering, generating a comprehensive list of value elements, and value elements are anything that affects the costs and benefits of the offering. Best (2000) makes the picture more clear as he sets the costs and the revenues at the customer side into monetary units in a sort of profit and loss account.

Second, business development through interactions with customers can be added to the basic foundation and analytical for understanding the general coordination processes (Håkansson, 1982, 1987; Håkansson & Snehota, 1995). The idea here is that also Internet-based ventures can be related to the same type of interactive processes. Thus, in value and business development processes, a broader range of sources of innovations should be considered, such as users, customers, distributors and suppliers. In accordance with these texts, these new value creation processes include, and should include, the customers. It should be viewed as a collaborative, value co-creation process extending over time.

Lastly, many different lines of research can be found in this tradition of internationalisation research. Models of companies' internationalisation processes have been drawn on in the underlying study of this chapter. The internationalisation process of the company is one of the central topics of international business research. Fletcher (2001) states that for the most part, this area of research has been devoted to the processes of internationalisation or to the factors causing the internationalisation. Due to changes in the environment — in our case the emergence of the Internet — more complex forms of international behaviour have evolved. One type of such new phenomenon is represented by the Internet-based companies, for which the market has been global from the very beginning, i.e. they are what has been named "Born Globals". From an inter-organisational network perspective, Sharma and Blomstermo (2003) have described the internationalisation processes of Born Globals in general. Among other things, they argue that such companies possess international market knowledge before their first foreign market entry, and their selection of foreign market entry mode is based on their existing knowledge and the knowledge supplied by their network ties. It can be assumed that such network ties could be important also for the types of Internet enterprises focused on in this chapter.

Medical Information Service over the Internet at the Swedish Market

A fast growing area for Internet-based ventures is medical information services. It is an important and information-intensive sector. There are many actors involved with different needs and interest. There are many different business ventures in progress and to a varying degree they rely on providing services over the Internet. Medical distribution supported by IT, prior to the Internet, has been one of the rare sectors that are well described and analysed during the 1980s (see e.g. Clemmons & Row, 1988; Konsynski & Vitale, 1988; Short & Venkatraman, 1992). The stake taken at that point of time was competitive advantage due to forward integration with different sorts of proprietary information technology.

Here we will focus on ventures and projects providing medical information provided over the Internet.

The Structure of the Swedish "Market" for Prescribed Medicine

When a person in Sweden falls ill he or she contacts with a medical doctor most often at the local medical centre. If seriously ill, the doctor recommends the patient to a specialist or a hospital where the patient is treated. All hospitals are coordinated regionally, and are administrated nationally under a public organ — Läkemedelsverket. Sweden is furthermore divided into regional County Councils that are funded by taxis and operates the regional sic-care. If possible, the doctor at the medical centre treats the patient locally, prescribes an appropriate medicine and gives the patient a prescription for the medical drug. The doctor acts on his or her skill when treating the actual illness with the best treatment medicine available. The doctors are also requested by the medical expertise from the National Board of Health to use certain treatments before others based on "evidence"-based research. They are also guided to choose an economical optimal treatment, i.e. they are supposed to choose the less expensive medicine when several are available.

At the Swedish market there is a law against advertising prescribed medicine to final users, hence the prescribing doctors are the targets for the pharmaceutical industry in their marketing effort.

The prescribed medicine is distributed by a public pharmacy in a legal monopoly position — Apoteket. The pharmacy has the responsibility to monitor the medical distribution in a number of aspects. They check that non-mixable medicines do not get mixed, that the prescriber has the authority to make the prescription and that the economically best choice is made. They also have the responsibility to inform the patient about the treatment, its medication and possible side effects. The patient hands over the prescription to the pharmacist who inspects the prescription and sells the medicine to the patient, within a system of publicly subsidised prices.

The last few years have turned up many ventures and projects within this area of providing medical information service. At the end of 1999 there were almost a hundred ventures in Sweden alone, aiming at providing medical information to end-users. Most of them had little success and were probably part of the dot.com euphoria at the time. Some have survived and yet more projects and ventures have emerged (see e.g. The National Board of Health and Welfare, 2002).

Our empirical case will illustrate a number of ventures and projects operating at the Swedish market. They all aim commonly at providing medical information over the Internet. Most of them have a medical information database called

"FASS" as a key service to provide. This database is a systematic collection of all prescribed medicines in Sweden. More than 125 pharmaceutical companies and about 5000 different medicines are represented. The database provides a brief description of, for example, the make, its major active components, its side effects and its different distribution packages, etc. This has since long (in paper format) been the guidebook for prescribers in their choice of medical treatments for a patient.

During the past years the has been flooded by various project, ventures and new companies providing various kind of medical information. The first www site in Sweden, and number 171 in the world, was MedicaLink that was launched in 1993. During 1999, we envisioned almost a hundred ventures of various ambition of serving medical information over the Internet. We followed two of them, PharmaPoint and Locus Medicus, in in-depth case research (see Andersson & Vilgon, 2000). During the last years of dot.com clean-up both of them failed to stay at the market as many other focusing at the same business.

These ventures and projects are naturally all different in their focus, ambition, history, position, etc., but they all, in common, aim at providing medical information based on some form of Internet distribution. Below we will describe a selection of these ventures and projects. We give a presentation of: NetDoktor.se, Vitea.se, Apoteket.se, Infomedica.se, Vårdguiden.se, PharmaPoint.com, LocusMedicus.net and the "JANUS-project".

NetDoktor.se

This venture was founded by the Danish physician Carl Brandt, who was working on the effects of informational content and formats provided by doctors to their patients. Brandt contacted a newspaper editor to get medial attention on his findings. They came to an understanding that they shared the common interest in creating a "new patient", a patient that is an informed patient, who actively seeks information about diseases and health. "The journalist and the doctor want to build a bridge between their respective professions to give birth to a new breed of well-informed patients using the Net as their tool" (from the web). The two decided to empower the patients and start an Internet-based company called NetDoktor.dk. The first website was launched in June 1998 in Denmark. The core of information, at the time, was two databases, one about diseases and conditions and the other on medicines. They also provided access to the world's leading medical database Medline. In addition to these sources of information, they provided an online debate, a list on and linkages to all national medical support groups. Furthermore, they provided information about waiting times for operations, health advice and an online bookshop focusing on medical/health literature.

Already from the start the service was a success. Within a few months they had more than 500,000 hits a month on their site and after a year 2.5 million. Media covered the progress and gave the venture its needed PR. A German news agency wrote about the venture, and a leading investment fund contacted the company with the offer of money to take the business to new markets. Soon five other European countries were added. In each country the same format as the Danish one was copied and launched. Later an extension has been added, the Pro version, focuses on the professionals in the industry, i.e. medical doctors and hospital personnel. Medical companies sponsored this part of the operation and therefore the public was blocked out, due to the legal restriction not to advertise prescribed medicine in, e.g. Sweden.

NetDoctor is currently running their services in Denmark, Germany, Sweden, Spain, Austria and the UK. There are plans for continuous market enlargement. They promote themselves as "the leading healthcare portal of Europe". The content is also developed into a community platform. They also cater to special interest groups such as asthma sufferers; diabetics and pregnant women, allowing easy access to relevant information and possible contact with experts and peers. NetDoktor also develop care services for disease management, monitoring of chronic patients and demand management services. Currently "NetDoktor aims to connect all players in the healthcare space and has set out to develop a single electronic medical record source that will be available to all parties, including the patient."

Vitea.se

Vitea.se was launched at the end of 1999 as a tool for patients to gain information about their health and medical status. One of the founders, Paul Källenius, had an experience of being of bad health and understood his own responsibility to become well, as he put it: "I had to become my own project leader of my curing". The aim was to provide a general guide of how to get well. Initially the one of the large Swedish pension funds, an investment bank and a bid insurance company, put up 210 MSEK and later one of the leading Internet companies, SOL joined the venture. Its initial revenue streams came from the investors and sales of banners mainly from the medical industry. They also began early to sell services to companies and thereby received fees on those services. From the beginning they had the plans to open up their service in France, Germany and UK.

Later Vitea.se has turned it business towards providing services to 50 companies in the mid-region of Sweden. They provide a large range of services connected to handling a sic employee, to both prevent employees from falling ill and as they may do they work with the logistics of treating and rehab them efficiently.

They idea and inspiration were from a US project called "Home Care". Currently they operate a call centre and an Internet site in providing the following services: cost analysis, health screening, rehab, access service and administration of health/sic-registration.

Apoteket.se, Infomedica.se and Vårdguiden.se

Apoteket is a state-owned monopoly in operating the retail part of the distribution of prescribed medicine in Sweden. They purchase from two wholesale companies: Kronans Droghandel and Tamro. Their assignment is to operate a cost-efficient distribution and to perform the regulated distribution in the whole of Sweden, in that they are responsible to monitor the function of prescriptions and to inform patients on the use of the prescribed medicine. In that sense, Apoteket is a natural actor in providing medical information, at least to the wider public audience. Apoteket also merchant an over-the-counter assortment aimed at the health sector, currently representing more than 10% of its sales. Apoteket has a public web, Apoteket.se, where information about the company, its distribution, job opportunities, store location, time when open and some health-oriented guidance are provided. Apoteket is planning to implement an e-recipe handling in order to dramatically increase its operational efficiency. They are also planning for an e-commerce module dedicated to the non-prescribed articles from their product range.

In the mid-1990s a local county council developed a project of providing health information on terminals located at the local pharmacies. After a few years, the project was abandoned but became the seed to a larger project. In 1999, six county councils developed an Internet-based service and launched in April 2000 after several delays. In the midst of the Internet boom, they perceived more than 35 competing ventures at the Swedish market. Infomedica though is the only not-for-profit venture reaching out to the public. Instead all of the nation's county councils supports with 1 SEK per inhabitant as Apotektet with 0.2 and the state provides a grant of 10 MSEK per year, giving the venture a budget of 22 million per year. There is an explicit choice of not accepting any financial support of commercial character, e.g. sponsorships or advertising even though several propositions have been presented. The general purpose of the venture is to strengthen the general public's position in utilising the medical care sector. Hence, Infomedica is the only "public-service" company for health care information on the Internet in Sweden. The target users are the Swedish public, but also schools and working medical personnel in the sector are supported and believed to benefit from the operation.

The process of developing content is done by almost 20 editors that select the topics to be developed and published. Then is the process of contacting medical doctors as expertise to write the content of the published material. Currently there are more than 600 articles. Another main component is the "ask a doctor" function where about 70 questions are answered daily. The database of such questions is close to 3000, meaning that many subjects are covered and the knowledge pool is build up. The venture had become bureaucratic and slow leading to a new organisation in which all mid-management was cast out. The number of visitors is low and the knowledge about the site is not widely spread. Without a large base of users the management does not believe the financiers to put up funds for further continuation of the venture. Therefore, the increase in unique visitors to the site is crucial for its long-term success. The venture does not do any major traditional marketing such as advertising but uses its creativity to be visualised and seeks various joint efforts via its financiers and partners.

The Stockholm county council has launched a health portal named vårdguiden.se. This is the previous paper-based magazine that provides basic information about the operations of the health care and also some stories about some popular subject as a teaser for reading the magazine. The web-based version has over time had the function to make the contact with the local medicare more efficient, and over time also developed into guiding the administrative interaction between patient medicare.

PharmaPoint.com/LocusMedicus.net

PharmaPoint describes the case of a completely new business venture on the web, where a new market for this kind of information is developed. The starting point was the fact that the primus motor of the venture, Sophia Salenius, defined it to be increasingly more difficult for prescribing doctors to keep control of all necessary information about the drugs; its contents, effects, interaction effects when used in combination with other drugs, etc. PharmaPoint.com was launched as a new web-based information platform for doctors in need of this type of information. It also connected various types of information suppliers, pharmaceutical companies, various public drug administration units and others in the attempt to become an informational platform for the doctors. Thus, PharmaPoint is the information broker on the web, which in the first step linked these suppliers with doctors, and other users of drug-related information. However, this was only one of the first steps in the business development process. Plans for PharmaPoint were also a number of other information-related services for the users. Another similar web venture, which was launched somewhat later, was LocusMedicus.net. Two physicians have developed a search engine that scans a large number of medical sources of information and present individualised presentations to subscribing users. The service also includes medicine information from the FASS database.

The venture is owned by the founders, an Internet consultant (Spray), a private medical company (Praktiertjänst), an investment company (Bure) and a VC company (Result Venture Comp.). The revenue is supposed to come from banners and later on fees on the services provided. The internationalisation process is so far only to Finland and in pipeline Holland.

The JANUS-project

This project has a history in an EC-supported project originated in the late 1980s. Over time, the project has emerged as a tool to support and direct prescribers at the Swedish market. The project is financed and run by the regional public health authority in Stockholm and Karolinska Institute. The aim is to aid and help prescribers making the best choice possible of the medicines available via a decision-support system and also direct them to choose the best medicine in both a national and economical sense. Currently the project is materialised under three components. One recent tool in the project is the computerised prescribing support system. A second component is a collection of sources and databases. These are independent from companies, such as information from the National Board of Health and Welfare and the Swedish Association of Pharmaceutical Industry (LIF). The value added is based on the databases in themselves and the combination effects of having them collected at one tool. And the third component of the project is an Internet-based knowledge support web.

As an attempt to summarise the illustration we visualise the industry and value chain, as in Figure 1. Here we can see the traditional value-chain actors (visualised as rectangular symbols): producer–distributor–user. As the market is for prescribed medicine, we also have the prescribing personnel and the society, running the societal functions. We have also added a dozen ventures and projects providing medical information over the Internet. These are illustrated as ovular symbols.

As we can see from Figure 2, there are actors placed at the same position in the distribution system as the above described. To some extent these are similar to those described, e.g. they focus at the same users of their services. Thus, NetDoktor.se has revealing ventures such as Doccu.se, Kroppsjournalen.se, PrimaVi.com and, before the strategy shift, Vitea.se. Currently, Vitea.se operates at the same customer as e.g. MittLiv.nu. Colife.se has another company focus as it supports the insurance company and its users as e.g. TryggHansa.se/halsa. There are several ventures focusing at the prescribers, e.g. Ronden.se that is operated by the medical doctors organisations, InternetMedicine.se and earlier Locus.Medicus.se. The pharmaceutical companies are becoming very active on their own, for example, launching dedicated information towards end users based

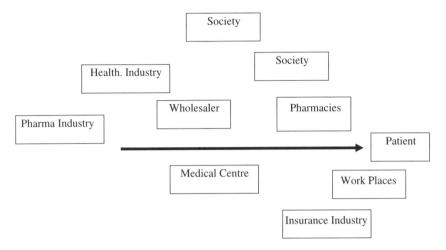

Figure 1: The distribution system of prescript medicine in Sweden.

on their skills and offers, illustrated by AstraZeneca's smarta.nu and we also see that the Phamaindustry provides direct contact over the net with prescribers, for example.

Analysing the Sector and the Cases

All the Internet-based ventures described, operate on their specific business model. It is by no means a simple task to find out how the new ventures make their money. They experiment and develop their business model over time and as the opportunities appear, by investigating who receives and utilises the information and services packaged at the venture and who providing the financial means or who is pay for the venture, we get an analytical framework. Thereby we need to identify the customers and the users. By customers we mean the ones who purchase the information or services provided. In a few cases, some attention has to be given to the financial situation of the venture, as some of them primarily focused at receiving financial funds or at least not necessarily committed to generate an economic gain in the short run. By user we mean those actors who utilise the service and information. The result is presented in a table (Figure 3). From this typology we propose 10 different types of ventures, 1a – 5. There are five main categories: (1) focus on patients as users, (2) work places as users, (3) insurance companies as users, (4) prescribing personnel as users and (5) society, for

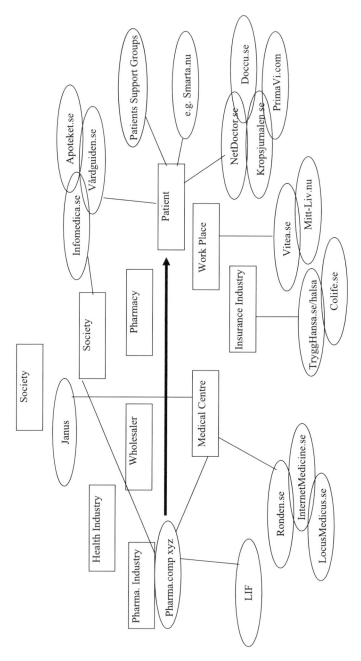

Figure 2: A schematic illustration of the 'market' and the actors described.

	Example company	Key customers	Key users	Venture focus	Key venture issue	Ownership
Type 1a	Infomedica.se	Society, the loc. medical regions & Apoteket	Patients, schools & medic. personnel	Exact information	Adoption & independence	Public
Type 1b	NetDoktor.se	Patients & health customers, pharma. & health industry, VCs	Patients & the medical sector	Empowererment of patients/ profit	Adoption	Private
Type 1c	Diabetolognytt.nu	"Society" & sponsors	A sub-group of patients	Sharing info. & experience	Trust & content	Cooperative
Type 1d	Smarta.nu	Apoteket	Patients	PR, info. & advertising	Legality & trust	Private
Type 2	Vitea.se	Companies, patients, society & VCs	Companies & patients	Reduced costs of illness	Delivery of appropriate info.	Private
Type 3	Colife.se	Internal, patients and companies	Patients	Reduced costs of illness	Delivery of appropriate info.	Private
Type 4a	"JANUS"	Society, medical centres & med. committees	Medical personnel & research	Efficient drug administration	Functionality, efficiency & adoption	Public
Type 4b	LocusMedicus.se	Pharma. industry & patients	Prescribes & patients	Profit & internationalisation	Trust & adoption	Private
Type 4c &5	Phama. company	Patients, pharmacies & med. society	Prescribers, patients & med. schools	Sales & education	Trust & access	Private

Figure 3: A classifying typology for the ventures.

example, medical schools, as users. Between categories 1 and 4 we suggest sub-groupings as a result of the classification.

The ventures presented to a large extent base their business, at least one part of their business, on one resource, the same database about prescribed medicine. Yet the variance of the business models identified varies significantly from each other. We also encounter an increase in the variance over time, i.e. the business focus of the ventures pinpoint new untapped opportunities as they learn about their customers and possibilities at the market.

In the fierce competition in an evolving market, the issue to capture a critical mass of users or customers, i.e. to become the dominant player in the field of medical information, time and timing, is crucial. In a fast developing area, the other actors move and development is important for what business opportunities may exist. It is therefore necessary to develop the venture fast, learn fast and be flexible enough to change and adapt to the most important issues at hand. It is also important to be somewhat right momentarily since there might not be time to do major changes in the business model and become the dominant player.

We find that some of the ventures have had one initial focus and later either changed that focus or added other focuses to their business. PharmaPoint, for example, focused initially on the medical doctors (prescribers) when the venture was launched and later patients were added, before it left the industry. At the same time, NetDoktor.se focused on patients and later added the pro version, focusing on hospital personnel, including the medical doctors. Vitea.se first focused their business on end-users and later on focused on companies for their administrative support. We can see that the JANUS project focused on the hospital sector and is developed within a "political sphere" as opposed to the PharmaPoint, for example, which aims at the same user but different customers. Then we have several web-based ventures focusing on the public in common, offering different information packages and services. Some ventures base their offering on a decision-support module while others, which we may label as portals offer less complex services or information about services.

Customer Value, Value Creation and Value Constellations

A cornerstone in this study has been the importance of the market side for understanding the venture's business and the development of the venture. The choice of customer and user is at the heart of guiding the development of the business. That is, the major choice of the entrepreneur is which customers to serve and develop the business towards. The development pattern of the business follows the needs of these customers and users. The problems and the need raised by these core customers and the ability to identify this by the venturing business are fundamental for explaining the actual business. That is, issues connected to what customer value is created in the business venture, the deliberate selection of those customers, the combination of various customers and users in each venture, etc., is of major importance. In choosing which customer and users to address the ventures have had to focus on certain offer attributes, delivery processes and value propositions, omitting other development paths. The knowledge about these was also developed in the interaction with these customers. Hence, there is a structure or even a structuring of the sector, dependent on the customer and user group that is targeted.

We found several paths of knowledge in the development of ventures. Several ventures were built up on knowledge gained in previous settings that were transformed into the ventures and the chosen strategy. In the cases of a venture failing to make it on the market, the knowledge gained was often carried on to the next venture, at times in new organisational settings. That is, the knowledge creation was built up and formed into various business organisations that often build on each other. There were also some provisions of information in a non-official form. It could, for example, be made reasonable to believe that the large medical companies in the pharmaceutical industry would like patients, i.e. potential end-users, to learn from their knowledge and their framing of the information developed to prescribers. It is also a simple procedure for an end-user to obtain access to the sites open only for prescribers, and thereby learn about the information specifically designed for professionals. Hence, a leakage may be built in. There is reportedly, also illegal distribution of highly popular drugs among end-users sold over the Internet.

We address different general strategies for the ventures observed (Figure 4). The rationale for the dichotomy administrative — commercial focus is that the former aims for cost efficiency and administrative tasks while the latter aims for sales at a profit. The rational for the relational/network — transactional mode is based on the conceptualisation of the venture. The former treats the venture as forming and upholding a large set of relations, while the latter treats its business as selling an offer within a market. As some of these new ventures are created within new actor constellations, focus will also be directed towards behavioural aspects such as power and control.

	Relational mode	Transactional mode
Administrative focus		
Commercial focus		

Figure 4: General strategies identified.

Internet-Based Marketplaces and the Internationalisation Connection

We also set out to search for the driving forces underlying the international dimension in the ventures. Some of them had the basic market reason for going to the international market in that there are potential customers to serve, and through the use of the Internet media there is a possibility to reach a larger market in a cost-efficient way. The economic argument is that there are large amounts of fixed costs that can be allocated on a larger customer base, i.e. there are more customers to take a share of this fixed cost as, for example, in the medical sector. During the dot.com era the ongoing international argument was key for getting venture capital funding. But since many of those ventures did not take off and did not make the market-test they have disappeared. There are a few exceptions in e.g. NetDoktor that both were venture-capital funded and had become a successful venture on several markets. On the other hand we encounter more and more of pharmacompanies that are fundamentally international in their operations and market coverage to both operate local web ventures of various kinds and supporting other ventures, at supposedly aiming to market their drugs. In enhancing their contact and supporting their PR activities, they are launching various web-based programs such as continuous learning programmes for medical doctors from e.g. Roche Pharma (see e.g. Liu, Wang, & Chan, 2004).

Conclusion and Discussion

This chapter is in part a description of the emergence of a new type of business ventures, a new sector, a process that extended over the last decade. There are a number of success stories, but also a series of business venture failures. The emergence of the sector as a whole can be divided into a number of loosely defined phases. In what might be called the pre-history, there were a number of ambitious attempts to run pre-Internet-technology programmes. Then, most ventures were drawn into the business boom and the venture capital driven frenzy of the late 1990s. The Internet-based ventures studied here were mostly aimed at the broad consumer market and the idea was to offer a cost-efficient business based on a multi-market strategy. There was also a belief that there existed various, previously unused, revenue sources to tap. Then, we witnessed a phase where many of these ventures either vanished or searched, and sometimes also found, in a "tinkering" process, a value-creating proposition that served as a paying market. At the time, the established actors began to launch ventures mimicking, but not coping, the existing entrepreneurial ventures. The pre-Internet business ventures were often focusing on the public sector. In this phase, they also got the necessary technology platform to develop important administrating tools. In this phase, the focus of the ventures was aimed at providing values to companies in many positions of value chains. Lately, we begin to see how the large, multinational, pharmaceutical industry is becoming active, launching web-based ventures in several areas on their own. Hence, we might witness the start of a new phase in the emerging sector for medical information services.

In the guiding research questions we set out to cover three interrelated questions regarding the development of new Internet-based ventures. The first question was about the patterns of coordination between companies launching the ventures. We found a number of cooperating companies working in new constellations. Furthermore, the pattern by which they related to each other changed over time. In other words, we encountered an industry, or several industries, in their making with a number of overlapping contacts between the networks of these industries. Hence, there were various reconfigurations of the alignment of the actors taking place in the process of establishing the new Internet-based medical information companies.

The second question concerned the ventures' international ambitions. We found that one group of the ventures could be defined as the so-called Born Globals but many of them failed to become international. (Many of them even failed to become national.) At the same time, the multinationals have, in later phases, become more and more active in launching local ventures. Hence, the international companies are developing local presence by launching various Internet ventures.

Finally, we set out to look into value propositions and the development of these ventures. We found that the initially fairly straightforward ideas presented by the companies of offering values have over time developed into a large variety of different offerings and expected customer values. This is explained partly by the fact that the companies were finding out more and more about each ventures' customers. They also managed to differentiate the offerings. Another part of the explanation is that companies managed to enrol more customer categories in the value chain. Hence, we encounter a large variation in market approaches over time of the medical Internet ventures.

This study leads us to identify some areas to investigate further. One area of special interest concerns issues connected to business development, especially concerning the value propositions developed in cooperation with other parties. Another interesting area concerns the international dimensions of the ventures and the emerging, new internationalisation phases of these ventures. On a more abstract level we think that the entrepreneurial opportunities are connected to the learning and knowledge accumulation in earlier settings. Hence, we suggest an approach that considers a combination of the Neo-Austrian view and the traditional Schumpeterian view on entrepreneurship to explain the evolution of the Internet-based ventures described.

References

Anderson, J.C., & Narus, J.A. (1999). *Business market management: Understanding, creating and delivering value.* Upper Saddler River: Pearson Education.

Andersson, P., & Vilgon, M. (2000). Implementing new logics for value creation the networking processes driving the emergence of electronic market places. Paper presented at the international marketing conference of the American marketing association, Universidad Torcuato di Tella, Buenos Aires, June 28–July 1, 2000.

Bakos, Y. (1991). Information link and electronic markets: The role of interorganizational information systems in vertical markets. *Journal of Management Information System,* *8*(2), 31–52.

Bakos, Y., & Brynjolfsson, E. (1999). Bundling information goods: Pricing, profits and efficiency. *Management Science, 45*(12), 1613–1630.

Best, R.J. (2000). *Market-based management: Strategies for growing customer value and profitability.* Upper Saddle River, NJ: Prentice-Hall.

Brynjolfsson, E., & Smith, M. (2000). Frictionless commerce? A comparison of internet and conventional retailers. *Management Science, 46*(4), 563–585.

Clemmons, E.K., & Row, M. (1988). McKesson drug company: A case study of ecnonomost — a strategic information system. *Journal of Management Information System, 5*(1), 36–50.

Essler, U., & Whitaker, R. (2001). Re-thinking e-commerce business modelling in terms of interactivity. *Electronic Markets, 11*(1), 10–16.

European Commission. Available at http://www.emarketservices.com/

Fletcher, R. (2001). A holistic approach to internationalisation. *International Business Review, 10*(1), 25–49.

Håkansson, H. (Ed.). (1982). *International marketing and purchasing of industrial goods.* Chichester: Wiley.

Håkansson, H. (1987). *Industrial technological development: A network approach.* London: Routledge.

Håkansson, H., & Snehota, I. (1995). *Developing relationships in business networks.* London: Routledge.

Konsynski, B., & Vitale, M. (1988). Baxter healthcare corporation: ASAP express. Harvard Business School case no. 9-188-080.

Liu, S.S., Wang, C.C.L., & Chan, A.C-F. (2004). Integration of multiple sales channels with web-based technology — A case of the pharmaceutical industry. *Journal of Business-to-Business Marketing, 11*(1/2), 131–148.

Mahadevan, B. (2000). Business models for internet-based e-commerce: An anatomy. *California Management Review, 42*(4), 55–69.

Malone, T.W., Yates, J., & Benjamin, R.I. (1987). Electronic markets and electronic hierachies. *Communications of the ACM, 30*(6), 484–497.

Nevaer, L.E.V. (2002). *The dot-com debacle and the return to reason.* Westport, CT: Quorum Books.

Porter, M.E., & Millar, V.E. (1985). How information gives you competitive advantage. *Harvard Business Review, 63*(4), 149–174.

Ramirez, R. (1999). Value co-production: Intellectual origins and implications for practice and research. *Strategic Management Journal, 20,* 49–65.

Sarkar, M.B., Butler, B., & Steinfield, C. (1998). Cybermediaries in electronic marketplace: Toward theory building. *Journal of Business Research, 41,* 215–221.

Shapiro, C., & Varian, H.R. (1999). *Information rules: A strategic guide to the network economy.* Boston, MA: Harvard Business School Press.

Sharma, D., & Blomstermo, A. (2003). The internationalization process of Born Globals: A network view. *International Business Review, 12,* 739–753.

Short, J.E. & Venkatraman, N. (1992). Beyond business process redesign: Redefining Baxter's business network. *Sloan Management Review, 34*(1), 7–21.

Stern, L.W., El-Ansary, A.I., & Coughlan, A.T. (1996). *Marketing channels* (5th ed.). Upper Saddle River, NJ: Prentice-Hall.

The National Board of Health and Welfare (2002). Health on the internet — a survey of Swedish websites 2002. ISBN: 91-7201-659-0 (http://www.socialstyrelsen.se/).

Timmers, P. (1998). Business models for electronic markets. *Electronic Markets, 8*(2), 3–8.

Timmers, P. (1999). *Electronic commerce: Strategies and models for business-to-business trading.* Chichester: Wiley.

Wigand, R.T. (1997). Electronic commerce: Definition, theory, and context. *The Information Society, 13,* 1–16.

Wind, Y. (1990). Getting a read on market-defined 'value'. *Journal of Pricing Management, 1*(Winter), 5–14.

Chapter 10

International Entrepreneurship and Customer Orientation in Globalizing Markets: A Study on Born Global Firms

Antonella Zucchella

Introduction: The New Spatial and Temporal Features of International Business

In the last two decades new business models emerged in the framework of glob-alizing markets; these models are characterized by growing precocity and speed in international orientation, and by focus on global market niches and customers rather than on foreign markets. These phenomena enriched the research field of international entrepreneurship, to which this contribution is addressed with the aim to identify its main drivers and characteristics. Two intertwined issues, the role of Information and Communication Technology (ICT) and the role of speed, seem at the core of these developments. The pervasive role of ICT is not just one of the drivers of world markets, interconnection and interdependence, but also the supporting factor for transaction costs reduction in foreign operations, and trade liberalization.

ICT constitutes the backbone of globalizing economies and societies (Kobrin, 1991). In the firm's perspective, ICTs support real-time information flows, enlarging and speeding up access to global sources of information, to global busi-ness opportunities, and make possible the management of international value chains, characterized by units located in different countries. The globally net-worked economy has the potential to create new ways in which firms can create and capture value (Brandenburger & Nalebuff, 1998) from being quick to respond to changes in the market and the environment (Einsenhardt, 1989; Zaheer & Manrakhan, 2001) to being able to profit from information scanning and inter-mediation (Evans & Wurster, 1999) and to create and exploit new knowledge (Dunning, 2000).

ICTs have been viewed mainly as a facilitator of internationalization processes and of international management issues, but since the end of 1980s their role in international business can be also regarded as one of changing firms' traditional patterns of growth in foreign markets (De la Torre & Moxon, 2001; Dunning & Wymbs, 2001). In particular, one of the key attributes of these technologies — speed (Nayyar & Bantel, 1994) — is currently applied to a growing number of new ventures aiming at international expansion. Born global firms have progres-sively called the attention of academic literature, practitioners and policy-makers since the beginning of the 1990s (Holstein, 1992; Oviatt & McDougall, 1994; Hordes, Clancy, & Baddaley, 1995). Customer relationships have been shaped accordingly as the advent of the internet provided any firm with cheaper and quicker ways — starting from the simplest tools like e-mails — to keep in con-tact regularly with actual and potential customers, to exchange and acquire infor-mation on the latter on a worldwide scale through websites, and more and more sophisticated search engines, while ICT developments coupled with statistical methodologies permitted firms to rely on Customer Relationship Management (CRM) tools to handle and manage customer relationships and their wealth in terms of marketing and relational intelligence.

We are currently facing a new and complex system of interactions between firms and foreign markets, where the two emerging issues of the globalizing scenery — ICT and time — play a dominant role and are deeply intertwined pro-ducing synergic effects. ICT is one of the enablers of early and fast international growth at different levels. First it contributes to developing an early international vision and orientation at a pre-entrepreneurial stage (cultural function), thanks to easy access to a worldwide economic web, thus opening up wider business oppor-tunities (entrepreneurial function), second it enables data collection on foreign markets and the identification of potential customers and suppliers (international business support functions). Finally, it permits a more effective and efficient management of customer relationships, foreign subsidiaries and global supply chain partners (international management support functions).

At the customer relationship level, ICT is the backbone of customer-centred internationalization strategies, as opposed to the traditional country-oriented ones. ICT tools allow firms to manage customer relationships across the globe efficiently and effectively, thus enabling also small and infant firms with no for-eign subsidiaries to be "close" to their customers. ICT cannot always completely substitute the role of direct contacts, as it happens for firms like Amazon or Ryanair, since in most businesses direct contacts must occasionally take place, especially when the product/service is tailored on specific clients, and/or pre–post sale assistance is needed (for example, machinery) and so on. Customer-centred strategies seem to be a common trait of many born global firms, which start up and develop through global customer orientation, rather than through a foreign market perspective (Zucchella, 2001).

According to the proposed interpretation framework, this chapter adopts the perspective of infant firms expanding in globalizing markets, where customer orientation is the core strategy — though not the only one — and ICT represents the main enabler — though not the only one — of such orientation to a global scale, supporting processes of fast and early international expansion. At the root of this common attitude there are some common drivers, which we would try to generalize in a general interpretation framework. These processes of early international orientation result in different performances, particularly in terms of effective internationalization. In the second part of this paper, we report the results of an empirical survey on 107 born global firms is reported, which was carried out in order to understand what are the most significant drivers of international entrepreneurship — as evidenced by the case of born global firms — and to verify their performance in terms of export intensity and geographical scope.

Industry- Versus Location-Specific Drivers of Early and Fast Internationalization: The Role of ICT

Born global firms could be the outcome of exogenous factors (industry- or location-specific ones, mainly), which acquired more importance in the last two decades in influencing accelerated international growth.

In the previous section, ICTs have emerged as one of the key drivers of globalizing economies, as a core context factor for business strategies and as a facilitator of international management and international business practices. From the latter point of view, they are one of the grounding elements of more pervasive, widespread and rapid internationalization processes, leading — among other factors — to the phenomenon of born global firms. In this section, ICTs are shown to be a factor conducive to the creation of new competitive arenas and new businesses dominated by ICTs. In particular, the purpose is to point out the relationship between the phenomenon of born global firms and a specific business context. The features of the globalizing economy push a growing number of activities and firms towards early internationalization, but this occurs much more massively and intensely in specific industries, where the impact of ICTs dominates or even shapes the business itself, as it happens in e-commerce-based businesses.

The digital economy has led to a progressive dismantling of barriers among industries, creating new competitive arenas, where previously separate industries converge progressively, mainly due to technological, and particularly ICTs' advances. In these enlarged arenas there is room for larger multi-business players and for smaller niche firms that are innovative and capable of dominating their specific sub-arena. To do so successfully they need to develop a global orientation since inception (Bell, 1995).

Three main conditions draw these firms into an early international expansion, viz. a tendency to operate within a narrowly defined market niche, which leads firms to enter an international market arena in order to break even; the high development costs typical of most businesses in the digital space; the speed of competition and product obsolescence, which leads firms with short product life cycles and intense competitive dynamics to choose simultaneous domestic and international market penetration. Empirical evidence shows that similar considerations apply to different business contexts, both high tech and traditional, where niche focusing and customer orientation represent a core strategy for international new ventures (Zucchella & Maccarini, 1999; McKinsey, 1993). Some studies suggest that born global firms could be also originated by location-specific, rather than industry-specific factors, which helps to explain why the number of international new ventures is significant also in traditional businesses (Maccarini, Scabini, & Zucchella, 2003). Geographical clusters — and districts in particular — are a special form of local network, characterized by high territorial concentration of similar and complementary economic specializations and high social cohesion. The territorial concentration of economic activities in globalizing markets begot the so-called "paradox of globalization" to indicate the growing spread of "sticky places in a slippery space" in the past two decades (Markusen, 1996).

There is a growing consensus in literature about the role of co-location of economic activities in early and fast international growth (Brown & Bell, 2001; Enright, 1998; Storper, 1992). The main points supporting such a correlation are the economies of agglomeration and the social capital available in the local cluster to any of its members. As far as the core issue of this chapter is concerned, co-location and local networking (of either a formal or an informal nature) enable small and infant enterprises to develop quickly and effectively an international market knowledge and exporting attitude, by sharing vision, experiences and investments (like those in trade fairs participation, in ICTs, etc.) with the other firms in the system (Cioccarelli, Denicolai, & Zucchella, 2004).

The performance of cluster-based firms is positively affected by the possibility of exploiting firm and territorial advantage to conquer foreign markets. The positive externalities provided by a local cluster lie in such factors as skilled and specialized labour, specialized services, access to "collective international knowledge" and easy access to information on the internationalization strategies of the main local competitors. The co-location of many similar and complementary businesses fosters inter-firm cooperation in order to share some investments. This allows small and infant firms to reduce both the liability of newness and financial and managerial constraints. The cost of participating in trade fairs and the organization of business contacts in foreign countries have been traditionally shared among the members of the cluster through export consortia and similar associations, and the same is happening lately for ICT investments. Some empirical findings (Rapporto Federcomin, 2003) report an impressive growth in the so-called "district digitization" in many Italian districts, even in those specialized in traditional businesses. Broadband and dedicated wireless connections are favoured by geographical concentration of economic activities and institutions. According to the above-mentioned survey, 40% of Italian district-based firms relies on their own website for informing potential customers and managing customer relationships, while the percentage is lower for non district-based firms (around 25%). At the moment, the most widely used tool for communicating with customers is e-mail. Supply-chain management tools are used by 25% of district-based firms.

Some information systems, e.g. Enterprise Resource Planning (ERP) systems, have a cost that could represent an entry barrier for small firms that want to manage and control their international value chain in real time. Location in a cluster allows them to bargain better conditions for adopting and implementing these systems through local associations and consortia, and the inter-firm exchange of information enables any entrepreneur to evaluate the costs and benefits of these investments more appropriately. Almost 70% of cluster-based firms declare that the local entrepreneurs' association is the main promoter of such ICT applications (Rapporto Federcomin, 2003). The adoption of ERP tools grew from 20 to 33% in the period of 2000–2003 in the case of district-based firms, while the percentage is much lower outside local clusters (Chiarvesio & Micelli, 2004).

The growing use of ICT in local clusters represents an additional element favouring cluster-based firms' early and effective international orientation. The importance of location-specific factors in the born global firm phenomenon is even more evident in the case of high-tech districts, where there is a geographical concentration of businesses involved in advanced technologies and related services. In such cases, the major ground for early and fast internationalization processes resides in the above-mentioned type of business- and location-specific factors.

Moreover, information technologies may provide an innovative and powerful tool for establishing and enforcing connections between distant locations, thus fostering the creation of networks among different districts. The above-mentioned study reports cases of Italian districts that have established similar local clusters in foreign countries and used ICT to keep dense connections between the originating district and its foreign spin-offs. Research on the use of the internet and e-commerce in Italian districts points to a considerable increase in the opportunities to establish new relationships, both inside and — in particular — outside the district (Previtali, Cioccarelli, & Denicolai, 2004). ICT may facilitate dispersal of activities that can be accomplished far away from regional clusters, while activities that depend on tacit knowledge, face-to-face interaction and trustful relations tend to remain in the clusters (Leamer & Storper, 2001). This may result in front-end or home-based activities remaining in the clusters, while other activities are increasingly outsourced worldwide, thus originating the so-called "double-edged geography" of the internet age (op.cit: p. 20), with its tendencies towards specialization and agglomeration, on the one hand, and spreading out on the other.

Born global firms are usually the most active in driving or accomplishing such phenomena and may represent the key connectors inside the cluster and among different clusters, due to their propensity to invest in ICT and their entrepreneurial attitude, as described below.

Firm and Entrepreneurial-Specific Drivers of Early and Fast Internationalization: The Role of Customer Orientation

Belonging to a given industry and/or a given territory is an exogenous factor, which could impact significantly on the firm's international growth. Firm-specific factors represent an endogenous perspective on born global firms (Harveston, Kedia, & Davis, 2000) and refer mainly to governance, financing and strategic orientation. The existence and importance of firm-specific drivers helps to understand why born global firms are neither an exclusive, nor probably a predominant outcome of high-tech businesses. Moreover, they are not necessarily the outcome of location-specific factors. The analysis of firm-specific factors driving early and rapid internationalization processes leads researchers to adopt, partly or entirely, the perspective of international entrepreneurship studies (Sahlman & Stevenson, 1991; Venkataraman, 1997; Brush, Greene, & Hart, 2001).

The entrepreneur's vision and his ability to translate it into a successful international expansion are drivers of early and fast internationalization, which have grown very much in the attention of academics and practitioners.

Studies carried out in different countries and at different periods have found out common traits in the firm-specific drivers at the root of the born global phenomenon

(Kuemmerle, 2002). Such factors stem primarily from the nature (education, experience, skills and attitudes) of the firm's founders and main shareholders, and in particular from their international vision and orientation (Madsen & Servais, 1997; Rasmussen, Madsen, & Evangelista, 1999). "Instant international" entrepreneurs' cultural (part of their life/education abroad, frequent travellers, curiosity and mind openness) or managerial background does not usually confine to the domestic market (Bloodgood, Sapienza, & Almeida, 1995; Kandsaami, 1998; Harveston et al., 2000). The presence of international partners among shareholders (Arenius & Autio, 2002; Zucchella & Maccarini, 1999) is another important factor that can explain fast international growth in infant firms, as they can provide knowledge of foreign markets, foreign customers and suppliers.

Born global business ideas and firms backed by venture capital represent another case explaining the importance of the firm's governance structure in international growth. Institutional shareholding can provide knowledge and vision on international operations together with start-up capital. In so doing, the debt/equity ratio is maintained at acceptable levels. Thanks to the provision of both knowledge and equity capital, the risk for born global firms is limited.

One of the features of international entrepreneurship is the attention to ICT as one of the supporting factors for fast international expansion, for managing and controlling dispersed value chains and for CRM.

The focus on global customers rather than on foreign markets is one of the dominant traits of many successful born global firms (Madsen & Servais, 1997; Zucchella, 2001; McKinsey, 1993). The capacity of the entrepreneur to identify worldwide business opportunities in terms of global customers rather than markets is an important feature of such firms, and outlines the role of international entrepreneurship in terms of "shaping" market niches according to a creative world market microsegmentation.

Empirical Evidence about Born Global Firms: A Survey on 107 Enterprises

The drivers listed above represent a theoretical framework that can orient empirical research on born global firms. In order to test this framework, verify its consistency and figure out the effective outcome of an early global orientation, an empirical research has been conducted in Italy involving 107 born global firms. The latter have been identified by extracting a sample representative of the overall population of the firms which had started selling abroad in the first 3 years of inception from the database of Italian exporters managed by the Chambers of

Commerce information system. The sample is representative of the Italian population of early exporting firms in terms of both size (with small scale largely prevailing) and industry stratification.

The objective of the survey was to outline some significant features of such firms, based mainly on quantitative information that could be obtained through a questionnaire. A better understanding of governance and strategic orientation issues was then obtained through semi-structured interviews. The latter aimed at collecting qualitative information in order to gain a better insight into the entrepreneurs' vision and international orientation. The semi-structured interviews involved 48 firms (approximately 50% of the firms of the overall data set), each interview lasted 60–90 min and the respondents were the entrepreneurs themselves (only in two cases an export manager), as in these small ventures ownership and management tend to coincide.

The definition of born global firm adopted in the study was mainly based on a temporal factor: born global firms are those which started going international in their first 3 years of life (for a literature survey on this parameter see Rialp-Criado, Rialp-Criado, & Knight, 2002). The concept of going international is typically referred to exporting, because small-scale firms usually adopt this entry mode first, and this is especially true for Italian firms, where very small (micro) enterprises dominate in terms of number of international firms.

The distribution of the 107 born global firms in terms of size, measured by two main parameters, viz. the number of employees and revenues reveals that born global firms appear to polarize into two main groupings: on one side there is a strong (dominant) concentration of such enterprises in the small scale, and particularly from 2 to 15 employees. This reflects the distribution of Italian exporters, as the dominant role of small-scale firms is confirmed. Compared with the overall population of enterprises (and, hence, including also non international ones) micro-enterprises (0–9 employees) are less represented in both the born global species and the overall exporters database. On the other hand, it is possible to observe a group of medium-sized born global firms (14%), i.e. those with a number of employees ranging from 50 to 199, a figure which is significantly higher than the average for the overall population of exporters (11%), which is already higher than the overall Italian average for all enterprises (6%), according to the Italian Chambers of Commerce database. Similar considerations hold good if we consider the stratification of born global firms in terms of sales volumes.

This feature is particularly interesting if we consider that born global firms are on average younger than the traditional ones, and, hence, we could expect a higher number of microenterprises. As mentioned above, many born global firms are not growth oriented, as they focus on small niches and prefer to maintain that market positioning over the years. The figures on the size of born global firms seem to suggest that either since inception their business has involved a more structured base than traditional firms or they must reach a certain size — though not a large one — rather quickly. The interviews to entrepreneurs and managers provided a number of reasons for such a growth path, e.g. the need for a fast global market positioning.

The Impact of a Globalizing Economy and the Role of Location-Specific Drivers: Sticky Places in a Slippery Space

Table 1 shows the firms' demography, distinguishing the figures relating to the overall sample and the two sub-groupings according to their location inside or outside a district. It emerges that two-thirds of born global firms were born in the past two decades, while only one-third was born before the 1980s.

District-based born global firms appear to be relatively older, thus reflecting the history of the districts, which in Italy have a long established tradition and were the first "natural" environment for Italian young firms' fast international-ization processes. The concept of district is much stricter than the concept of clus-ter, because we adopted the definition of district laid down in the Italian regulation. Such "sticky places" tend to develop very strong interconnections with foreign markets: among the many outcomes of these interactions we can mention the high and growing level of foreign sales reported by districts (Maccarini et al., 2003), and more recently the increasing amount of semi-fin-ished and even finished goods imported, qualifying a transition of the district from local concentration of the different phases of the value chain towards the organization of global value chains. Such a transition gave rise to the concept of

Table 1: The period of birth of born global firms, district versus non district-based ones.

	Overall sample		District-based		Non district based	
	No.	%	No.	%	No.	%
During 1990s	35	32.71	12	21.05	23	46.00
During 1980s	36	33.64	16	28.08	20	40.00
Before 1980s	36	33.64	29	50.87	7	14.00
Total no. of firms	107	100.00	57	100.00	50	100.00

digital district (Rapporto Federcomin, 2003), i.e. a district where the connectivity inside the district and — most important — with firms and other clusters scattered all over the world but belonging to the same value chain is supported by ICT platforms, devices and services.

Non-district-based producers appear to be younger, their birth concentrating from the 1980s on, i.e. when the globalization of the world economy became more and more evident. An important issue arises from the analysis of these figures: in statistical terms the large majority of born global firms is district-based confirming the importance of location-specific factors, but in a dynamic perspective the role of agglomeration economies and co-location in born global attitude seems to fade. From this point of view, the role of ICT could be an important enabler of early internationalization by making access to information on foreign markets and potential customers and partners easier and wider, partly substituting the role of the local knowledge base available in clusters and districts. The growing spread of born global firms outside local clusters suggests that much of the knowledge needed to approach foreign markets can be codified and made accessible via ICT. This is demonstrated by the growth of online information and consulting services offered by Chambers of Commerce (Globus and Info-export are very good examples) and other public sector service providers to internationalizing firms.

On the other hand, tacit knowledge remains an important ground of internationalization strategies, but such knowledge base can be conveyed not necessarily by the local context alone but also by the entrepreneur and the start-up firm human resources, as described better in the following pages. In the past two decades, a new class of entrepreneurs has grown, which appears to be characterized by a stronger international vision and a sounder foreign market expertise than the former entrepreneurial generations.

The Role of Industry and Business-Specific Issues

Among the 107 sample firms, the main industries are mechanics and steel products (18%), machinery (14%), shoes and leather products (13%), food and beverages (9%), textiles and apparel (6%), then followed by many other industries with decreasing shares. The percentage of knowledge-intensive industries is 2%, covering a range of businesses involving high technologies and advanced know-how, by aggregating different sub-sectors of the National Bureau of Statistics standard. The figure seems to demonstrate that born global firms are not necessarily an offshoot of the high-tech and knowledge-intensive industries.

The most interesting issue arising from an industry perspective is that most born global firms do not fit very well into traditional industry classifications, due to the very high specialization of their products. For this reason, no detailed classification of our sample in terms of industry is provided, as many distinctions based on the National Bureau of Statistics standard classes would not provide any useful tool to understand sample firms' productive specialization.

It seems that technology plays a major role for born global firms as a cross-industry enabler or facilitator: in particular, information and telecommunication technologies definitely support these firms' global orientation since start up, even though the tools and options they adopt may vary a lot, from simple communication to occasional information exchanges, to stable supporting of international networks to electronic commerce. The information was obtained by visiting all the firms' websites and holding interviews.

Even though the distribution by industry of the surveyed firms is similar to the weight of the respective industries in the Italian manufacturing system, it seems that the percentage of born global firms exceeds the industry weight in the "made in Italy" businesses on one side and in high-tech businesses on the other. This could be interpreted as a result of the combined effect of two different factors affecting an early exporting attitude: on one side the effect of the former experience of the entrepreneur in similar businesses and of location-specific factors (traditionally made in Italy productions concentrate geographically, and in clusters/districts spin-off phenomena are predominant) and on the other, the mentioned features characterizing them as belonging in innovative industries, which seems to favour early and fast internationalization. Anyway, the industry-specific perspective was not found to be particularly significant in order to understand drivers and features of born global firms. The perspective of business-specific drivers, namely niche orientation, appears to be much more significant. It partly involves some industry influence, but most of all involves a dominant role of the entrepreneur's vision and competencies.

Table 2 shows that there are 69 niche firms over 107 born globals (64.5%), which seems to prove the importance of niche orientation in explaining the precocity of internationalization. Operationalizing the concept of niche orientation involved using some information obtained from the questionnaire, in particular product and market segment descriptions.

Operating within a narrowly defined market niche leads to look at an international market horizon in order to break even, since the domestic horizon alone — at a small niche level — does not allow firms to achieve adequate sales volumes. All over the world, niche firms share some fundamental similarities: they possess unique assets, focus on narrow global market segments, are strongly customer orientated and the entrepreneur's vision and competencies are of a crucial importance. Ultimately, being a strong exporter does not seem to be an option but a necessity for niche firms. They are pushed into globalization by global customers

Table 2: Business-specific drivers of early internationalization: The role of niche orientation.

	Overall sample (107 born global firms)		Niche firms (69 born global firms)	
	No.	%	No.	%
0 employees	3	2.80	0	—
1 to 9 employees	44	41.12	38	55.07
10 to 49 employees	43	40.19	19	27.53
50 to 249 employees	16	14.95	12	17.39
Over 250 employees	1	0.93	0	—
Total	107	100%	69	100%

and prohibitively small national/regional market segments. They can sustain their immediate global reach, thanks to entrepreneurial vision and competencies. Niche-oriented firms can be found in both traditional and innovative industries. From the interviews, the role of ICT emerges mainly as a cross-industry enabler rather than in terms of a distinctive industry where born global firms are found. Niche-oriented firms demonstrate a higher propensity to utilize a wide array of ICT services, and the motivations for such an attitude are to be found in the global reach that these firms typically have and in the customer-oriented approach they pursue. In fact, they offer a highly specialized and very often tailor-made product/service to a number of global customers located in very different and distant countries. As a consequence, they need a well-developed system of ICT-based tools and services to maintain a customer-centred approach — involving frequent communications, concurrent engineering, exchanges of information and assistance services — on a global scale.

Many interviewees declared that they do not plan and build their international expansion in terms of countries but mainly in terms of global customers. They admit that country differences may affect international expansion, especially when artificial barriers and industry standards are involved, but they donot feel so much affected by psychic distance issues in terms of countries' cultural diversities, since their products tend to focus on market niches (or more frequently deep niches) were the customer evidences worldwide common expectations and requirements. Being deeply niche-focused/global customer oriented allows the smallest firms to be global players (see Table 2).

Firm and Entrepreneurial-Specific Drivers

If we consider new ventures, firm- and entrepreneurial-specific issues tend to coincide, due to the dominant role of the entrepreneur in shaping the strategic orientation and organizational architecture of the start up. Investigating the role of the entrepreneur is one of the most promising fields in the research agenda about the born global firm phenomenon, since it is not well explored yet and presumably is one of the most (maybe the most) influential drivers of early internationalization processes. In order to investigate the role of entrepreneurial factors properly, it was necessary to rely most on the direct interviews to 46 firm owners and two export managers. In fact, the questionnaire provided only some quantitative information about the knowledge of foreign languages (89% of entrepreneurs) and the possession of specific competencies, as measured mainly by previous experiences in international firms (59%) (see Table 3). Developing an international vision is not necessarily the result of spending part of one's own life or education abroad, but is more often the outcome of previous work experience in international firms. This phenomenon is very common in districts, where spin-offs are very frequent. If, as mentioned earlier, location-specific factors represent an important driver of a born global attitude, a new generation of entrepreneurs is growing outside districts, characterized by a strong international vision, even without any previous experiences. These entrepreneurs are on average younger than the earlier ones, have a higher education and have developed their international attitude by being embedded in a global "atmosphere" and being heavy ICT users mainly, rather than by being embedded in a local network with a strong exporting attitude. Their international orientation stems much more from a vision than from an experience, which makes them lack an adequate knowledge base to

Table 3: The entrepreneur's profile in born global firms.

	Overall sample (107 born global firms)	
	No.	%
Good knowledge of one foreign language	95	88.78%
Good knowledge of two foreign languages	34	31.77%
Good knowledge of three or more foreign languages	8	7.48%
Previous experience in international firms	63	58.88%
Part of life/school career abroad	6	5.61%
Total	107	100%

ground the growth of the born global firm in foreign markets. For this reason, they seem to be more willing to use external support services for their international growth. An entrepreneur declared that his joint venture with a Chinese partner occurred only 3 years after the birth of his firm, when his only foreign operations consisted of some export activity in France and Germany. The joint venture was part of the entrepreneur's vision, but it was planned and realized with the major support of the industry association.

In some cases, namely innovative businesses, the entrepreneurial vision is complemented by venture capitalists, who provide not only financial capital but also know-how and support to international growth. A high-tech firm entrepreneur revealed that he had conceived his business as international since the beginning, but his vision was much strengthened by the venture capitalist who encouraged the firm to plan on a global scale and accompanied the international business plan implementation.

In commenting the role of globalization and localization forces in the world economy, it was found that markets integration, ICT developments, local network opportunities and knowledge base are all factors influencing more (the latter) or less (the former) directly the firms' early and fast international growth, but the entrepreneur's vision and competencies can better explain why a growing number of born global firms is found outside local clusters and how a firm can interpret a globalizing environment, and exploit the opportunities it offers through a serial growth in foreign markets. Moreover, the issue of how firms interpret such opportunities was also considered in industry- and business-specific drivers. The main outcome of the survey was that a niche orientation characterizes born global firms much more than belonging in a high-tech industry. Once again, such strategic orientation is mainly the result of the entrepreneur's vision, as the interviews highlighted that a global niche is the result of a cognitive and decisional process of the entrepreneur, and not a passive acceptance of a given market segmentation.

The Performance of Born Global Firms: Precocity, Export Intensity, Geographical Scope and Entry Mode Variety

The performance of born global firms can be analysed according to a set of parameters, namely precocity, intensity and scope. It is important to notice that the two fundamental performance indicators adopted for firms, i.e. growth and profitability, are not applied here. The reasons for this choice are many:

- Growth, as measured by sales/employees/assets increases over the years, is not a key target for many born global firms. In particular niche firms focus on a very narrow world market segment and are usually not affected by growth needs, because they tend to reach their optimum sales volume relatively quickly and then stabilize it over the years. The interviews seem to confirm that entrepreneurs of niche firms (a dominant category in born global firms) are not growth oriented.

- Profitability measures are frequently misleading, especially when new and small firms are considered. In addition to this, both growth and profitability measures would involve the availability of a significant observation period, and since many born global firms are relatively recent it was impossible to work on comparable data sets for the different firms.

- The analysis carried out in this research deals primarily with the internationalization process of firms, so it appears more coherent to measure the direct outcome of that process in terms of internationalization intensity, geographical scope and mode variety. Before measuring the outcome of serial internationalization processes, it was necessary to complete born global firm profiling in order to better understand — in addition to the drivers analysis carried out above — what are the features of the firms involved in early/instant international growth.

A first important measure is the precocity of such growth. In fact, we defined born global firms as those going international within 3 years of inception — according to a widely accepted parameter. Table 4 shows that almost 60% of such firms were actually instant international ones, since they started selling abroad in the same year of their inception. The figure is slightly higher for niche firms, since presumably the need to reach a tiny market segment of the global market pressures firms to go international very soon, in order to break even. A higher figure is reported for district-based firms, thanks to the local system positive externalities for international growth discussed earlier in this paper.

Exporting represents the major form of internationalization for small firms and is largely prevailing, in particular, in the case of infant firms, where it is usually the only approach such firms establish with foreign markets. For this reason, the

Table 4: Internationalization precocity.

	Overall sample		Niche producers		District-based firms	
	No.	%	No.	%	No.	%
Same year of inception	63	58.88	43	62.31	41	71.92
Within 3 years of inception	107	100.00	69	100.00	57	100.00

measure of export intensity was considered to be particularly relevant to the purpose of the research, in order to verify how effectively born global firms were grounding their business on foreign markets sales. According to one of the first empirical surveys on born global firms (McKinsey, 1993), such concept involves that at least 25% of revenues are made in foreign markets. Applying this parameter to our sample reduces the number of born global firms to only 34 over 107, nearly one-third. This result suggests that the majority of firms which started exporting within 3 years of inception did not reach appreciable levels of export intensity. This may be due to difficulties encountered at the outset of their activity in reaching the planned level of foreign sales, or to their willingness to adopt a more gradual international commitment. This involves that many firms are born global based on the temporal parameter, but are not so based on foreign sales intensity.

Another question regarding the concept and effective internationalization of born global firms is related to their geographical scope. Some studies have identified a minimum number of countries where the firm operates for it to be considered born global (Oviatt & Mc Dougall, 1994). The applicability of such definition should rest on minimum standards of both foreign sales intensity and geographical scope (number of countries). In particular, the latter parameter should help in distinguishing true global from merely international players, whereby the former show a broader reach and the ability to operate beyond their neighbouring regional area. This latter question is particularly important in a European perspective, as the European Union (EU) is progressively undergoing a transformation into an integrated internal market characterized by a continental size. An Italian firm operating with one or more countries, all belonging to the EU market area, will be considered less and less as being an international one (Zucchella & Maccarini, 1999). In addition to the traditional approach proposed by previous empirical studies on the geographical scope of born global firms usually using the number of countries in which they operate as a measure, the approach suggested here is to also distinguish among regional areas, and in particular between EU and extra-EU markets.

The absolute majority of born global firms operates in at least two countries (103 over 107), but their number drops to 53 and 23, if one considers those exporting in at least three and four countries, respectively. The born global firms in the sample show a prevailing attitude to focus on the EU market, similarly to the overall population of Italian exporters. Only when the number of countries involved is more than three do born global firms show a prevailing non-EU orientation. The main partners of born global firms show the same distribution as the population of Italian exporting firms, the most important country of export destination being France, followed by Germany. As to non-EU markets, there is a wide and dispersed variety of countries, depending mainly on the nature of the product. It is interesting to note that district localization has an impact on the geographical scope too, as firms located in the same district show similar geographical orientation. This is due to product specialization and the collective international knowledge cumulated by local systems, which based on past experience and success, and the exploratory capabilities of district collective institutions — notably export consortia and industry associations — shape avenues for firms' expansion in foreign markets. This also explains why firms located in districts show a larger geographical scope and a higher propensity to expand in extra-EU markets.

Firms showing the highest performances in terms of geographical scope and export intensity also showed the highest propensity to invest in ICT, and especially in advanced tools, like ERP systems. This emerged clearly from the interviews held in the framework of our survey, outlining an international entrepreneur's profile where the awareness of ICT opportunities in international business and management was greater.

A final international performance measure is the variety of entry modes in foreign markets. From this point of view the research found a low propensity to establish formal agreements (only 19 firms), both equity, like joint ventures (only two), and non-equity ones (the remaining 17 cases, among which 14 were commercial agreements and only three were productive ones).

The semi-structured interviews permitted us to better outline the reasons leading born global firms to establish the agreements, and the role of business versus location-specific factors.

Commercial agreements typically characterize born global firms with high export to sales ratios, and are considered as a complement to their export strategy by the concerned firms. Commercial agreements aim at strengthening foreign sales in strategic markets for the firms and seem to be consistent with the strong customer orientation of niche firms. In particular they provide a good answer to the requirement of guaranteeing local assistance and spare parts for exported (and frequently customized) machinery. District-based born global firms evidence a higher frequency of such agreements and, based on the interviews, possible explanations lie in imitative behaviours on one side (follow the local competitor) and the local availability of specialized services (associations, consortia, consultants) on the other.

Niche orientation explains the lack of productive agreements among the absolute majority of firms: the uniqueness of a firm's product is consistent with the decision to export what they produce in the home country, with limited or no production de-localization, since the exclusive know-how behind the product makes the organizational and productive hubs of the firm coincide. Uniqueness is often the result of business competencies and creativity associated with "territorial competencies" (specialized workforce, services).

Customer orientation is a powerful instrument to increase the knowledge base and boost its imperfect uniqueness. Small scale, flexibility and deep niche positioning are all factors explaining this attitude. Moreover, it is strong customer orientation that pushes for continuous product and process innovation.

The latter concept seems to be confirmed by the two research agreements in joint venture form reported in the survey. The global niche approach does not in fact imply that there is any stable niche protected from competition. The dynamism of markets, the transversality of new technologies, and the newly acquired ability of large firms to respond with flexible strategies and penetrate the market at the niche level (also by acquiring small firms) create a continual challenge for small enterprises. In both cases, the research agreement stemmed from the need to explore new technological opportunities with a foreign partner. The underlying need was to reach a better and faster product adaptation to foreign customer needs, and to learn from the foreign context in order to improve their technology to respond to local customers' needs and conditions. This knowledge is not bound to be used in the concerned foreign market alone, but can have important fallouts on the overall firm product strategy.

Conclusion

The reality of born global firms has known significant improvements along the years, thanks to a growing interconnection and interdependence among countries and markets across the world, the facilitating role of ICT, the development of high-tech and niche businesses, where a global reach is a condition of success, the clustering of economic activities with its economies of agglomeration. Correspondingly, also the knowledge of born global firms has improved through a number of both theoretical and empirical studies carried out in the past decade. Despite these considerations, the phenomenon of born global firms still needs more empirical investigation and lacks a complete theoretical framework.

The present contribution proposes an integrated approach to the development of these firms, taking into consideration not only factors like globalization versus localization, ICT, technology-based industries, i.e. environment or market-specific issues, but also the emerging and promising field of entrepreneurial issues.

The international entrepreneurship approach offers an interesting perspective to integrate environment- and business-specific issues with the entrepreneur's vision and competencies, to understand the spread of born global firms, and their global customer versus foreign markets orientation. This perspective of analysis is helpful in trying to provide an answer to the question of the possibility of survival and success of born global firms. Like any other new venture, the latter has in fact to face a considerable default risk, which could increase with the entry into a global competitive arena, due to the managerial and organizational complexities involved in this choice. Understanding the differences between international new ventures and successful born global firms is a relevant research issue, as Oviatt and McDougall (1994) outlined in their pioneering work. Entrepreneurial factors coupled with other managerial resources or "external knowledge suppliers" (associations, export consortia, private and public service providers) offer the possibility of better understanding successful born global firms.

One of the main managerial implications of this study is that in some cases being a born global firm can be the result of external conditions (location in a cluster, industry-specific factors) to some extent, but being a successful born global firm, capable of achieving a broad geographical scope and a high foreign sales ratio — sustainable over time — involves developing an international vision, opening up to world market opportunities and being able to identify groups of global customers to be targeted with a unique offer (creative world market segmentation and customer orientation). The possibility of making and sustaining this fast and intense global effort depends also on the attitude of the firm towards ICT. Exploring opportunities in world markets and understanding global customers are both supported by the global access to information made possible by the internet. Managing customer relationships on a global scale and controlling dispersed value chains require adequate ICT investments.

References

Arenius, P., & Autio, E. (2002). *International social capital and its effects on resource acquisition in born global firms*. Helsinki University of Technology Working Paper.

Bell, J. (1995). The internationalization of small computer software firms: A further challenge to "stage" theories. *European Journal of Marketing, 29*(8), 60–75.

Bloodgood, J.M., Sapienza, H.J., & Almeida, J.G. (1995). The internationalisation of new high potential ventures: Antecedents and outcome. *Frontiers of Entrepreneurship Research, 4,* 7–11.

Brandenburger, A.M., & Nalebuff, B.J. (1998). The right game: Use game theory to shape strategy. *Harvard Business Review, 73*(4), 28–39.

Brown, P., & Bell, J. (2001). Industrial clusters and small firm internationalization. In: J.H. Taggart, M. Berry, & M. McDermott (Eds), *Multinational in a ew era* (pp.10–26). Basingstoke: Palgrave Publishers.

Brush, C.G., Greene, P.G., & Hart, M.M. (2001). From initial idea to unique advantage: the entrepreneurial challenge of constructing a resource base. *Academy of Management Executive, 15*(1), 64–78.

Chiarvesio, M., & Micelli, S. (2004). L'impatto delle tecnologie di rete sui distretti industriali italiani, Primo Forum Regionale sulla Società dell'Informazione, 2 aprile 2004, Regione Marche.

Cioccarelli, G., Denicolai, S., & Zucchella, A. (2004). Reputation, trust and relational centrality in Italian districts — an empirical study. *Proceedings of the 20th EGOS onference*, 1–3 July, Liubljana, SLO.

De la Torre, J., & Moxon, R.W. (2001). E-commerce and global business: The impact of the information and communication technology revolution on the conduct of international business. *Journal of International Business Studies, 32*(4), 81–90.

Dunning, J. (Ed.). (2000). *Regions, globalization and the knowledge-based economy.* Oxford, UK: Oxford University Press.

Dunning, J., & Wymbs, C. (2001). The challenge of electronic markets for international business theory. *International Journal of the Economics of Business, 8*(2), 21–28.

Eisenhardt, K. (1989). Making fast strategic decisions in high velocity environments. *Academy of Management Journal, 32*(3), 54–60.

Enright, M. (1998). Regional clusters and firms strategy. In: A.D. Chandler, P. Hangstrom, & O. Solvell (Eds), *The dynamic firm: the role of technology, strategy, organizations and regions* (pp.35–49). New York: University Press.

Evans, P., & Wurster, T.S. (1999). Blown to bits: *How the new economics of information transforms strategy.* Boston, MA: Harvard Business School Press.

Harveston, P.D., Kedia, B.L., & Davis, P.S. (2000). *Internationalization of born global and gradual globalizing firms: The impact of firm specific advantage.* Babson College-Kauffman Foundation 20th annual conference on entrepreneurship, Boston.

Holstein, W.J. (1992). Little companies, big exports. *Business Week*, April 13, 70–72.

Hordes M., Clancy J., & Baddaley, J. (1995). A primer for global start ups. *Academy of Management Executive, 9*, 7–11.

Kandsaami, S. (1998). Internationalisation of small and medium sized born global firms: A conceptual model. Singapore: International Council for Small Business World Conference on Entrepreneurship.

Kedia, B.L., & Harveston, P.D. (1998). *International entrepreneurship: An examination of born global and gradual globalising firms.* Babson College-Kauffman Foundation entrepreneurship research conference, Boston.

Kobrin, S. (1991). An empirical analysis of the determinants of global integration. *Strategic Management Journal, 12*(17), 28–34.

Kuemmerle, W. (2002). Home base and knowledge management in international ventures. *Journal of Business Venturing, 17*, 99–122.

Leamer, E., & Storper, M. (2001). The economic geography of the internet age. Journal of *International Business Studies, 32*(4), 88–94.

Maccarini, M., Scabini, P., & Zucchella, A. (2003).Internationalisation strategies in Italian district-based firms: Theoretical modelling and empirical evidence. *Proceedings of clusters, industrial districts and firms:The challenge of globalization. Conference in honour of Professor Sebastiano Brusco.* Modena: University Press

Madsen, T.K., & Servais, P. (1997). The internationalization of born globals: An evolutionary process? *International Business Review*, 6/6, 561–583.

Markusen, A. (1996). Sticky places in slippery space: A typology of industrial district. *Economic Geography*, 72(3), 293–313.

McKinsey (1993). Emerging exporters: Australia's high value added manufacturing exporters. Melbourne: Australian Manufacturing Council.

Nayyar, P.R., & Bantel, K.A. (1994). Competitive agility: A source of competitive advantage based on speed and variety. In: P. Shrivastava, A.S. Huff, & J.E. Dutton (Eds), *Advances in strategic management: Resource-based view of the firm* (pp.29–40). Greenwich, CT: JAI Press.

Oviatt, B.M., & Mc Dougall, P.P. (1994). Toward a theory of international new ventures. *Journal of International Business Studies*, 25, 45–64.

Previtali P., Cioccarelli, G., & Denicolai, S. (2004). Blind enterprises and inter- organisational forms in Italian districts: An empirical analysis in the jewellery sector.*Proceedings of the 20th EGOS conference* , Ljubljana.

Rapporto Federcomin (2003). *Distretti produttivi digitali*. Rome: RUR-Censis

Rasmussen, E.S., Madsen, T.K., & Evangelista, F. (1999). *The founding of born global company in Denmark and Australia: Sensemaking and networking*. Odense: Odense University Proceedings.

Rialp-Criado, A., Rialp-Criado, J., & Knight, G.A. (2002). The phenomenon of international new ventures, global start ups an born globals: What do we know after a decade (1993–2002) of exhaustive scientific inquiry? *Proceedinngs of the 28th EIBA conference*, Athens.

Sahlman, W.A., & Stevenson, H.H. (1991) *The entrepreneurial venture*. Boston: McGraw-Hill.

Storper, M. (1992). The limits to globalization: Technology districts and international trade. *Economic Geography*, 68, 60–93.

Venkataraman, S. (1997). The distinctive domain of entrepreneurship research. In: J.A. Katz, & R.H. Brockhaus (Eds), *Advances in entrepreneurship, firm emergence and growth* (Vol. 3, pp. 230–245). Greenwich, CT: JAI Press.

Zaheer, S., & Manrakhan, S. (2001). Concentration and dispersion in global industries: Remote electronic access and the location of economic activities. Journal of International Business Studies, 32(4), 104–121.

Zucchella, A., & Maccarini, M.E. (1999). *I nuovi percorsi di internazionalizzazione*. Milan: Giuffrè.

Zucchella, A. (2001). The Internationalisation of SMEs: Alternative hypotheses and empirical survey. In: J.H. Taggart, M. Berry, & M. McDermott(Eds), *Multinationals in a new era* (pp. 47–60). Basingstoke: Palgrave.

Chapter 11

The Acquisition of Foreign Market Knowledge – A High-Tech SME's Usage of ICTs

Sara Melén

Introduction

In order for a company to internationalise, the accumulation of knowledge about foreign markets is a crucial process. The lack of foreign market knowledge, as for example a lack of knowledge in foreign markets and foreign customers, is regarded as an obstacle in the company's internationalisation (Johanson & Vahlne, 1977; Eriksson, Johanson, Majkgård, & Sharma, 1997). For small, entrepreneurial companies that sell high-technological products in new, emerging and specialised niche markets, international business is often a crucial consideration from the first day of a company's establishment, or soon thereafter (Crick & Jones, 2000; Yli-Renko, Autio, & Tontti, 2002; Saarenketo, Puumalainen, Kuivalainen, & Kyläheiko, 2003; Sharma & Blomstermo, 2003; Melén, Rovira, & Sharma, 2004; Rovira, Melén, & Sharma , 2005). The process of acquiring foreign market knowledge is, therefore, an important but also a challenging process for these companies, when a company must start to acquire knowledge about foreign markets soon after it is established.

Prior studies of small and medium-sized enterprises' (SMEs[1]) internationalisation, and in particular SMEs operating in high-tech businesses, such as software and

---

[1]The Swedish national entrepreneurs' federation defines small and medium-sized enterprises (SMEs) as enterprises with 1–199 employees.

---

biotech, have demonstrated the importance of a company's network of relationships (Coviello & Munro, 1997; Madsen & Servais, 1997; Coviello & McAuley, 1999; Chetty & Blankenburg Holm, 2000; Ellis, 2000; Yli-Renko et al., 2002; Saarenketo et al., 2003; Sharma & Blomstermo, 2003; Melén et al., 2004). The network of relationships, such as relationships to customers, suppliers, partners and competitors, can provide an SME with important foreign market knowledge. Prior studies of small, high-tech companies that start to operate in international markets from the first day of their establishment, have demonstrated that foreign market knowledge is acquired in the company's interaction with its foreign customers (Sharma & Blomstermo, 2003; Rovira et al., 2005). This study will expand on this research by means of a more in-depth study of a high-tech SME's acquisition of foreign market knowledge, in its interaction with existing and new customers in a foreign market. In this study, a high-tech SME is defined as a knowledge-intensive SME that sells high-technological new products in emerging, international and often specialised niche markets (Crick & Jones, 2000; Saarenketo et al., 2003).[2]

When studying an SME's interaction with foreign customers, a factor that has come to influence an SME's opportunities for doing business and interacting with foreign partners, is its usage of Information and Communication Technologies (ICTs) (Hamill, 1997; Hamill & Gregory, 1997; Moen, 2002; Sadowski, Maitland, & van Dongen, 2002). This factor must, therefore, be considered in this study. In analysing SMEs' usage of ICTs, some studies only refer to a single element of ICTs, such as the usage of e-mail or the Internet (Moen, 2002), while other studies are more ambitious in studying a full spectrum of ICTs, such as audio/video conferencing, CD-ROM, Web-based communication, etc. (Sinkovics, Bell, & Deans, 2004). In a report[3] by the Swedbank Föreningssparbanken and the Federation of Private Enterprises in Sweden, Sweden's small companies were asked about their usage of the Internet. The results demonstrated that small companies used Internet most often for communication (e-mail) and searching for information. The findings also showed that companies that were dependent on export used Internet to a higher extent than the domestic oriented companies. Based on the result of this report and prior studies on SMEs' usage of ICTs, a high-tech SME's ICT usage will be considered as searching the Internet for international information or using e-mail as a communication medium with customers and partners.

---

[2]Within the literature, these kinds of companies have been given several names, such as Born Globals (Sharma & Blomstermo, 2003) and Born Global SMEs (Melén et al., 2004; Rovira et al., 2005).
[3]The report, "Småföretagsbarometern," has investigated companies with 1–49 employees (http://www.foretagarna.se/pdf/BAR_Vt_2004/EU_Internet.pdf).

The purpose of this study is, therefore, to analyse how a high-tech SME acquires foreign market knowledge in its interaction with existing and new customers within a foreign market. In doing so, a high-tech SME's usage of ICTs will be considered and this study, thereby, contributes to the research of the Internet's impact on international business, which is an area where more research is required (Petersen, Welch, & Liesch, 2002).

In defining foreign market knowledge, Eriksson et al.'s (1997) definition of experiential market knowledge is used as a point of departure. These authors define foreign business knowledge as experiential knowledge of clients, the market and competitors (Eriksson et al., 1997, p. 343). In analysing a high-tech SME's acquisition of foreign market knowledge, this study focuses on the acquisition of knowledge about foreign clients and a foreign market.

For the purpose of this study, a case study of a small Scandinavian biotech company has been conducted. The company produces and sells specialised niche products in international markets and is defined as a high-tech SME. The study is limited to the company's interaction with existing and new customers within a specific foreign country market.

The chapter starts with a short literature review of SMEs' internationalisation. The characteristics of knowledge and its acquisition are then discussed. An analysis framework for studying a high-tech SME's acquisition of foreign market knowledge, in its interaction with its foreign customers, is outlined at the end of the theoretical part. After describing the research methodology and data collection, the empirical findings are presented and discussed. Finally, concluding remarks, future research and managerial implications are presented.

The Internationalisation of SMEs

The theoretical part starts with a short review of prior studies in SMEs' internationalisation and how SMEs use ICTs. The aim of the review is not to summarise all the studies that have been written within the area, but to draw some conclusions about SMEs' internationalisation and how these companies acquire knowledge about foreign markets.

The Importance of SMEs' Network of Relationships

In order to understand the internationalisation process of small, often resource-constrained companies, researchers have found network theories to be successful (Coviello & Munro, 1997; Madsen & Servais, 1997; Coviello & McAuley, 1999; Chetty & Blankenburg Holm, 2000; Ellis, 2000; Yli-Renko et al., 2002; Saarenketo et al., 2003; Sharma & Blomstermo, 2003). From the relationships to foreign customers, suppliers, distributors, etc., these companies are able to acquire important knowledge about markets abroad (Coviello & Munro, 1997; Chetty & Blankenburg Holm, 2000; Ellis, 2000; Sharma & Blomstermo, 2003). The knowledge that is acquired can be exemplified by knowledge of opportunities in foreign markets (Ellis, 2000) and knowledge of foreign business partners' needs and demands (Sharma & Blomstermo, 2003).

For SMEs that produce a high-technological product and operate in international niche markets, often directly after the company is founded, prior studies have indicated that the network of relationships might play an even more decisive role for the company's ability to engage in foreign businesses (Saarenketo et al., 2003; Sharma & Blomstermo, 2003; Melén et al., 2004; Rovira et al., 2005). Saarenketo et al. (2003) argue that a rapid internationalisation requires rapid learning, and this is partly enabled by the company's increased use of partners and networks. Sharma and Blomstermo's (2003) theoretical study of small knowledge-intensive companies that start to engage in international operations from the first day of their establishment, emphasises that the internationalisation process of these companies is driven by the knowledge supplied by the company's network. More specifically, Sharma and Blomstermo (2003) describe that a company selling a product that is high-tech and new in the market might need to teach its customers how to use the product. Due to the customers' need for knowledge on the product, its uses and its reliability, a direct contact with the customers is achieved. These feedback processes provide the small, knowledge-intensive and rapidly internationalising company with new knowledge of foreign clients and markets. Sharma and Blomstermo (2003), therefore, emphasise this two-way flow of information between a high-tech company and its customers. Supporting the findings of Sharma and Blomstermo (2003), Rovira et al. (2005) also demonstrate that the feedback provided by a company's customers has given the small, high-tech company important knowledge about the foreign customers.

So, prior studies have indicated that high-tech SMEs acquire important foreign market knowledge in their network relationships, and the interaction with foreign customers is one of these important network relationships.

SMEs' Usage of ICTs

When arguing that a high-tech SME's interaction with foreign customers is important for the company's acquisition of foreign market knowledge, a factor that has come to influence an SME's opportunity for interacting with foreign network partners is its usage of ICTs. Several studies have emphasised the new opportunities that have come with ICTs, and how these technologies can facilitate small companies in their internationalisation process (Hamill, 1997; Hamill & Gregory, 1997; Poon & Swatman, 1997; Moen, 2002; Spence, 2003; Saarenketo et al., 2003). ICT is shown to facilitate small companies' search for information about the international market (Moen, 2002), and communication with foreign customers and partners (Hamill, 1997; Hamill & Gregory, 1997; Poon & Swatman, 1997; Sadowski et al., 2002). Authors point out that information can now be distributed at an almost costless expense (Madsen & Servais, 1997; Petersen et al., 2002). Poon and Swatman (1997) found that small Australian companies perceived the key function of the Internet as being a medium for human communication. To accomplish this communication e-mail was used, primarily to communicate with customers and business partners. In contrast to telephone and fax, e-mail could overcome both time and geographical limitations. These advantages of using e-mail for communication were also emphasised in a study by Sinkovics et al. (2004), who describe e-mail as a technology that enables efficient, quick, and well-documented communication and is particularly useful for cheap, long-distance communication across international boundaries and time zones. Sinkovics et al. (2004), therefore, state that for international entrepreneurs, e-mail can improve the communication with network partners and contribute to a faster response to and from clients, prospects and suppliers. In a study of the Internet and international marketing, Moen (2002) found that the companies using information technology intensely in support of their export activities were young, in the sense of being relatively newly established, operating in growth markets, and were extremely niche focused and technologically advanced. Moen (2002), furthermore, found that several of the SMEs in his study considered it important to be able to keep in intensive contact with agents/distributors, and customers in export markets. ICTs were then used to support and strengthen these relationships. In another study by Moen, Endresen, and Gavlen (2003), the small software companies that were studied were using the Internet extensively for support and post-purchase activities. These activities and the Internet were important for small software firms in order to generate trust and long-term relationships. In support of Moen's (2002) findings, Quelch and Klein (1996) highlight the opportunities that the Internet has given small companies offering specialised niche products, as the Internet enables these companies to find their critical group of customers in the world. The authors point out that the Internet will facilitate both finding markets for new products and developing products for new markets. New product announcements on the Internet can generate immediate demand, and the Internet's new communication capabilities might speed the local adaptation and customization of products. In contrast to these arguments, Moen et al. (2003) argue that the Internet is not suited for marketing and promoting more complex and customised software. They find, rather, that inexpensive and standardised software is most suited for purchasing over the Internet.

In sum, prior studies of SMEs' usage of ICTs indicate that the Internet and e-mail can facilitate a high-tech SME's interaction with foreign customers.

Knowledge and Information – How Can It be Acquired?

In order to study a high-tech SME's acquisition of foreign market knowledge, the question of what knowledge is about and how it can be acquired, must first be discussed. In doing so, some attention will be paid at the start to the area of knowledge management. Within this research area, definitions of knowledge, information and data are a central issue.

Van Beveren (2002) is one of the researchers who discusses what knowledge is about and what differentiates knowledge from information. In doing so, he starts by defining data as raw facts (Van Beveren, 2002, p. 19). Information is then created when the data is given some context (Van Beveren, 2002, p. 19). Within an international business context, information is, for example, data about the number of potential clients in a specific country market. But in order to be able to make inferences from the information, to understand and interpret it, a person needs skills, experiences, beliefs, memories and a stock of information. This is what differentiates knowledge from information and data, whereas the latter can exist outside the human brain, knowledge must be processed within a person's brain. Van Beveren (2002) uses the words of Alexander, Schallert, and Hare (1991) when describing knowledge as referring to an individual's stock of information, skills, experiences, beliefs and memories (Alexander et al., 1991, p. 317). Similar to Van Beveren's (2002) way of describing the distinction between information and knowledge, Alavi and Leidner (2001) say that information is converted to knowledge once it is processed in the mind of individuals, and knowledge becomes information once it is articulated and presented in the form of text, graphics, words or other symbolic forms (Alavi & Leidner, 2001, p. 109).

In international business literature, the concepts of tacit and explicit knowledge, as well as experiential and objective knowledge, are widely used. Explicit and objective knowledge can be described as having similar characteristics, as this kind of knowledge can be expressed in formal, systematic language and, therefore, be acquired from libraries, databases, market research, product specification, etc. In contrast to explicit and objective knowledge, tacit and experiential knowledge has a personal quality, which makes it hard to formalise and communicate. This kind of knowledge is, therefore, acquired through action, involvement and commitment in a specific context, such as from personal experience of operating in a foreign market (Johanson & Vahlne, 1977; Eriksson et al., 1997; Nonaka, 1991, 1994). In discussing tacit knowledge, Nonaka (1994), furthermore, divides this knowledge into a cognitive and a technical element. The cognitive element helps an individual to perceive and define the world, and is described as an individual's images of reality and visions for the future. The cognitive element, therefore, has similar characteristics to Van Beveren's argument that knowledge must be processed in the human brain. The other part of tacit knowledge is the technical element, which involves concrete know-how and skills that apply to specific contexts.

Even though different terms are used in the discussion of what knowledge is about, I will, in line with several researchers, emphasise the similarities in the different terms. As, for example, Van Beveren (2002) argues that explicit knowledge is no more than information. Information, i.e. explicit knowledge, can then be used to create new knowledge within peoples' own brains and, thereby, contribute to solving unfamiliar problems. A similar standpoint is argued by Mårtensson (2000), namely that explicit knowledge is expressed as being identical to information, and this information cannot be considered to be knowledge until it has been processed in the human brain.

So, by considering the thoughts of researchers within knowledge management, and connecting these thoughts to the arguments made by researchers within international business, a fruitful distinction between information and knowledge and their acquisitions is offered. I will distinguish between information and knowledge by using Van Beveren's (2002) definition of information. Information is then data within a context, and it can be acquired via databases, market research, country reports, etc., when information is easy to transfer. In contrast to information, knowledge must be processed in the human brain. The acquisition of knowledge is, therefore, connected to involvement and experience in a specific context, and the knowledge that is acquired is of a more tacit kind and difficult to transfer.

Knowledge Acquisition via the Usage of ICTs

After distinguishing between information and knowledge, the two concepts will now be discussed in relation to the usage of ICTs. Whether knowledge can be acquired via ICTs has frequently been discussed within knowledge management research. Several researchers argue that information technology is not capable of creating knowledge in itself. In order to acquire knowledge, some human involvement is needed (McDermott, 1999; Mårtensson, 2000; Van Beveren, 2002). For example, Van Beveren (2002) argues that information technology has contributed to faster, more efficient methods for accessing information, but it is a mistake to equate information with knowledge.

Within international business research, Petersen et al. (2002) have presented an article about how the Internet may affect companies' foreign market expansion, and to what extent the Internet will facilitate the creation and transfer of tacit knowledge. The authors do not come to a definitive conclusion on this question but rather discuss different predictions about its effect. One of the predictions highlights the Internet's shortcomings in providing experiential knowledge. The Internet has the potential to facilitate firms' acquisition of objective knowledge, but whether experiential knowledge can be acquired is much more questionable. The authors, however, also come up with a more optimistic proposition regarding the Internet's facilitation of experiential and tacit knowledge. This prediction states that when operating in foreign countries via the Internet, the staff of a company will develop techniques for handling foreign clients and cross-cultural exchanges. This experiential learning provides critical feedback into the ongoing activities of internationalising companies.

In sum, the question of whether or not tacit and experiential knowledge can be acquired via the Internet is still not solved. For the purpose of this study I will argue that by communicating via e-mail or searching for information via the Internet, a high-tech SME can only acquire information about foreign markets and foreign customers when information can be transferred. When this information is processed in the human brain and combined with a person's involvement and experience in a specific context, foreign market knowledge, i.e. knowledge about foreign markets and customers, can be acquired. In accordance with Petersen et al.'s (2002), more optimistic proposition of the Internet's facilitation of experiential and tacit knowledge, I argue that even though the involvement and experience in a foreign market has only occurred via the ICTs, important knowledge can be acquired. This knowledge is then of a more tacit kind, that will help a high-tech SME to perceive and define a foreign market, and know how to best approach specific foreign customers.

Interaction Processes in Business Relationships

In order to study a high-tech SME's acquisition of foreign market knowledge in its interaction with foreign customers, it is useful to refer to the research that has been conducted in the European International Marketing and Purchasing (IMP) group. Researchers have then described a relationship between a seller and a buyer as a business relationship that evolves through interaction processes between the parties (Håkansson, 1982; Blankenburg Holm, Eriksson, & Johanson, 1996). Based on the interaction model (Håkansson, 1982), two related interaction processes, i.e. the exchange and adaptation processes, can be distinguished (Johanson & Mattsson, 1987). For the purpose of this chapter, these processes offer a useful point of departure in analysing a high-tech SME's interaction with its foreign customers. Even though the buyer and the seller company are two distinctive units, several researchers have emphasised the need for not analysing the two parties in isolation from other companies that might be connected to these two parties (Anderson, Håkansson, & Johanson, 1994; Blankenburg Holm et al., 1996). As described in Anderson et al. (1994), the two companies that are of interest, i.e. the supplier and the customer company, can be directly or indirectly connected with other relationships that may influence the two parties. In taking this aspect into consideration, this study focuses on a high-tech SME's interaction with a group of German customers, but in doing so the other customer relationships that are seen to influence these interactions will also be considered.

In discussing the exchange processes, the exchange can be distinguished in terms of product and service exchange, as well as in information, financial and social exchange. As pointed out in Håkansson (1982), the product or service is often the central exchange element, and its characteristics will, therefore, be likely to influence the relationship. Furthermore, Håkansson (1982) emphasises that the content of the information that is exchanged, whether it is technical, economic or organisational questions that dominate the exchange, might also be of importance for the relationship. The financial exchange and the quantity of money exchanged is an indicator of the economic importance of the relationship. Whether social exchange is evident in the relationship has important implications. The social exchange process can contribute to maintaining the relationship in periods where no transactions are taking place, by contributing to building up trust in the relationship. The need for social exchange and mutual trust can, however, vary depending on the elements that are exchanged in the relationships (Håkansson, 1982).

The other form of interaction processes are the adaptation processes that can take place in different dimensions. Technical adaptations are, for example, modifications of product and production processes. Logistical adaptations may concern delivery systems or stock levels. Further forms are administrative and financial adaptations, which deal with adapting payments in special ways. As pointed out by Johanson and Mattsson (1987), the exchange and adaptation processes are related and the more intensive the exchange processes between the companies, the stronger are the reasons for the involved companies to make adaptations. The type of elements that are exchanged in the relationship can, furthermore, also influence the characteristics of the adaptations made (Johanson & Mattsson, 1987).

For the purpose of this chapter, the two interaction processes that have been outlined above must be connected to a high-tech SME's usage of ICTs. Prior studies have indicated that these technologies facilitate a high-tech SME's interaction with foreign customers and its acquisition of information. In the analysis framework presented in Figure 1, the exchange processes are analysed in order to

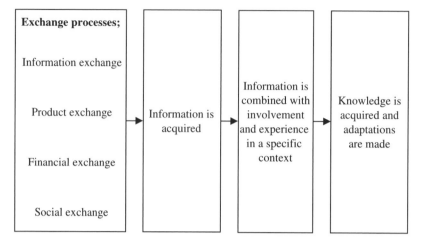

Figure 1: An analysis framework of how a high-tech SME can acquire foreign market knowledge when interacting with its foreign customers via the Internet and e-mail.

study how information is acquired. The analysis framework highlights that when information has been acquired, it must be combined with a person's involvement and experience in a specific context, in order for knowledge to be acquired. In this study, the adaptations that are made will be regarded as an indicator of what knowledge a high-tech SME has acquired.

Research Methodology

In order to gain a deeper understanding of a high-tech SME's acquisition of foreign market knowledge when interacting with its foreign customers, a case study proved to be a suitable research methodology. I was interested in receiving the stories and perspectives from those people within a high-tech SME who were engaged with the task of managing foreign customer relations. In-depth interviews were, therefore, conducted.

The case selected for this study is a company that operates within the biotech industry and manufactures high-technological products. In selecting the company for this study, five criteria were set up. The company's founder should still work in the company, as the founder of small entrepreneurial enterprises has been shown to play an important role in the company's first years of internationalisation (Madsen & Servais, 1997). The second and third criteria assured that the company produced and sold a high-technological product on a foreign market. The company should, furthermore, be a small or medium-sized enterprise that used ICTs as a tool in its internationalisation process. In order to keep the company studied anonymous, it is called Epsilon in this chapter.

As mentioned by Eisenhardt (1989), case studies typically combine different kinds of data collection methods, such as archives, interviews, questionnaires and observations. The main source for this study is five face-to-face interviews and one telephone interview. Complementary data were found in annual reports, newspaper articles, databases and Web pages.

In April 2004, the first interview was conducted at Epsilon. During the following 12 months, another five interviews were conducted with people involved in managing the foreign customer relationships in the company. The interviews that were carried out at the company had slightly different objectives. The first interview had the objective of acquiring an overview of the company's internationalisation process. The second interview was made in order to follow up the company's international business. From the first two interviews, it was found that Epsilon used the Internet extensively in its collaboration with foreign customers. The third, fourth and fifth interviews, therefore, had the objective of investigating how Epsilon managed its collaboration with customers by using the Internet.

Five of the six interviews made at Epsilon were conducted with the founder of the company, who also holds the position of the company's CEO. The CEO has had the main responsibility for managing the company's foreign customer relationships and, furthermore, is the person with the technological knowledge in the company. He is, therefore, the person who can answer customers' questions about how to use the products. The sixth interview was conducted with a German person, who was employed at Epsilon for a 6-month period in order to manage the German customer relations.

Each face-to-face interview lasted for about 2 h. All the interviews were semi-structured. An interview guide was used but was departed from when interesting topics came up during the interview. The face-to-face interviews were conducted at the company's office, where the company also runs its production. I, therefore, got access to another source for data collection, i.e. direct observation. I spent more than 2 h at the company's office on each interview occasion, and I have been guided around its production units. The informal chats and the opportunity to observe how it was organised gave me a better understanding of the company.

A Case Study – Epsilon's Interaction with Customers in the German Market

Epsilon was established in the mid-1990s, and is a small Scandinavian biotech company specialised in producing biochemical products. Since the year it was founded, Epsilon has grown from a one-person company to a company of 10 employees in 2003. Within 2 years of the company's establishment, Epsilon sold its products to customers in Germany, Great Britain and the USA. By 2003, Epsilon was also exporting its products to several European countries and Japan. Epsilon manages its sales through the company's headquarter, and in some countries international distributors are used. The existing customers are both small and large companies that are mainly found in the area of biotech and diagnostics. This study focuses on Epsilon's expansion into the German market, and on one group of German customers that purchase Epsilon's product. In 2003, Germany was Epsilon's third largest export market, and during the last 2 years Epsilon has started to direct a great deal of resources to the German market.

The customer companies that are the focus for this study are a group of German veterinary clinics. The first German veterinary clinic came into contact with Epsilon about 2 years after the company's establishment. Since the first clinic started to use Epsilon's product, several German clinics have contacted Epsilon to order the product as well. In 2003, Epsilon exported its product to about 30 veterinary clinics in the German market. Even though these veterinary clinics do not generate any large revenues for Epsilon, they have been a target market for the company and a lot of resources have been invested in these customers. The product that the German clinics purchase from Epsilon is a specialised diagnostic kit. In contrast to the existing products in the market, Epsilon's diagnostic kit is equipped with a certain parasite that is fairly unknown in the market. The product is, therefore, more specialised than the common tests available. The veterinary clinics work with animals, and when treating the animals the clinics often use several test procedures. Epsilon's specific diagnostic kit is one of these test procedures. In selling the diagnostic kit, Epsilon does not make any special customer modifications and every kit is the same to all customers.

The veterinary clinics can be differentiated based on their size. The smaller kinds of clinics usually employ one or two doctors, and have additional two or three employees. The other group of clinics is represented by the larger clinics that are more like centres of doctors. The number of doctors is often three to twelve, and to each doctor one or two assistants are employed. The number of employees can then vary from 10 to 50 people.

Apart from the German veterinary clinics, Epsilon also sells its products to other customers in the German market. In contrast to the veterinary clinics, these customers might be larger companies and buy the other products that Epsilon manufactures. This chapter will focus on Epsilon's interaction with the German veterinary clinics but in doing so, Epsilon's other German customer interactions will also be considered.

The CEO Manages the Communication with the German Customers

During the period from 1996 to 2003, the CEO of Epsilon managed the contacts with the German veterinary clinics. When the small veterinary clinics had problems using the product, the CEO had great deal of contact with these clinics. The clinics needed support when starting to use the product. Epsilon has, therefore, made a special box for these clinics with all the accessories needed to start using the product. Those clinics that had used the test for several years bought the ready to use kit. Epsilon even considered making a video film in order to support new clinics when starting to use the product. Even though Epsilon has had rather a lot of contact with some of its clinics, the CEO does not know the customers at all and Epsilon has never met anyone from the clinics. The CEO believes that Epsilon's product has been recommended to the German veterinary clinics by other veterinary clinics in Germany, when the clinics participate in congresses and similar activities. The clinics then contact Epsilon via e-mail or telephone.

During this period of communication, the parties communicated in English when no one at Epsilon was able to speak German. The information material and instructions that were available for the customers were also in English. Difficulties in understanding the customers could, however, arise, due to language difficulties and problems in finding the right terms for the technical expressions. The contact was, therefore, mostly managed via e-mail. Epsilon also perceived that the German customers wanted to have the instruction material in the German language, instead of in English. Epsilon understood that the inability to speak the German language was an impediment for the company.

In September 2003, Epsilon employed a German student for a period of 6 months. The German employee was going to sell Epsilon's products in the German market and work with the German veterinary clinics. The employment implied that the German student would now handle some of the tasks that had previously been managed by the CEO, and Epsilon was hoping to be able to develop better relations with the customers in Germany, as the company would now be able to have a direct contact with these customers.

During the autumn of 2003, Epsilon was hoping to find new customers in the German market. The first step was to find more veterinary clinics, and the second step was to start looking for a distributor in the German market that could sell one of Epsilon's other products in Germany. When the German student began working at Epsilon, the CEO perceived that the German customers really appreciated being able to communicate in German.

The German Student Manages the Communication with German Customers

In September 2003, the German student began working at Epsilon. However, she lacked prior knowledge and experience in the biotechnology area. Her first task was to do some research about the German market and potential veterinary clinics. By using a German Internet site and different databases that displayed all the German veterinary clinics, she found about 600 addresses to potential veterinary clinics. The 600 addresses mostly represented the smaller kinds of clinics, the clinics which were in greatest need of this product. The German employee found the German market to be large, and she was not able to do research about the whole market by herself. In describing the market, the student expresses: "I could have sat down for ages and found more addresses to these kinds of small clinics." Even though the diagnostic kit that Epsilon sells is based on a common procedure, the kit is specialised towards a certain parasite that few clinics are aware of. The situation implies that even though Epsilon had several addresses to potential clinics, only a few of these would need the test. An even smaller number of clinics would be aware of Epsilon's specific kit, and the clinics that are not aware of the specific parasite will not buy it. The market and product characteristics imply that although the immunology sector within which Epsilon works is large, the doctors and researchers that both need and are aware of this specific parasite are rather limited.

During her work at Epsilon, the German student tried to come in contact with new German customers, not only veterinary clinics, by telephone or direct mailing. This was, however, more difficult than Epsilon expected. Epsilon experienced that if a company did not know about Epsilon, it was difficult to sell the product.

The German student, therefore, found that it is always the customers that contact Epsilon. The veterinary clinics most likely become aware of Epsilon through word-of-mouth. The German student explains: "If some clinics have used the product and they were satisfied with the product, then they will talk about this test to other companies that will ask where they have bought the test and then more customers want to come in contact with us."

The German student, furthermore, argues: "Brings me also back to the point that you need to build up a network. A person just believes you if another person tell the first person that we are trustworthy."

When new veterinary clinics become interested in Epsilon, the clinics most often contact the company by e-mail or telephone. The clinics that become interested in Epsilon are usually already aware of the product and, therefore, know about the common procedure upon which the test is based. Some clinics also know about the specific parasite that is unique to Epsilon's product. When a new clinic e-mails or telephones Epsilon for the first time, the questions, therefore, often concern more general matters, such as the price and how many tests the customer can do with the kit. The clinics do not ask about how to work with the kit, the questions rather concern matters such as whether they can read the test in accordance with the common, already known procedure. The clinics often ask Epsilon how reliable the test is, i.e. whether Epsilon can guarantee that the customer will attain certain results. These kinds of questions are asked before a customer purchases the product. The questions are most often responded to by Epsilon via e-mail. If Epsilon, however, receives questions from a customer and the questions indicate that the customer does not understand the product, the German student can telephone the companies just to say that she will send them the instructions via e-mail. The telephone call does not include that much information but the customer often feels satisfied with it.

When communicating with the clinics, the German student talks with the doctors. She wants to come into contact with the doctors, because these are the people who ought to know most about the immunology area and, thereby, understand most of the matters. The German student has, however, experienced that the small clinics lack an in-depth knowledge about the tests. The small clinics should know about the common procedure but they may not know about the specific parasite.

When clinics receive the product, proper instructions and explanations are included. By following the instructions, the customer is introduced to the specific parasite and to the common procedure used when performing the test. After a customer has ordered the product once, Epsilon most often does not hear anything from the customers for 1 or 2 years. The clinic can use the product for 1 or 2 years before they need to order again. The German student explains: "And that is not because they are impolite or that we are impolite, it is just that it is no need for having more contact. And everything that is needed is told by the instructions that are sent out to customers."

The German student also mentions that she once tried to contact the existing customers, to ask if they had any problems or if they were interested in ordering again. She also introduced Epsilon's other products. The telephone call resulted in her sending most of the customers a prospect of Epsilon's other products.

Working with the veterinary clinics and the specialised diagnostic test was the German student's first project during her time at Epsilon. The German student summarises her work by saying that: "The German market has a great potential but we must figure out how to go into the German market without having personal contacts. It is a huge disappointment."

Discussion

The purpose of this paper was to study a high-tech SME's acquisition of foreign market knowledge in its interaction with existing and new customers within a foreign market. By taking a high-tech SME's usage of the Internet and e-mail into consideration, the case study has given some indications about how the interaction processes and a high-tech SME's acquisition of foreign market knowledge have been facilitated by the use of ICTs. Even though the group of German customers that have been studied in this chapter does not generate any large revenues for Epsilon, and the financial exchange, thereby, is rather limited, interesting findings regarding the other exchange processes will now be discussed.

Knowledge Acquisition in the Information Exchange Process

In the communication between the CEO of Epsilon and the clinics, it is indicated that an exchange of technical information has characterised the relationships. The customers have had problems in starting to use the product, and an exchange of information concerning the product has taken place. From the CEO's exchange of technical information with the clinics, Epsilon acquired knowledge about the customers' capability in using the product and the customers' needs and demands. This knowledge resulted in a technical adaptation, i.e. the special box that Epsilon made to support new customers. An administrative adaptation was also made, which is demonstrated in Epsilon's employment of the German student. The German student could meet the German customers' requirements of having instructions in the German language instead of in English.

The German student has, more specifically, described the exchange processes in the relationships with the German veterinary clinics. As most of the clinics that contact Epsilon are well aware of the test procedure that the kit is based upon, the situation described by the German student shows that there seems to be no need for any intensive exchange of information. The well-informed clinics have some questions about the reliability of the product and its usage, but after the order has been made, the clinics usually do not need any further information. Some clinics, mostly the smaller ones, however, lack an in-depth knowledge in the area and need more technical information from Epsilon. A more intensive information exchange might be necessary in these relationships.

Even though the intensiveness of the information exchange is seen to be rather low in most relationships, e-mail is used to manage most of the information exchange when customers start using the product. E-mail has, thereby, facilitated this kind of technical information exchange, and in the CEO's interaction with the clinics, there are some indications that e-mail has facilitated the information exchange when language difficulties and technical expressions made it more difficult to understand each other on the telephone. When the information that was acquired via e-mail was combined with Epsilon's experience and involvement in the German market, Epsilon acquired important knowledge about the exiting veterinary clinics.

Knowledge Acquisition in the Product Exchange Process

Epsilon's product is standardised, in the sense that all customers buy the same product, and by following the instructions that come with the product, most of the customers are able to use it without any intensive need of help. When the product has been received, the clinic can generally use it for 1 or 2 years before another product needs to be ordered. As pointed out in Johanson and Mattsson (1987), the need of industrial activities will influence the interaction processes. In this case, the product characteristics are seen to contribute to the limited information exchange that takes place in most customer relationships. The diagnostic kit is, however, specialised towards a certain parasite and few clinics are shown to be aware of this specific test. These characteristics of the product are shown to influence Epsilon's ability to initiate a product exchange with new potential customers in the German market. This is illustrated in Epsilon's use of the Internet in order to find new potential clinics. The information that was acquired gave Epsilon an overview of the market and the German veterinary clinics. When this information was combined with Epsilon's experience and involvement in the market, Epsilon acquired knowledge about the number of customers that both needed and were aware of the product, which differed from the information that was acquired via the Internet. The German student also tried to initiate a product exchange with new customers in the German market, by using the telephone and e-mail. The German student experienced that Epsilon needed to have personal contacts in potential customer companies in order to initiate a product exchange. As expressed by the German student, "… A person just believes you if another person tell the first person that we are trustworthy."

So, in trying to initiate a product exchange with new potential customers, Epsilon acquired knowledge about how to best approach potential German customers. To approach a new customer required Epsilon to have some personal contacts in the potential customer company. Epsilon has also acquired knowledge about how the clinics are connected to each other and how the clinics have received information about the company.

The case, therefore, indicates that the characteristics of the product have influenced Epsilon's opportunities for initiating a product exchange with new customers. Even though the Internet and e-mail have facilitated the existing and new veterinary clinics' initiation of a product exchange, it is seen that these ICTs have not facilitated Epsilon's initiation of a product exchange with new customers.

Knowledge Acquisition in the Social Exchange Process

In trying to initiate a product exchange with new German customers and in understanding how the veterinary clinics are connected to each other, elements of trust and personal relationships are seen to be crucial for Epsilon in their interaction with existing and new German customers. Epsilon's lack of personal contacts in potential customer companies and the need for trust have made it more difficult for Epsilon to use e-mail in trying to initiate new customer relationships.

As pointed out by Epsilon's CEO, the company has never met the veterinary clinics and the CEO does not know them at all. The CEO's argument highlights that there has been a rather limited social exchange in the relationships. Epsilon has, however, made some adaptations in order to better satisfy the needs of the clinics, and these adaptations have contributed to the development of trust between Epsilon and the clients. The German student also points out that she could sometimes use the telephone when the questions indicated that customers did not understand the product. A telephone call solely for the purpose of exchanging some general information is shown to be appreciated by the customers and, therefore, also contributes to the development of trust in these relationships.

Concluding Remarks and Future Research

This study has demonstrated how a high-tech SME has acquired foreign market knowledge in its interaction with new and existing customers in a foreign market, and how the usage of ICTs has facilitated this interaction and the acquisition of knowledge. The analysis has indicated that e-mail has facilitated the exchange of technical information in customer relationships, even though the information exchange is rather limited in the relationships. In support of several prior studies of SMEs' ICT usage in its internationalisation process (Poon & Swatman, 1997; Sinkovics et al., 2004), this study shows that e-mail is an important ICT for Epsilon in order to acquire information about foreign customers and markets. When the information has then been combined with Epsilon's involvement and experience in the German market, foreign market knowledge has been acquired. Considering Petersen et al.'s (2002) different predictions, this study has taken a rather optimistic standpoint in ICTs' facilitation of experiential and tacit knowledge acquisition. This standpoint can be seen in contrast to several knowledge management researchers' opinions in this question.

In light of this optimistic finding regarding the ICTs' facilitation of knowledge acquisition, the case also points to the shortcomings of ICTs in Epsilon's attempt to initiate new customer relationships, as few potential customers are aware of Epsilon's specialised kit. The Internet has contributed to Epsilon's search for addresses to new potential customers, but in order to initiate a product exchange with new customers, personal relationships are needed. Prior studies have highlighted the ICTs' usage among small, high-tech companies, producing specialised niche products (Quelch & Klein, 1996; Moen, 2002). The case of Epsilon has indicated that difficulties may come in selling these products in international markets by using ICTs, where few customers are aware of Epsilon's specialised products. Elements of trust and personal relationships are seen as being important in order to sell these products in foreign markets. In the case of Epsilon, Internet, e-mail and telephone are the only technologies used in interacting with existing and potential German customers. In his study of the Internet and SMEs' international marketing, Moen (2002) points out that the companies in his study were using ICTs to support customer relationships and partners in export markets, but that the ICTs could not replace or reduce the personal involvement and market presence. In order to provide more detailed knowledge about how a high-tech SME's product characteristics are related to the level of e-mail interaction that occurs in customer relationships, and how these aspects then influence a high-tech SME's acquisition of foreign market knowledge, quantitative research can be used.

As shown in this case, there is mostly no need for any intensive information exchange in the customer relationships. When connecting this finding with the arguments in Sharma and Blomstermo (2003), it is shown that the two-way flow of information, emphasised as important for a small high-tech company's acquisition of foreign market knowledge, is rather limited in most of Epsilon's relationships with veterinary clinics. Furthermore, the information exchange has, to a large extent, been initiated by the customers, with their questions about the product. The customers with more questions will initiate a more intensive and extensive information exchange, which could result in Epsilon acquiring more specific knowledge about these customers' needs and demands. However, this case has only provided indications about the relationships between the customers' need for information, the level of intensity in the information exchange and a high-tech SME's acquisition of foreign market knowledge. Quantitative research could provide more detailed knowledge in this area.

Managerial Implications

This case study has shown that small, high-tech companies, operating in international markets, can acquire important knowledge of new and existing customers in foreign countries by using the Internet and e-mail. However, managers must be aware of the differences between information and knowledge. The information that can be acquired via the Internet and e-mail communication must be combined with a person's experiences and involvement in a specific context, in order to acquire knowledge.

The knowledge that can be acquired in the interaction with foreign customers is important for the company's expansion in foreign markets. It is, therefore, crucial for managers to keep an intensive and extensive exchange of information with the customers, especially when customers do not frequently place an order. In those situations, the managers of a small high-tech company might need to think even more about maintaining the interaction with the customers.

Acknowledgment

I gratefully acknowledge the financial support of the Jan Wallander and Tom Hedelius' Foundation, Handelsbanken, Sweden.

References

Alavi, M., & Leidner, D.E. (2001). Review: Knowledge management and knowledge management systems: Conceptual foundations and research issues. *MIS Quarterly*, *25*, 107–136.

Alexander, P.A., Schallert, D.L., & Hare, V.C. (1991). Coming to terms: How researchers in learning and literacy talk about knowledge. *Review of Educational Research*, *61*, 315–343.

Anderson, J.C., Håkansson, H., & Johanson, J. (1994). Dyadic business relationships within a business network context. *Journal of Marketing*, *58*, 1–15.

Blankenburg Holm, D., Eriksson, K., & Johanson, J. (1996). Business networks and cooperation in international business relationships. *Journal of International Business Studies*, *27*, 1033–1053.

Chetty, S., & Blankenburg Holm, D. (2000). Internationalisation of small to medium-sized manufacturing firms: A network approach. *International Business Review*, *9*, 77–93.

Coviello, N.E., & McAuley, A. (1999). Internationalisation and the smaller firm: A review of contemporary empirical research. *Management International Review*, *39*, 223–256.

Coviello, N.E., & Munro, H. (1997). Network relationships & the internationalization process of small software firms. *International Business Review*, *6*, 361–386.

Crick, D., & Jones, M.V. (2000). Small high-technology firms and international high-technology markets. *Journal of International Marketing*, *8*, 63–85.

Eisenhardt, K. (1989). Building theories from case study research. *Academy of Management Review*, *16*, 532–550.

Ellis, P. (2000). Social ties and foreign market entry. *Journal of International Business Studies, 31*, 443–469.

Eriksson, K., Johanson, J., Majkgård, A., & Sharma, D.D. (1997). Experiential knowledge & cost in the internationalization process. *Journal of International Business Studies, 28*, 337–360.

Hamill, J. (1997). The Internet and international marketing. *International Marketing Review, 14*, 300–323.

Hamill, J., & Gregory, K. (1997). Internet marketing in the internationalization of UK SMEs. In: J. Hamill (Ed.), Special Edition on Internationalization. *Journal of Marketing Management, 13*, 9–28.

Håkansson, H. (1982). *International marketing and purchasing of industrial goods: An interaction approach.* New York: Wiley.

Johanson, J., & Mattsson, L.-G. (1987). Interorganizational relations in industrial systems: A network approach compared with the transaction-cost approach. *International Studies of Management & Organization, XVII*, 34–48.

Johanson, J., & Vahlne, J.-E. (1977). The internationalization process of the firm – A model of knowledge development & increasing foreign market commitments. *Journal of International Business Studies, 8*, 23–32.

Madsen, K.T., & Servais, P. (1997). The internationalization of Born Globals: An evolutionary process. *Internationalisation Business Review, 6*, 561–583.

Mårtensson, M. (2000). A critical review of knowledge management as a management tool. *Journal of Knowledge Management, 4*, 204–216.

McDermott, R. (1999). Why information technology inspired but cannot deliver knowledge management. *California Management Review, 41*, 103–117.

Melén, S., Rovira, E., & Sharma, D.D. (2004). Knowledge management in Born Global SMEs within the biotech industry. In: Y. Cader (Ed.), *Knowledge management: Theory and application in a twenty-first century context* (pp. 31–52). Australia: Heidelberg Press.

Moen, Ø. (2002). The Internet and international marketing, an empirical analysis of small and medium sized Norwegian firms. *Quarterly Journal of Electronic Commerce, 3*, 31–41.

Moen, Ø., Endresen, I., & Gavlen M. (2003). Executive insights: Use of the Intenret in international marketing: A case study of small computer software firms. *Journal of International Marketing, 11*, 129–149.

Nonaka, I. (1991). The knowledge-creating company. *Harvard Business Review, 69*, 96–104.

Nonaka, I. (1994). A dynamic theory of organizational knowledge creation. *Organization Science, 5*, 14–36.

Petersen, B., Welch, L.S., & Liesch P.W. (2002). The Internet and foreign market expansion by firms. *Management International Review, 42*, 207–221.

Poon, S., & Swatman, P.M.S. (1997). Small business use of the Internet. *International Marketing Review, 14*, 385–402.

Quelch, J.A., & Klein, L.R. (1996). The Internet and international marketing. *Sloan Management Review, 37*, 60–75.

Rovira, E., Melén, S., & Sharma, D.D. (2005). The internationalisation of a Born Global SME in the high-tech business – A longitudinal case study. In: J.-W. Lee, A. Hadjikhani, & J. Johanson (Ed.), *Business networks and international markets*. South Korea: Brain Korea Publishing Ltd.

Saarenketo, S., Puumalainen, K., Kuivalainen, O., & Kyläheiko, K. (2003). Dynamic knowledge related learning processes in internationalizing high-tech SMEs. *International Journal of Production Economics, 89*(3), 363–378.

Sadowski, B.M., Maitland, C., & van Dongen, J. (2002). Strategic use of the Internet by small- and medium-sized companies: An exploratory study. *Information Economics and Policy, 14*, 75–93.

Sharma, D.D., & Blomstermo, A. (2003). The internationalization process of Born Globals: A network view. *International Business Review, 12*, 739–753.

Sinkovics, R.R., Bell, J., & Deans, K.R. (2004). Using information communication technology to develop international entrepreneurship competencies. *Journal of International Entrepreneurship, 2*, 125–137.

Spence, M. (2003). International strategy formation in small canadian high-technology companies – A case study approach. *Journal of International Entrepreneurship, 1*, 277–296.

Van Beveren, J. (2002). A model of knowledge acquisition that refocuses knowledge management. *Journal of Knowledge Management, 6*, 18–22.

Yli-Renko, H., Autio, E., & Tontti, V. (2002). Social capital, knowledge, and the international growth of technology-based new firms. *International Business Review, 11*, 279–304.

Chapter 12

Face-to-Face Interaction in an Age of Information — Necessary or Not?

Emilia Rovira

Introduction

> History will pity the managers of the 1990s. The Internet touched
> down intheir midst like a tornado, tearing up the old game book,
> disrupting every aspect of business, and compelling them to man-
> age for a new economy   (Brown & Duguid, 2000, p. 1).

The emergence of Internet and information technology (IT) certainly changed the
prerequisites for conducting business in a fundamental way. The new technology
enabled companies to store, transmit and process information in a quicker and
more efficient manner than before. In a global perspective Internet also emerged
as a great equalizer, since it rolled back some of the constraints of location, scale
and time zones (Hill, 2001). The fact that Internet allowed companies to expand
their global presence at a lower cost than ever before also changed the opportunities for resource constrained, small and medium-sized enterprises (SMEs)[1] to
internationalise in a rapid manner.

---

[1]The EU definition of SMEs that is currently in use is based on three criteria. The first criterion states
that an SME is an enterprise with less than 250 employees. The second criterion states than an SME
shall have an annual turnover that is no greater than ECU 40 million (about US$49.3 million), or alter-
natively that its balance sheet total should be no higher than ECU 27 million (about US$33.2 million).
The third criterion states that an SME must be independent. An enterprise is considered as being independent unless 25% or more of the capital or of the voting rights are owned by one enterprise falling
outside the definition of an SME, or owned jointly by several such enterprises (Szabo, 2003).

Even though the use of information technology has doubtless proved to be a positive force in the daily operations of organisations, a rearview perspective sometimes shows that new technology, like IT-solutions, have not always conveyed the success that was expected from them (Mårtensson, 2000; Storey & Barnett, 2000). As a consequence of this, a vast number of researchers have started to discuss the importance of complementing pure-technology solutions with personal interaction (Nonaka, 1994; Malhotra, 1998, 2000; Soo et al., 2002). Personal interaction between individuals, like face-to-face communication, is, for instance, believed to be particularly necessary in business situations where feelings of uncertainty, ambiguity and risk are involved (Nohira & Eccles, 1992). Many researchers, furthermore, see a connection between face-to-face interaction and the evoking of trust in relationships (Nohira & Eccles, 1992; O'Hara-Devereaux & Johansen, 1994; Handy, 1995; Hunter, 2000).

Even though Internet and information technology have created new opportunities for SMEs to internationalise in a rapid manner, these kinds of companies still face the challenge of balancing their communication with customers between the utilisation of IT communication and face-to-face interaction. The aim of this chapter is to investigate the role that face-to-face interaction with customers still plays for a particular kind of SME, namely Born Global[2] SMEs, which compete in high-tech markets. The study, more specifically, attempts to investigate the question of how face-to-face interaction influences the factors of trust and uncertainty in the relationships between Born Global SMEs and their customers.

Previous studies of Born Global SMEs indicate that these kinds of companies increasingly seem to utilise partners and networks in order to learn about and obtain access to foreign markets sooner (Saarenketo, Puumalainen, Kuivalainen, & Kyläheiko, 2004). This makes the relationships of Born Global SMEs and their international customers an interesting area to study. The main reason for choosing to base this study on Born Global SMEs in the high-tech business is that these kinds of companies face particularly interesting challenges in their interaction with customers. Since Born Global SMEs in the high-tech business must often operate on completely international markets almost directly from their start in order to survive, they are generally known to utilise information technology to a great extent, in order to communicate with their more remote customers. At the same time, it is very important for these kinds of companies to be able to make their customers trust them, since they are often forced to convince their customers to take the risk of investing in brand new technology. The Born Global SMEs

---

[2]A Born Global is a firm that adopts an international or even global approach right from its birth or very shortly thereafter (Madsen & Servais, 1997).

must find a way to reduce their customers' uncertainties about conducting business with small, new and, for them, often unknown enterprises.

Even though researchers such as Coviello and Munro (1997), Jones (1999), Crick and Jones (2000), and Saarenketo et al. (2004) have contributed to research with studies that discuss the internationalisation of high-tech SMEs, no previous research has, to my knowledge, focused on how high-tech, Born Global SMEs' interact with international customers. As the number of Born Global SMEs grows, the need for knowledge and research about various aspects of these kinds of enterprises increases. By using empirical data from two Born Global SMEs in the Scandinavian biotech business, the study aims at contributing to the research area that investigates Born Global SMEs' business activities towards customers in international high-tech markets. Since the literature of Born Global firms is relatively new (Chetty & Campbell-Hunt, 2004), this study also endeavours to extend the empirical scope of Born Global literature.

The chapter opens with a presentation of the theoretical background that has been chosen in order to perform the study, after which the method is discussed. The characteristics of the companies that are to be investigated are treated, thereafter, and the empirical data is introduced and analysed. Finally, a concluding discussion is presented.

Theoretical Review

The theories that are addressed in this chapter have been chosen in order to enable a discussion of how Born Global SMEs communicate with their customers in international high-tech markets. The first theories that are to be reviewed in this section of the paper discuss how the emergence of information technology has changed the prerequisites for the small companies' internationalisation processes, thus enabling the evolvement of Born Global companies.

The Changed View of Internationalisation

The emergence of IT has certainly revolutionised the business world as we knew it. The Internet gives a majority of actors in business access to a tremendous wealth of information and contacts (Papows, 1998), as well as facilitating communication through new channels, namely via e-mail and other electronic procedures (Prescott & Slyke, 1997). As a consequence of these new possibilities, many researchers have started to notice the opportunities that information technology offers for small and middle-sized enterprises in particular (Oviatt &

McDougall, 1994; Coviello & Munro, 1997; Jones, 1999; Jeffcoate, Chappell, & Feindt, 2000; Lituchy & Rail, 2000; Fernández Jurado & Bilbao Calabuig, 2001; Hill, 2001; Feindt, Jeffcoate, & Chappell, 2002). Researchers like Hill (2001), for example, argue that the Web has emerged as a great equalizer that allows both small and large businesses to expand their global presence at a lower cost than ever before (Hill, 2001). Information technology can, furthermore, be used to gather information about markets and competitors, and cut a company's communication costs. The utilisation of IT can also help an SME to sell products all around the world, thus becoming a mini-multinational company (Fernández Jurado & Bilbao Calabuig, 2001).

As the emergence of IT enables even small and resource-constrained firms to internationalise, it has changed the old game book on international trade. This development of small firms' rapid internationalisation has also led researchers to abscond from traditional internationalisation models that describe internationalisation as an incremental process. The most commonly cited conceptual and empirical base for research, which argues that firms expand into international markets in incremental, stepwise manners, is Johanson and Vahlne's internationalisation process model from 1977 (Coviello & Munro, 1997). This model is based on behavioural theories of internationalisation.

Johanson and Vahlne (1977) suggest that a firm's initial internationalisation activities are targeted to psychologically close markets, i.e. markets that share a similar culture, language, political system, trade policy, etc. to the internationalising company. This manner of international expansion poses a low risk for an internationalising firm, and enables it to learn about new markets and improve its foreign market knowledge. Over time and through experience, firms become able to increase their foreign market commitment and expand to more psychologically distant markets, thus conducting incremental internationalisation.

One study suggesting that traditional incremental internationalisation theories are unable to explain the internationalisation processes of SMEs is the article of Lituchy and Rail (2000). They argue that Johanson and Vahlne's internationalisation process model from 1977 no longer applies to small businesses, because of the improved communication systems, for instance Internet, that are in place today. Even though small businesses that used the Internet may have existed before the development of websites, they could, nevertheless, not have been considered to be the global start-ups there are today. Also Crick and Jones' (2000) study of small, high-tech firms repudiates the incremental approach. Crick and Jones argue that certain small firms, especially in the high-tech business, often possess the competence, capability and experience that is needed to operate on distant international markets early in their development.

In accordance with Crick and Jones (2000), Saarenketo et al. (2004) argue that the internationalisation process of small high-technology firms often differs from the internationalisation process of more mature industries. They specifically point out that there is an increasing amount of evidence that many firms within high-tech industries do not follow the incremental paths to international markets. On the contrary, these companies aim at international markets from their very first day of existence. These kinds of companies can be considered to be Born Globals, and show very rapid and intensive international growth by the use of external resources such as partners and networks. Saarenketo et al.'s (2004) study indicates that firms increasingly seem to utilise more partners and networks and that this enables high-tech, Born Global SMEs, with limited resources, to learn about and reach foreign markets sooner.

The theoretical discussion of this study has hitherto indicated that the emergence of information technologies has developed the research area of internationalisation. Recent theories challenge traditional, incremental approaches to internationalisation, and remark that IT has enabled even small and resource-constrained companies to internationalise quickly. The literature discussed in the next section of this chapter addresses the limitations of IT utilisation and the importance of face-to-face interaction.

The Importance of Face-to-Face Interaction

> Marketing functions are performed under a hypermedia-computer-mediated-environment where interactivity and connectivity are replacing the traditional mode of "face to face negotiation" and communication. Internet allows interactivity between buyers and sellers to create a shared real time common marketplace. Connectivity links buyers-sellers worldwide creating a shared global market-space.
> (Khatibi, Thyagarajan, & Seetharaman, 2003, p. 77)

The quotation above gives the impression that a problem no longer exists for even the smallest company to compete in international markets; that the world is an oyster for any company not afraid of participating in the hypermedia-computer-mediated-environment, and that face-to-face interaction between individuals can easily be replaced by other means of communication. But is this world-view really a good representation of reality? Many researchers beg to differ.

In a study about network organisations, Nohira and Eccles (1992) argue that an electronically mediated exchange can only substitute face-to-face interaction when the identities of the interactants are not very important. An electronically mediated exchange should therefore only be used when the circumstances at hand are certain and unambiguous, and the actions necessary are standard and routine, and also when ongoing interaction does not depend on a robust structure of relationships. Nohira and Eccles (1992) also argue that face-to-face meetings are essential for forming the mental images of others that facilitate the development of a strategy for interacting with them. Strong feelings of like or dislike, trust or distrust, attraction or repulsion and so forth are often formed in the first face-to-face interaction. Face-to-face communication therefore plays an essential role in establishing and maintaining the kind of multidimensional and robust relationships necessary for effective interaction and co-ordinated action, in situations of uncertainty, ambiguity and risk.

Apart from the research of Nohira and Eccles (1992), numerous additional studies have, over the years, been carried out in order to investigate what kind of communication ought to be most effective in different situations (Rice, 1992; Suh, 1998; D'Ambra, Rice, & O'Connor, 1998; Roberts, 2000). Many of these studies have been based on the widely known and used media richness theory (Daft & Lengel, 1984, 1986). In the media richness theory, Daft and Lengel (1986) describe face-to-face interaction as the richest medium of communication. The reason that face-to-face interaction is the richest medium is because it provides immediate feedback, so that interpretation can be checked. Face-to-face interaction furthermore provides multiple cues via body language and tone of voice, and message content is expressed in natural language. The difference between rich media and media of lower richness is that rich media are personal and involve face-to-face contact between managers, while media of lower richness are impersonal and rely on rules, forms procedures, or databases (Daft & Lengel, 1986).

The theories above have indicated that face-to-face interaction is an important means of facilitating the communication between individuals. Previous research has, furthermore, emphasised that a connection exists between the utilisation of face-to-face interaction and the evoking of trust and reduction of uncertainty in relationships. The next section of this chapter will further discuss this area of research. The reason that the discussion of media choice consequences is limited to the subjects of trust and uncertainty in this study, is that the inducement of customer trust and reduction of uncertainty is instrumental for Born Global SMEs that compete in international high-tech markets. In order for customers to take the risk of investing in brand new technology, they must be able to trust that their suppliers can deliver what they have promised. Companies have to be able to reduce their customers' uncertainties in order to get the opportunity of doing business with them.

The Importance of Building Trust and Reducing Uncertainty

> Trust, though a rather elusive concept, is, however, highly impor-
> tant for the efficient operation of a knowledge-based economy,
> since the market exchange of knowledge gives rise to a high level
> of risk and uncertainty. These risks and uncertainties are reduced
> by the presence of a high level of trust.
>
> (Roberts, 2000, p. 433)

Even though the concept of trust is popular to use, there is no consensus about what the definition of trust is. There are, in fact, dozens of definitions of trust to be found (McKnight & Chervany, 2001–2002). For the purpose of this study, the commonly used trust definition by Moorman, Deshpandé, and Zaltman (1992) will be utilised, namely that trust is the willingness to rely on a business partner in whom one has confidence.

In their book from 1994, O'Hara-Devereaux and Johansen (1994) argue that face-to-face meetings are virtually irreplaceable for building interpersonal bonds between individuals. They argue, furthermore, that face-to-face interaction is very important for building trust in relationships. Voice-mail and video conferencing can provide ongoing support for maintaining trust because they convey some of the emotional context and interaction impossible in text only technologies like e-mail. Even so, face-to-face meetings are usually essential to establish trust in the first place (O'Hara-Devereaux & Johansen, 1994).

Once trust has been established in a relationship, it plays a central role in help-ing individuals overcome the perceptions of risk and insecurity (McKnight, Chodhury, & Kacmar, 2002). Trust helps to reduce the uncertainty that individuals may feel. For the purpose of this chapter, Levine's (1997) definition of uncertainty will be used. Levine describes one sense of uncertainty to be that "I am uncertain when I think something is true about the world, especially the likely future shape of events, but acknowledge that I could be wrong" (Levine, 1997, p. 7).

The Reduction of Uncertainty through Information and Knowledge Means

In an article, Kollock (1994) introduces the dimensions of information and knowledge into the discussion of uncertainty. He argues that the lack of informa-tion about the motivations of others is the ground on which uncertainty is built. Sellers and buyers both face risks in an uncertain situation, but buyers face much greater risks because they are always in danger of being exploited by sellers because of their lack of knowledge about the quality of the goods.

The discussion of information and knowledge will, for the purpose of this study, be limited to the effects that these two concepts have on the reduction of customer uncertainty. Information is defined as data within a context, where data are raw facts that can be shaped and formed to create information (Van Beveren, 2002). Knowledge, on the other hand, refers to an individual's personal stock of information, skills, experience, beliefs and memories (Alexander, Schallert, & Hare, 1991). Information becomes knowledge when it is acquired through the senses of an individual and processed in the human brain. During this processing of information new knowledge can be acquired or created for future use (Van Beveren, 2002).

In accordance with Kollock, Shepherd, and Zacharakis (2003) argue that knowledge decreases uncertainty. Knowledge represents the first stage in the decision-making process and can help to decrease a customer's uncertainty regarding a specific product or service. In their article the authors discuss the concept of cognitive legitimacy, a concept that includes the uncertainty and ambiguity that is associated with a customer's purchase decisions. Shepherd and Zacharakis' (2003) study shows that the two factors that affect customers' cognitive legitimacy most is their knowledge of a supplier's product or management team. The less knowledge that a customer has about these two factors, the lower the level of cognitive legitimacy, and, therefore, the less likely consumers are to purchase a new venture's market offerings. Another factor that influences customers' cognitive legitimacy is their knowledge about a supplier's organisation.

The theories above indicate that trust plays an important role for individuals in overcoming their uncertainties. Apart from trust, information and knowledge can help to decrease individuals' uncertainties about specific organisations, people, products or services. The next section of this chapter consists of a description of the method that has been used to gather information about the companies studied in this chapter. Thereafter, follows a section that describes and analyses the firms studied.

Method and Data Collection

In this chapter, the case study method is used to investigate the international development of two Born Global SMEs in the Scandinavian biotech business. Case studies typically combine various forms of data collection methods (Eisenhardt, 1989), and before starting to gather qualitative data about the investigated companies, details about the companies were collected from databases, masters' theses and websites. This provided a broad description of the companies being studied. In order to investigate the companies further, in-depth interviews have been conducted with different employees, concerning the companies' creation and internationalisation. The interviews conducted were semi-structured, since I wanted to give the interviewees the opportunity to speak freely. According to Rubin and Rubin (1995), the semi-structured interview is also suitable when the understanding, knowledge and insights of the interviewee are of interest. Depending on what was said in the interviews, follow-up questions were asked. A questionnaire had, however, been prepared beforehand to make sure interesting and important facts were included in the interviews.

All of the interviews were conducted by two researchers, who were able to alternate the tasks of asking the questions and writing notes. This method gave one interviewer the perspective of personal interaction with the informant, while the note-taker retained a more distant view (Eisenhardt, 1989). According to Eisenhardt (1989), the use of multiple investigators may enhance the creative potential of a study, since complementary insights increase the richness of data. Multiple investigators may also build confidence in the findings and increase the likelihood of surprising findings. All of the interviews were conducted at the head-offices in Scandinavia of the companies being studied, and this, furthermore, provided the opportunity of observing how the work at the companies was performed. The researchers also had the opportunity of observing the company's organisational structure, during a guided tour of the companies' premises. Twelve interviews have hitherto been conducted with staff at the two companies. The cumulative interview time has amounted to about 24 h, and the interviews have been conducted over a period of 13 months. As well as hand-written notes, a tape recorder was also used during the interviews. With the help of both the tapes and the hand-written notes, transcripts of the interviews were written. After the interviews, the data were briefly analysed and interesting themes about the subject of this chapter were identified.

The main reason that this chapter is built on more than one case is that my research interest ultimately relies on the phenomenon of Born Global SMEs in high-tech businesses, and not on an individual case. In accordance with Stake (1994), I believe that we cannot understand one case without knowing about other cases. The cases in this study are chosen because understanding them will lead to better understanding, and perhaps better theorising, about a still larger collection of cases.

Born Global SMEs in High-Tech Businesses — What Are They About?

The empirical data on which this study is based is collected from two Scandinavian biotech companies, Alpha and Beta.[3] Both these companies are relatively young Born Global SMEs that have focused on selling their products in international

---

[3]To maintain anonymity, the companies studied are represented by aliases.

Table 1: The Born Global SMEs.

Company alias	Year of foundation	Number of staff	Business alignment	Means of performing international sales
Alpha	1997	28	Alpha develops, manufactures and sells micro-systems. Different product applications are also developed in close collaboration with the company's customers	Exports products from headquarters in Scandinavia
Beta	2001	25	Beta develops, manufactures and sells diagnostic products with in the area of veterinary medicine and food safety. Beta specialises in the selling of test-kits for veterinary medicine testing	Exports products directly from headquarters in Scandinavia, but focuses on selling their products through 17 international distributors

high-tech markets from the start. The companies, furthermore, conduct their own research and development, and have at least one product out on the market. Both companies also have at least one international customer in their portfolio.

Even though the two companies are similar in many ways, they are slightly different in terms of age and number of employees. The largest differences between the two companies studied are, however, their products on offer and the contact they have with the end users of their products (Table 1).

Alpha

Alpha is a company that has specialised in manufacturing micro-components in plastic. Micro-components are traditionally made from silicon, which is a much more expensive material to utilise than plastic. Alpha is, furthermore, able to manufacture a plastic component in a fraction of the time that it takes to manufacture a similar micro-component in silicon. Alpha's production technology, with a large series of products that can be manufactured cheaply, fits well for one-time products in biotechnology or electronics. Even though Alpha can manufacture large quantities of products, different product applications must be developed in close and long-term collaborations with the customers/end users before the manufacturing phase can begin. Alpha, furthermore, only sells products from their headquarters.

Beta

Beta manufactures and sells laboratory products that are utilised to analyse animal diseases. Traditional technology in the area of veterinary medicine requires that analytical tests be sent to external laboratories for testing. In contrast to traditional technology, Beta has developed test-kits that speed up the test-procedures and even enable veterinarians to test animals on location. The test-kits that Beta manufactures aim to be easier to use and have a shorter assay time than traditional technology. Unlike Alpha, Beta does not need to develop product applications in cooperation with their customers. The test-kits that the company manufactures are ready to use instantly. Beta can therefore let distributors manage most of the company's international sales, even though the company also sells products directly to end users from their headquarters.

High-Technology, Exploration and Exploitation

Both Alpha and Beta are considered to be high-tech companies, since they belong to and compete in a high-tech business. Instead of merely offering a broad definition of the term high-tech, Gardner, Johnson, Moonkyu, and Wilkinson (2000) make an effort to define the difference between high- and low-tech products. They argue that "…traditional or low technology products are those that employ familiar and accepted technology and whose acceptance and use are generally understood. Likewise, high technology products are those that employ turbulent technology in their use, manufacture and/or distribution, and are seen to require significant changes in usage patterns" (Gardner et al., 2000, p. 1056).

Gardner et al.'s explanation of the difference between high-tech and low-tech products, gives an indication that it is somewhat complicated to label a company as a fully-fledged manufacturer of high-technology products. Gardner et al. (2000) also emphasise that the distinction between high- versus low-tech products should not be considered as a matter of type, but as a matter of degree. In order to differentiate between products of different technical degrees, the terms exploration and exploitation will be used for the purpose of this study.

Figure 1: The placement of the companies on an exploration/exploitation continuum.

When the degree of newness in both technology and market is high, firms are mainly involved in a phase of exploration. When the degree of newness in technology and markets are low, firms mainly are involved in a phase of exploitation. For high-tech firms, the exploitation phase is possible when they have explored new technologies, developed innovative processes, products or services and developed a market for their innovation (Bengtsson & Holmquist, 2000).

Taking as a point of departure the terms exploration and exploitation, Alpha could be considered to be in an exploration phase whereas Beta is in an exploitation phase (Figure 1). One of the main reasons for this difference between the two companies is that Alpha has developed new technology and offers unique technological applications to their customers. Alpha's products are, thus, so new that the company constantly faces the challenge of informing actors in international markets about the functions of their products. Beta's technology, on the other hand, is accepted and frequently utilised by both customers and competitors. Beta, therefore, has access to a developed market in which to sell their products. Even though Beta's technology is better known than Alpha's newly developed technology, Beta's products cannot be considered to be low-tech since their acceptance and use are not generally understood. Employees at Beta relate that they or their distributors must still assist customers occasionally.

It is not only differences in technology that separates Alpha from Beta, but also the contacts that the companies have with their end users. In contrast to Beta, a company that still mainly uses distributors to sell its products, Alpha uses a great deal of resources keeping in contact with their most important end users themselves. The next section of this chapter will discuss the means of communication and technical aids that Born Global SMEs, like Alpha and Beta, can utilise to improve their relationships with and information about foreign business partners.

The Impact of Information Technology

In accordance with researchers that emphasise the opportunities that information technology offers for small and middle-sized enterprises (Oviatt & McDougall,

1994; Coviello & Munro, 1997; Jones, 1999; Jeffcoate et al., 2000; Lituchy & Rail, 2000; Fernández Jurado & Bilbao Calabuig, 2001; Hill, 2001; Feindt et al., 2002), the people that have been interviewed for the purpose of this study see information and communication technologies as helpful tools in their companies' international operations. Alpha's founder gives an example of how he has used the Internet to acquire information about potential customers in the USA:

> The choice of interesting potential clients is to a large extent a randomly performed process. In order to find potential customers in the USA I have used a homepage called Biospace.com that lists the American bio-companies. This homepage enables me to sort the companies after their area codes. This information is useful when I travel on scouting journeys in the states. With help of the area codes and the companies' homepages I can contact the most interesting of these companies that are situated along my travel route.

Besides using Internet to acquire information about foreign businesses, staff at the companies investigated regarding e-mail as an important complement to the telephone when it comes to keeping in touch with business partners. Beta's Product Manager relates:

> I handle most of my distributor relationships both through e-mail and telephone. The telephone is most useful for playing around with new ideas whereas technical queries more easily are handled through e-mail contact.

Also one of Alpha's Account Managers relates:

> E-mail is a useful tool because it documents everything that is going on in the relationship and clarifies what one of the parties want from the other. E-mail is also useful to communicate with customers situated in the USA because it solves the time difference problem. Also the telephone is a convenient tool in the early stages of a customer relationship.

Internet and e-mail are used as tools to obtain information and partake in communication with international business partners. Since resource-constrained, Born Global SMEs are often forced to compete in completely international markets almost directly from the outset, information technology offers an important means for them to conduct business in an inexpensive manner. The next section of this paper will further discuss the means of interaction that drive international relationships.

The Role of Face-to-Face Interaction

In accordance with the research that emphasises the significance of face-to-face interaction (Daft & Lengel, 1986; Nohira & Eccles, 1992; O'Hara-Devereaux & Johansen, 1994), employees in the two companies investigated discussed the importance of having face-to-face interaction with customers, but to different degrees. Unlike Beta, which mostly keeps in touch with their distributors via the telephone or e-mail, Alpha frequently interacts with their customers on a face-to-face level. Besides the contact as per e-mail and telephone, Alpha's Account Managers try to meet the customers for which they are responsible every 6–8 weeks. One of Alpha's Account Managers relates:

> It is essential to meet customers face-to-face. You can always start communicating with a customer through e-mail, but a deal can never be made before you meet somebody face-to-face. Products and services are sold between companies, but a deal is made with a specific person.

In accordance with the statement above, another of Alpha's Account Managers relates:

> To visit the customers is an important part of a seller's tasks. Good projects demand that companies see each other and build up a feeling for one another, especially in the beginning of a customer relationship. If we want to get our customers to return after the first project, the contacts between the customers and us must be physical, not only through e-mail and the phone .... The only way to understand what customers need is to sit down with them. Homepages and the Internet can provide certain information but not enough.

Since Alpha develops their products in close collaboration with their customers, it is important that the company's staff interact on a personal basis with individuals at the customer companies. Initially, Alpha's visits also give their customers an opportunity to evaluate whether Alpha's staff are people with whom they want to work together or not. Beta has not focused on developing unique technology, like Alpha, and does not need to meet their customers often in order for the cooperation to work. Even so, employees at Beta believe that personal interaction is important for building lasting relationships. Beta's Product Manager relates:

> One of the targets of our marketing department is that the distributors on the most important target markets shall be followed up once a year. This follow up meeting shall be face-to-face and not through e-mail or the telephone …. It is easier to cooperate with a distributor that you have a personal relationship with.

Even though the frequency of face-to-face meetings with customers differs between Alpha and Beta, individuals in both the companies investigated emphasise the importance of meeting customers in person. Face-to-face interaction is, however, a very time consuming and expensive means of communicating with international customers. One journey to visit the company's different American customers for a week costs Alpha about US$ 6500 per person. Disregarding the financial costs, extensive travelling is, furthermore, associated with stress and is also a burden for the travellers' families. (Boutellier, Grassmann, Macho, & Roux, 1998) The companies investigated, themselves, seldom receive visits from their customers, since the customers also have to keep within their budget.

One of the reasons that Alpha, in particular, visits their customers regardless of the high cost, is that it is important for the company to get to know their customers on a personal level. Meeting through face-to-face interaction is a way for Alpha to induce trust in their customers, and thereby reduce the customers' uncertainty about cooperating with Alpha. The next section of this chapter will discuss what companies can do to further portray themselves as trustworthy.

The Inducement of Trust and Reduction of Uncertainty

> The customer visits are, of course, important for building trust.
> (Extract from interview with one of Alpha's Account Managers)

Born Global SMEs must frequently overcome many challenges that larger and more established international companies can often disregard. In order to convince their international customers to take the risk of investing in brand new technology, small and unknown companies face the challenge of proving that they can be trusted. In order to do this, it is important to increase the level of information directed towards the customers (Kollock, 1994). It is particularly important for companies to provide additional information about their product and management team to their customers (Shepherd & Zacharakis, 2003).

Since the products that Beta sells are based on a rather established technology, there is often not much need to provide their customers with more information about the company's products than they already have. Beta's CEO relates:

> Many of our products are so well known that the customer does not need too much information before testing the products. In these cases our sellers do not have to visit companies to demonstrate how the product works. If the customer, on the other hand, has problems with their products, it is important that the distributor has the technical knowledge to help the customer.

Since Alpha's products are based on brand new technology, the company faces the important challenge of presenting their technology in an understandable manner to their customers. One of Alpha's Account Managers relates:

> It is not enough just saying that we have an interesting potential technology, we have to prove this somehow…. We must therefore develop application examples to show the customers. We cannot show the customers fully developed products, but we develop them so far that we can show them something.

Besides providing necessary information about products, Alpha also provides their customers with information about their management teams by including high-level staff in the sales activities. Alpha's Head of Marketing and Applications relates:

> We want to introduce relationships with customers on at least two different levels. The idea of introducing Account Managers is that they shall move beyond the interaction with technical personnel at the customer company and leave these contacts to be managed by the technical project leaders. The roles of the Account Managers are instead to cooperate with the marketing representatives in the customer companies. Hopefully our founder will be able to enable a third relational level using his contacts with different individuals in the customers' management teams.

The quotations above indicate that it is a more important task for Alpha to provide their customers with additional information about their product and management teams, than for Beta, that exploits a more commonly accepted and standardised technology. When Alpha's customers receive information about the company's products and employees, they get the chance to process this information into additional knowledge about the company. According to Shepherd and Zacharakis (2003), even unflattering knowledge about a company's product and management is better than no knowledge at all. The old saying "Better the devil you know than the devil you don't know" can, therefore, be true when companies make purchase decisions with an unknown venture. Since knowledge reduces customer uncertainty, the additional information that Alpha provides to their customers may increase the chances of the customers wanting to do business with that company.

High-Tech = High-Touch?

In the companies investigated, the level of face-to-face interaction with customers is related to the level of uncertainty that the customers feel. The fact that Alpha's technology is rather new on the market, whereas Beta's technology is more widely used, also influences the customers' understanding of the two companies' respective technologies. The more uncertainties that the decision-making staff at a customer company feel and the less they know about the product and management of a supplier, the more information they need to acquire in order to reduce their uncertainties. When suppliers meet customers face-to-face the latter are provided with a rich source of information (Daft & Lengel, 1986; Nohira & Eccles, 1992). If a customers' face-to-face interaction with a supplier involves people at different levels at the two companies, customers can create a picture for themselves of the knowledge that resides in a company, how the organisation works and what experience the management group possesses. Face-to-face interaction, furthermore, provides opportunities for customers to reflect over the multiple cues that suppliers display, and this makes it easier for the customers to interpret their counterparts as trustworthy or not.

Alpha's customers feel great uncertainty about the company's products since the technology around which Alpha is built is new and unknown. Alpha, therefore, has to spend a great amount of resources on interacting with its customers on a face-to-face level in order to reduce their uncertainties. Beta, which has based its products on better-known technology, does not need to go to the same length to reduce its customer's uncertainties and seldom has to meet its customers on a face-to-face level (Figure 2).

Concluding Discussion

Instead of following incremental paths to international markets, Born Global SMEs in the high-tech business are generally forced to operate in foreign markets almost directly from their start, in order to survive. Because of the fact that Born

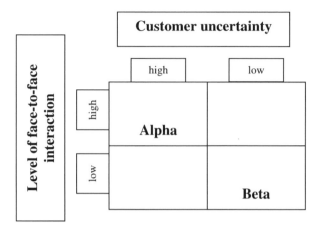

Figure 2: The companies' level of face-to-face interaction with customers related to the customers' uncertainties.

Global SMEs have to internationalise in a rapid manner, it is common for them to use tools like the Internet and e-mail, to collect information about, and keep in touch with international customers. Even though these tools are very helpful, previous research indicates that they cannot work as a substitute for face-to-face interaction in all situations. Face-to-face interaction is, for instance, considered to be an important foundation when it comes to the inducement of trust and the reduction of uncertainty in the establishment and maintenance of business relationships.

The aim of this chapter was to investigate what role face-to-face interaction with customers still played for Born Global SMEs in the high-tech business, and how face-to-face interaction influenced trust and uncertainty in the relationships between Born Global SMEs and their customers. Even though no generalised results can be drawn from the empirical material in this chapter, the study indicates that a company's level of face-to-face interaction with customers is related to the level of uncertainty that the customers feel about working with the company. Customer uncertainty can, however, be reduced if the company provides useful information to their customers.

The results of the study, furthermore, indicate that the inducement of trust and the reduction of uncertainty are important tasks for certain Born Global SMEs that compete in international high-tech markets, since these kinds of companies must be able to convince their international customers to take the risk of investing in brand new technology. The inducement of trust and reduction of uncertainty is particularly important for companies that are in an exploration phase of their development, and act in a market that is signified by fast technological change. Companies that exploit a more commonly accepted and standardised technology, on the other hand, do not need to focus as much on inducing trust in their customers.

The utilisation of IT communication and face-to-face interaction are not mutually exclusive, and most Born Global SMEs that compete in high-tech businesses still use both in their endeavours to communicate with international customers. Since all companies, however, are different in terms of speed of technological change, producer difficulty in developing and manufacturing products and customer understanding of technology, there is a need for more research about how IT solutions and face-to-face interaction with customers ought to be balanced in accordance with different kinds of companies' needs. More research is also needed about other factors that influence the relationships between Born Global SMEs and their international customers. Quantitative research could provide more detailed knowledge about these areas of research.

Managerial Implications

Even though IT offers good and cost-effective opportunities for resource-constrained and small companies to find information about, and communicate with international customers, it may be of vast importance for companies that are in an exploration phase of their development to uphold frequent face-to-face interaction with customers. This is in order to improve the customers' level of trust in the companies and reduce uncertainties. Companies that compete with businesses that are signified by fast technological change and sell technology that is new and unknown must, therefore, be prepared to invest more resources in face-to-face interaction with customers than companies that compete in more established markets.

Even though it is generally less expensive to communicate with international customers with the help of IT solutions, in comparison to face-to-face meetings, companies that only utilise this means of interaction risk losing important opportunities. Face-to-face interaction with foreign customers can, for instance, lead to closer relationships with foreign business partners and an increased amount of knowledge about foreign markets.

Acknowledgements

I gratefully acknowledge the financial support of the Jan Wallander and Tom Hedelius' foundation, Handelsbanken, Sweden. I also wish to thank the anonymous reviewers for their helpful comments on the two earlier drafts of this chapter.

References

Alexander, P.A., Schallert, D.L., & Hare, V.C. (1991). Coming to terms: How researchers in learning and literacy talk about knowledge. *Review of Educational Research, 61*(3), 315–343.

Bengtsson, M., & Holmquist, C. (2000). Dynamic capabilities and entrepreneurial drives in situations of encompassing technological change. Paper presented at competence 2000: The 5th international conference on competence-based management, June 10–14, Helsinki, Finland.

Boutellier, R., Grassmann, O., Macho, H., & Roux, M. (1998). Management of dispersed product development teams: The role of information technologies. *R & D Management, 28*(1), 13–25.

Brown, J.S., & Duguid, P. (2000). Balancing act: How to capture knowledge without killing it. *Harvard Business Review, 78*(3), 73–80.

Chetty, S., & Campbell-Hunt, C. (2004). A strategic approach to internationalization: A traditional versus born global approach. *Journal of International Marketing, 12*(1), 57–81.

Coviello, N., & Munro, H. (1997). Network relationships and the internationalization process of small software firms. *International Business Review, 6*(4), 361–386.

Crick, D., & Jones, M.V. (2000). Small high-technology firms and international high-technology markets. *Journal of International Marketing, 8*(2), 63–85.

Daft, R.L., & Lengel, R.H. (1984). Information richness: A new approach to managerial behaviour and organisation design. In: B.M. Straw, & L.L. Cummings (Eds), *Research in organisational behaviour* (pp. 191–233). Greenwich, CT: JAI Press.

Daft, R.L., & Lengel, R.H. (1986). Organizational information requirements, media richness and structural design. *Management Science, 32*(5), 554–571.

D'Ambra, J., Rice, R.E., & O'Connor, M. (1998). Computer-mediated communication and media preference: An investigation of the dimensionality of perceived task equivocality and media richness. *Behaviour and Information Technology, 17*(3), 164–174.

Eisenhardt, K. (1989). Building theories from case study research. *Academy of Management Review, 16*(3), 532–550.

Feindt, S., Jeffcoate, J., & Chappell, C. (2002). Identifying success factors for rapid growth in SME e-commerce. *Small Business Economics, 19*, 51–62.

Fernández Jurado, M.Y., & Bilbao Calabuig, P. (2001). The impact of electronic commerce on small and midsized Spanish companies. *IAER, 7*(1), 91–99.

Gardner, D.M., Johnson, F., Moonkyu, L., & Wilkinson, I. (2000). A contingency approach to marketing high technology products. *European Journal of Marketing, 34*(9/10), 1053–1077.

Handy, C. (1995). Trust and the virtual organisation. *Harvard Business Review, 73*(3), 40–50.

Hill, C.W.L. (2001). *International business: Competing in the global marketplace-international edition.* New York: McGraw-Hill.

Hunter, M. (2000). Survey finds people want advice delivered face-to-face. *American Banker, 165*(102), 8.

Jeffcoate, J., Chappell, C., & Feindt, S. (2000). Attitudes towards process improvement among SMEs involved in e-commerce. *Knowledge and Process Management, 7*(3), 187–195.

Johanson, J., & Vahlne, J.E. (1977). The internationalization process of the firm — a model of knowledge development and increasing foreign market commitments. *Journal of International Business Studies, 8*(1), 23–32.

Jones, M.V. (1999). The internationalization of small high-technology firms. *Journal of International Marketing, 7*(4), 15–41.

Khatibi, A., Thyagarajan, V., & Seetharaman, A. (2003). E-commerce in Malaysia: Percieved benefits and barriers. *Vikalpa: The Journal for Decision Makers, 28*(3), 77–82.

Kollock, P. (1994). The emergence of exchange structures: An experimental study of uncertainty, commitment, and trust. *The American Journal of Sociology, 100*(2), 313–345.

Levine, D.P. (1997). Knowing and acting: On uncertainty in economics. *Review of Political Economy, 9*(1), 5–17.

Lituchy, T.R., & Rail, A. (2000). Bed and breakfasts, small inns, and the Internet: The impact of technology on the globalization of small businesses. *Journal of International Marketing, 8*(2), 86–97.

Madsen, K.T., & Servais, P. (1997). The internationalization of born globals: An evolutionary process. *Internationalisation Business Review, 6*(6), 561–583.

Malhotra, Y. (1998). Deciphering the knowledge management hype. *Journal for Quality and Participation, 21*(4), 58–60.

Malhotra, Y. (2000). Knowledge management for e-business performance. *Information Strategy: The Executives Journal, 16*(4), 5–16.

Mårtensson, M. (2000). A critical review of knowledge management as a management tool. *Journal of Knowledge Management, 4*(3), 204–216.

McKnight, D.H., & Chervany, N.L. (2001–2002). What trust means in e-commerce customer relationships: An interdisciplinary conceptual typology. *International Journal of Electronic Commerce, 6*(2), 35–59.

McKnight, D.H., Chodhury, V., & Kacmar, C. (2002). Developing and validating trust measures for e-commerce: An integrative typology. *Information Systems Research, 13*(3), 334–359.

Moorman, C., Deshpandé, R., & Zaltman, G. (1992). Relationships between providers and users of market research: The dynamics of trust within and between organisations. *Journal of Marketing Research, 29,* 314–329.

Nohira, N., & Eccles, R.G. (1992). Face-to-face: Making network organizations work. In: N. Nohira, & R.G. Eccles (Eds), *Network and organisations* (pp. 288–308). Boston, MA: Harvard Business School Press.

Nonaka, I. (1994). A dynamic theory of organizational knowledge creation. *Organization Science, 5*(1), 14–36.

O'Hara-Devereaux, M., & Johansen., R. (1994). *Global work: Bridging distance, culture, and time.* San Francisco, CA: Jossey-Bass.

Oviatt, B.M., & McDougall, P. (1994). Toward a theory of international new ventures. *Journal of International Business Studies, First Quarter,* 45–64.

Papows, J. (1998). The rapid evolution of collaborative tools: A paradigm shift. *Telecommunications: Americas Edition, 32*(1), 31–32.

Prescott, M.B., & van Slyke, C. (1997). Understanding the internet as an innovation. *Industrial Management and Data Systems, 97*(3), 119–124.

Rice, R.E. (1992). Task analyzability, use of new media, and effectiveness: A multi-site exploration of media richness. *Organisation Science, 3*(4), 475–500.

Roberts, J. (2000). From know-how to show-how? Questioning the role of information and communication technologies in knowledge transfer. *Technology Analysis and Strategic Management, 12*(4), 429–443.

Rubin, H.J., & Rubin, I.S. (1995). *Qualitative interviewing, the art of hearing Data.* Thousand Oaks, CA: Sage.

Saarenketo, S., Puumalainen, K., Kuivalainen, O., & Kyläheiko, K. (2004). Dynamic knowledge related learning processes in internationalizing high-tech SMEs. *International Journal of Production Economics, 89*(3), 363–378.

Shepherd, D.A., & Zacharakis, A. (2003). A new venture's cognitive legitimacy: An assessment by customers. *Journal of Small Business Management, 41*(2), 148–167.

Soo, C., Devinney, T., Midgley, D., & Deering, A. (2002). Knowledge management: Philosophy, processes, and pitfalls. *California Management Review, 44*(4), 129–150.

Stake, R.E. (1994). Case studies. In: N.K. Denzin, & Y.S. Lincoln (Eds), *Handbook of qualitative research* (pp. 236–248). Thousand Oaks, CA: Sage.

Storey, J., & Barnett, E. (2000). Knowledge management initiatives: Learning from failure. *Journal of Knowledge Management, 4*(2), 145–156.

Suh, K.S. (1998). Impact of communication medium on task performance and satisfaction: An examination of media-richness theory. *Information and Management, 35*, 295–312.

Szabo, A. (2003). The development of the SME sector in the various regions of the OSCE. *3rd OSCE Parliamentary Assembly conference on sub-regional co-operation: Small and medium-sized businesses*, 14–15 May, Swiss Parliament, Bern.

Van Beveren, J. (2002). A model of knowledge acquisition that refocuses knowledge management. *Journal of Knowledge Management, 6*(1), 18–22.

Chapter 13

IT and Innovations in Multinationals: Experiences from Product Development at SCA and IKEA

Enrico Baraldi and Francesco Ciabuschi

Introduction

Successful innovations, in terms of new products and production technologies, for example, are increasingly recognized as the key to competitive advantage (Tidd, Bessant, & Pavitt, 2001), in particular for multinational corporation (MNCs) (e.g., Cantwell, 1989; Doz, Santos, & Williamson, 2001). Developing and leveraging innovations through the internal network of geographically dispersed subsidiaries is identified as a critical issue for MNCs (Bartlett & Ghoshal, 1989), and their actual ability in such processes is believed to be the reason for their existence (Kogut & Zander, 1992, 1993).

Since the 1960s, information technology (IT) has been applied to most business activities (Davenport & Short, 1990). This holds also, increasingly, for the management of innovations (Bessant & Buckingham, 1993). MNCs have invested in a large variety of IT solutions, ranging from Intranets to CAD/CAM and ERPs,[1] with the purpose of improving their performance in innovation tasks

---

[1]CAD/CAM stands for "Computer-aided Design" and "Computer-aided Manufacturing," respectively. CAD is a set of software tools employed to produce electronic drawings, while CAM is a set of programs employed to support and steer the operations of manufacturing equipment. ERP stands for "Enterprise Resource Planning" and is a breed of IT systems employed for administrative purposes ranging from production planning to cost accounting and from order management to payroll administration.

---

and even their control on the innovation process (Tidd et al., 2001, pp. 113–114). However, studies concerned with the actual role and potential of IT systems to the innovation process are underrepresented (Dewett & Jones, 2001) in both IT and business literature, and the limited empirical investigations have either too wide or too narrow a focus.

In this paper we look at IKEA and SCA, two large Swedish-based MNCs, which are not exceptions to the trend of IT investments to support innovations. Interestingly, these two firms often use specific IT systems in different and unexpected ways, and their role in the innovation process is far from being clear-cut and unequivocal. The underlying question of this study is: *What concrete role and contribution do heterogeneous IT solutions play in a firm's innovation efforts (e.g., in product development)?* More precisely, we deal with the two questions: *What role do IT tools play in the various phases of an innovation process?* and *What affects the role played by IT in each of these phases?*

Answering these questions requires, first of all, making clear what is meant by IT, with a focus on specific types of IT solutions and their functions. Secondly, it requires clarification of what is meant by innovation and identification of its key dimensions. Innovations and IT are, in fact, broad and complex phenomena that must be qualified and treated within a structured framework.

Therefore, the aim of this paper is twofold: (1) providing this framework and (2) applying it to two empirical settings where specific IT solutions are used in innovation work. This paper is nonetheless just a first step toward answering the question on the role of IT systems in innovations, since that question can only be fully answered by investigating a great variety of empirical settings. Moreover, among the factors that affect IT's role during the innovation process (e.g., type of innovation or IT tool features), we restrict our empirical investigation and analysis to the factors found in the *inter- and intra-organizational context* where the innovation process unfolds.

In the second section we present our theoretical framework on IT and innovation development. The theoretical discussion is followed, in the third section, by two empirical accounts: SCA's innovative activities on customized packaging solutions, and IKEA's work on developing one of its best-selling products, the "Lack" sofa table. We apply here our theoretical framework in order to tackle the two research questions stated earlier. The fourth section compares and discusses the two cases according to our theoretical framework. The paper concludes with a set of relevant issues for research and practice about the role and potential of IT tools in the innovation process.

The empirical material was collected through personal in-depth interviews with over 40 individuals for both the SCA and IKEA cases. For the SCA case, interviews were made at several subsidiaries (users of the focal IT system) and at divisional HQs (developers of the IT system) between 2002 and 2003. For the IKEA case, visits and interviews, covering also key suppliers, were conducted in the period 2001–2003 as part of a larger case study (Baraldi, 2003).[2] Respondents were identified by means of snowballing, that is, by referrals from previous interviewees, who indicated the person most knowledgeable about the topic at hand. For instance, specific product development projects and IT tools were traced and investigated in this way. Interviews lasted between 30 minutes and 2 hours and were tape-recorded. Each interview was based on a different and very general guide, in order to leave space to respondents to provide new insights on the interview topics (e.g., an IT tool or a typical problem in using it). The interviews and visits were complemented with on-site demonstrations and other first-hand unedited sources, such as printouts from the relevant IT tools, and with edited company sources, such as brochures and IT user manuals.

A Theoretical Framework for the Role of IT in Innovations

Our basic assumption is that an IT system is a tool whose concrete role in innovative efforts, such as product development, although based on its inner characteristics, is largely dependent on factors outside the tool itself. Thus, each IT solution's internal technical features are certainly important, but they must be confronted with what surrounds the IT tool: for instance, where and when this is utilized, for what purpose, and by whom (Baraldi, 2003, pp. 5–6).

To understand the innovations occurring in firms, one must be clear on what is innovated (the innovation object), how and when it is innovated (the characteristics and phases of the innovation process), and where and within which firms it is innovated (the innovation context). Our theoretical framework therefore stresses these three factors and the tight interplay between them. In this paper, we focus on the role of IT within the innovation process, but at the same time take into account the other two factors, the innovation object and context. First, we need to identify the dynamics of the innovation development process and how it proceeds. Second, we need to consider the specific characteristics of the innovation object. Third, we need to frame the process in its intra-organizational and inter-organizational context. Only after recognizing the characteristics and interdependencies of these three aspects, can we discuss their influence on the actual role of IT within the innovation process.

---

[2]A full listing of these empirical sources, together with others not employed for this paper, is provided in Baraldi (2003, pp. 246–248).

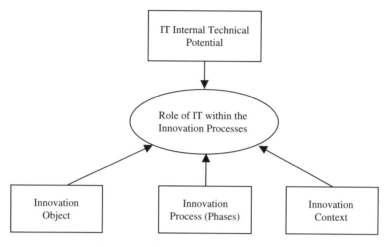

Figure 1: The theoretical framework.

Figure 1 illustrates the framework for exploring the role and utilization of IT in the innovation development process.

In the next section, we shall develop this theoretical framework by first considering IT tools and their potential. We move then to the issue of innovation, starting from the need to specify its process-like nature and, subsequently, its object and context.

Information Technology as Tools

We consider the IT component as a unique solution or series of tools used during the various phases of the innovation process. Like any other tool, IT has technically defined internal potentials but is also attributed great expectations for stimulating and enabling innovative processes. The range of IT solutions is nonetheless so broad that both potentials and expectations vary widely. Despite being increasingly integrated, such IT applications as CAD systems differ greatly from (for example) ERPs or Intranet platforms. Moreover, integration creates strong interdependencies among IT tools that make it difficult to separate the effects of one from the others; nonetheless, we need to deal with the single IT system and to stress its unique functions and effects. This uniqueness holds especially for their influence on the innovation process and its outcomes. We therefore restrict our empirical investigation to single specific IT solutions, by considering the abstract technical potentials, expectations, and actual use for each of them.

The *potential* functions of IT tools for businesses are suggested by informatics and the computer sciences. Examples are data collection and processing, process and output monitoring or steering, inter-system and inter-individual communication, simulation, and informative functions to sustain decisions by managers (Simon, 1977). Some recent studies (Dewett & Jones, 2001; Davies & Brady, 2000) describe, for instance, how IT employment in knowledge management may lead to efficiencies and synergies of information as well as promoting learning and innovation. A precondition for learning is absorptive capacity (Cohen & Levinthal, 1990), and a proper IT system may support the fundamental requirements of knowledge assimilation and integration. IT tools can also become the necessary precondition for the performance of key business routines.

However, the specific internal potential of any given IT system does not necessarily correspond to the actual utilization patterns of such a tool: the specific innovation process, its object and its context are all fundamental issues to be taken into account. Although potentials feed expectations and are usually nurtured by IT developers and top management, often a mismatch between potential and expectation results in the concrete applications of the tool in different phases of the innovation processes.

Innovations: the innovation process, object, and context   The possible roles of IT in the innovation process can include enabling, speeding up, focusing, directing, and integrating, but these roles may also leave unaffected or even restrain the whole process — or just specific phases of it (e.g., Huber, 1990; Alavi & Leidner, 2001; Dewett & Jones, 2001). It all depends on the actual characteristics, object, and context of the innovation process.

The innovation process   A better understanding of the role of IT in innovations requires considering the ways a specific IT tool can impact on the different phases of the innovation process (see Figure 2). This impact depends on how and when the tool comes onto the scene of the innovation process. We therefore present a generalized description of the phases characterizing the innovation process, inspired by Van de Ven, Polley, Garud, and Venkataraman (1999, pp. 23–62, 182–184), Tidd et al. (2001, pp. 52–59), and Normann (1971, p. 203). This nonlinear and path-dependent process (Rosenberg, 1994) starts from *idealization* and moves through spirals of *concretization* leading to the *emergence* of a viable innovative solution. The innovation process proceeds then with *introduction* and *spatial diffusion* leading to local utilization by firm-internal or external users. While being modified and adapted to local contexts, the innovation is *exploited* until it decays or is so substantially changed to be no longer recognized as the

Innovation Process

Figure 2: Generalized sequence of the phases in the innovation process.

"original" innovation. We claim that any single IT solution plays very different roles in, for instance, idealization as compared to exploitation.

The innovation object   The nature of the innovation object (e.g., product vs. process and incremental vs. radical innovation) and its characteristics (complexity, tacitness, novelty, etc.) affect the way IT solutions intervene in the innovation process. As pointed out by Tidd et al. (2001), some conceptualizations of innovations are too wide, whereas others distinguish between invention, that is, any novel idea, and the commercial exploitation of an idea, which is an innovation in proper terms (Teece, 1986). In this study, we refer to innovation as the entire process of linking any new problem-solving ideas to actual uses (Kanter, 1988). However, this article does not investigate how IT tools and the innovation object affect each other, because we chose to keep the innovation object in the background and to regard it as given. We focus instead on the relevance of the innovation context for the role and use of the IT solutions in the innovation process.

The innovation context   This context is expressed by the firm's *internal network* of subsidiaries, including the focal unit (e.g., Bartlett & Ghoshal, 1987; Hedlund & Rolander, 1990; Ghoshal & Nohria, 1997), and by the surrounding external *business network* (e.g., Håkansson & Waluszewski, 2002; Håkansson & Snehota, 1995; Andersson, Forsgren, & Holm, 2001; Forsgren, Johanson, & Sharma, 2000). On a more detailed level, the innovation context is textured in terms of organizational structures (Bartlett & Ghoshal, 1987; Hedlund & Rolander, 1990; Gupta & Govindarajan, 1991), specific routines (e.g., Nelson & Winter, 1982; Grant, 1996), integrative mechanisms (Martinez & Jarillo, 1989), cultural cues, knowledge and capabilities (Kogut & Zander, 1993; Nelson & Winter, 1982; Grant, 1996; Spender 1996), and specific external business relationships (e.g., Håkansson & Snehota, 1989, 1995). It is important to notice that factors influencing the innovation process are found both internally and externally to the MNC boundaries (Brown & Eisenhardt, 1995; Frost, 2001; Andersson, Forsgren, & Holm, 2002). *We argue that each specific IT solution plays very different roles for a given phase of the innovation process, depending on the specific innovation context.* This is because the way the MNC is internally organized, the initiating unit characteristics, the level of corporate and external embeddedness (e.g., Andersson et al., 2002; Andersson & Forsgren, 1996) all intervene in affecting how the IT solutions we focus upon are concretely used, irrespective of their technical features and the managerial expectations about them.

Experiences with Innovations at SCA and IKEA

Customized packaging solutions at SCA packaging   SCA produces and sells absorbent hygiene products, packaging solutions, and publication papers.[3] SCA net sales amount to more than 9 billion Euros annually. At the beginning of 2002, the number of employees were approximately 40,000, in some 40 countries.

SCA Packaging division is Europe's leading producer of corrugated board and containerboard, and one of the world leaders in "customized packaging solutions." About 35 million packaging units are delivered daily from SCA's more than 220 plants in Europe, North America, and Asia. Customers range from food companies to retailers and producers of industrial products. These packaging solutions are the *objects of innovation* efforts by SCA Packaging. They differ one from the other in terms of characteristics (e.g., size and design), applications, and functions. Differences in product innovation are mainly due to the specificity of customer needs.

SCA uses IT systems throughout the value chain, from the development stage to the final product. IT is used for online sales, logistics, supplies, communication, and administration. SCA Packaging perceives IT potentialities to be very high, especially for product development activities. Today, IT influence on innovation processes is mostly in terms of speed of the development, but major steps have already been taken to improve quality and content of the innovations and their processes. "MIDAS" is one of the most interesting information systems used within SCA Packaging. This IT system is a tool that helps designers to develop and tailor optimal packaging solutions for the many different customers needs. Although IT solutions at SCA are usually independently chosen and managed by the single unit, MIDAS is a clear exception. It has been developed in-house by SCA Packaging HQs and it has been adopted by almost all the subunits in the division. It is composed of an extensive database of CAD drawings, user instructions, properties and material details, and basic box characteristics. All this enables designers to have the necessary information available when developing a new "packaging solution."

---

[3]SCA business areas are: SCA Hygiene Products, SCA Packaging, and SCA Forest Products.

The *innovation object* is incremental product development with rather low complexity and explicit nature. SCA consumer and industrial packaging solutions use, in fact, basically the same materials, i.e., corrugated board and container-board.[4] They have also similar components, but very specific functions (protect, carry, store, display, etc.), which, depending on the specific solution and customer, could be more dominant than the others (e.g., strength and corrugated container resistance are fundamental for industrial machinery transport boxes).

The *idealization* of new packaging solutions starts in one of the many units distributed in the different countries and does not involve any participation of SCA Packaging HQs. The solution is clearly customer-driven and its *concretization* is the result of the interaction between the customer and SCA local unit's development team. Thus, SCA Packaging units develop their solutions by relying on: (a) their capabilities, resources, and previous experience; (b) the interaction with the customer; (c) SCA's internal network of information and resources. Information is obtained through interaction with other sister units dealing with similar customers and through the access to different product solutions already existing and made available via MIDAS. Resources such as raw materials are mainly provided by SCA Packaging mills (testliner and kraftliner) and by SCA Forest Products (pulp and recycled paper). The new packaging solution created is then *sold* to the specific customer, but *introduced* in many different markets. This is because the innovated package follows the customer's products and production facilities. Moreover, by *sharing* the new solution developed (and its documentation) with the other SCA Packaging sister units, there are good chances of finding other customers for the same packaging solution, through the other units' local markets and networks. It is in this way that the innovation of one unit is *exploited* in many different markets and by many other SCA units, for many more customers.

Approximately 800 persons are involved with R&D, an effort that awarded SCA with more than 4000 patents. R&D resources and responsibility are distributed to the various business areas. At SCA Packaging, R&D specifically focuses on product development with emphasis on improved performance, cost effectiveness, and better design. SCA Packaging has a large decentralized network of resources devoted to product development, which operate close to the customers, and a central, more traditional R&D center, which conducts mainly basic research on raw materials. The cooperation with suppliers is very limited, and almost all the efforts are dedicated to the interaction with customers, mostly face-to-face. This is mainly due to the very nature of developing "customized solutions."

---

[4]Although they might be sold with other packaging materials, such as plastics, metal or glass.

What is MIDAS's role in the overall innovation process of customized packaging solutions? During the early stage of *idealization*, ideas come from the very intense interaction with customers and the understanding of their needs. In the following phase of *concretization*, customers still play a central role for determining the functions and applications of the packaging solution. But it is through MIDAS that the package characteristics are determined and finally *emerge*. Because of the CAD database and the interactive applications that MIDAS withholds, this IT tool became fundamental for the integration, diffusion, and exploitation of new products information,[5] and for the development of the final blueprint. MIDAS covers mainly technical details of products, but very little on production process specifications or marketing information. To summarize, MIDAS does not appear to be useful or used in: (a) the *early stage* of idealization, since the SCA unit mainly interacts with the customer; (b) the introduction, which is managed by personal interaction with customers; or (c) utilization, since customers have no access to MIDAS. But it largely contributes in the specification, concretization, and product emergence phases. MIDAS, moreover, plays a sustaining role in the internal diffusion of the innovation.

IKEA and the "Lack" Table

IKEA is a worldwide leader in furniture retailing, with sales in 2001 of over 10 billion euros. IKEA employs over 65,000 people in its retailing, warehousing, and product development operations. Its home furnishing products are distributed through a worldwide network of 180 retail outlets. IKEA's business idea relies on developing and procuring, in close connection with over 2000 suppliers, furniture products that reunite "form, function and affordability" and that are made available to over 200 million consumers in self-service showrooms. IKEA's strategic centre, "IKEA of Sweden," is in charge of developing each of its over 10,000 products.

IKEA is a production-led retailer   IKEA of Sweden neither picks suppliers' already existing products nor designs products without taking into account the available production facilities. IKEA of Sweden is instead constantly involved with suppliers and develops products that are engineered for manufacturing in order to obtain as low production costs as possible. This is particularly important for a product manufactured in large volumes like the "Lack" sofa table, one of IKEA's absolute bestsellers reaching the 2.5 million units sold yearly. Lack was launched over 20 years ago, but its retail price has been kept constant through all

---

[5]MIDAS-generated documents are then stored and made available for the entire network of sister units.

these years. The secret behind this miracle has been a continuous work of product development where IKEA of Sweden and its suppliers are constantly involved. Innovation efforts around Lack aim at marginal improvements of materials, production technology, and colors.

One of IKEA's central information systems is named "PIA" (Product Information Assistance). This system was introduced in 1998 also to support product developers at IKEA of Sweden in the management of innovation projects, such as those around Lack. For this purpose, PIA is equipped with a database including a large amount of product-related information: supplier identities and contracts, production technology and quality certifications, technical descriptions of Lack, and the related CAD files. PIA also includes an application that allows product developers to electronically launch each innovation project they start on (such as Lack). They can set dates, budgets, and goals for the project. By compiling regularly a series of flaps they can actively follow up each single project from start to conclusion, when the product is launched in retailing. PIA is fundamental for innovation efforts around Lack especially because of a particular internal routine at IKEA: each product modification, before being introduced to the retailing units, must be preceded by a PIA-borne message called "News" and by a detailed "Technical Description" that can be produced only by using PIA. These documents are the information base from which to create product-related information material for sale points and for packaging. Without News and Technical Descriptions no product can be sold in the IKEA universe.

The object of this innovation at IKEA is marginal product modifications, with low complexity but relatively high tacitness. The innovation process starts from idealization at IKEA of Sweden and becomes concretized in a development project that specifies goals, dates, and budgets. At this stage of the project, suppliers of materials, lacquers and Lack manufacturers are engaged in the innovation process. The specific technical solutions adopted emerge in the interaction between IKEA of Sweden and these various actors. The innovated Lack, e.g., with a new type of veneering material, is introduced to all IKEA retail units around the world, in absolutely standard form. In this way, the marginally new Lack is spatially diffused and gets locally utilized by each IKEA store. During a certain period of time, the specific new Lack is exploited by retailing units to sustain their sales volumes. After a while IKEA of Sweden considers the time ripe for further modifications of this product, which signals the decay of the one currently present in retail stores. The innovation process can thus start again in a cyclical fashion.

The innovation context typical for marginal developments of Lack includes IKEA of Sweden as a driving actor. This unit involves actively its external network of suppliers in finding technical solutions to achieve project goals that it usually defines rather independently. To find concrete solutions, face-to-face meetings are usually held, especially on the factory floor. IKEA of Sweden then pushes the new Lack in unvaried and standardized shape to all retail units all over the world. The only possibility retail units have to affect product development is during the periodic meetings with IKEA of Sweden. But retail units give only feedback on the already introduced modifications of Lack, rather than suggesting future ones. IKEA would, in fact, never be able to cope economically with all the requests for adaptations and new features suggested by local retail units.

What concrete role does PIA play in the innovation process involving Lack? Product developers claim that they never use PIA in the idealization phase, since ideas derive from other sources, such as meetings with suppliers, retail units, or personal intuition. The same holds for the concretization of the innovation project goals, dates and budgets, even though some Lack-related projects are actually inscribed into PIA at this stage. But soon, product developers escape from PIA and avoid it through the phase of emergence of concrete solutions, during which they instead interact with their supplier network. Only as soon as a new solution emerges, because of the News and Technical Description routines, PIA becomes instead fundamental for the introduction of the new Lack to the retail units. Spatial diffusion and local utilization depend largely on the local context in terms of retail unit interest and consumer tastes. But still, PIA-borne documents are presented to and used by these units, also in handling physically Lack inside the store. Moreover, consumers are reached by PIA-borne information in the form of assembly instructions, price tags, and packaging information. Finally, also the famous IKEA catalogue relies for advertising information and product pictures on key documents generated inside PIA. All in all, PIA contributes, quite unexpectedly, much more to the phases of innovation introduction, diffusion, and utilization, rather than to idealization, concretization, and emergence.

Analysis and Discussion

The two empirical descriptions highlight the different roles of specific IT tools in the innovation process, not only at two different firm sites, but also within two different innovation contexts. Moreover, MIDAS and PIA are dissimilar in terms of potentials and functionalities and they affect differently the innovation process and its various phases at SCA and IKEA (see Table 1). While MIDAS speeds up and directs concretization and emergence of innovations, PIA leaves these phases substantially unaffected. Conversely, while PIA enables innovation introduction, diffusion and exploitation, MIDAS almost disappears from the scene in these phases.

Table 1: A comparative table on MIDAS's and PIA's role in the innovation process.

	Ideali- zation	Concreti- zation	Emergence	Intro- duction	Diffusion	Exploi- tation
MIDAS	No/yes*	Yes	Yes	No	No/yes†	No
PIA	No	No	No/yes‡	Yes	Yes	Yes

* MIDAS intervenes in the late idealization phase, after a customer has already specified its needs, by presenting and combining already existing packaging solutions.
† MIDAS intervenes in the diffusion of the developed packaging solution between sister units.
‡ PIA intervenes at the end of the emergence phase to record the actual technical features emerging as results from technical tests.

But what do these different patterns of effects and roles of the IT tools depend on? The theoretical framework presented in the second section points at three main issues:

(1) MIDAS's and PIA's different potentials and technical functionalities;
(2) the different innovation contexts at SCA and IKEA, in terms of routines and intra- and inter-organizational networks;
(3) the different innovation objects (e.g., customized vs. standard products).

And, to further complicate things, the innovation context (and to a certain extent even the innovation object)[6] changes from one innovation phase to the other: these context dynamics account for why the inner technical functionalities of the very same IT tool play a major or minor role (or no role at all) in the different phases of the innovation process. It is therefore helpful to continue our analysis by discussing the ways in which the two IT solutions presented in the empirical sections interplay with the contexts in each phase of the innovation processes. In this way, we shall be able to identify potential matches and mismatches of IT tools with these dynamic contexts. Our findings are summarized in Table 2.

For simplicity, we chose to describe the context within each phase of the innovation process in terms of only two distinct features: (a) the degree of interaction with other organizational units (inside or outside the MNC) that is necessary to move through a certain phase; and (b) the extent to which rigid routines and structured procedures are in place to sustain the performance of tasks during a certain phase. For instance, the idealization phase at SCA is highly interactive, because

---

[6]As mentioned in the second section, we decided to regard the innovation object as given and not to investigate its effects on the role of IT tools for the innovation process.

Table 2: MIDAS's and PIA's role in the phase-specific innovation contexts.

	Idealization	Concretization	Emergence	Introduction	Diffusion	Exploitation
MIDAS	No/yes	Yes	Yes	No	No/yes	No
SCA context ↔	Interactive but structured (constraints)	Less interactive and more structured	Single-unit and structured (routines)	Interactive and unstructured (face-to-face)	Multi-unit but structured knowledge	Single-unit, but outside MIDAS
Impact on IT's role	IT focuses specifications	IT suggests re-corded solutions	IT used to draw solutions	IT too rigid vs. personal sale	IT as central info collector	IT does not cover this
PIA	No	No	No/yes	Yes	Yes	Yes
IKEA context ↔	Single-unit but very unstructured	Interactive and unstructured (no routines)	Interactive but more structured	Single-unit and structured (routines)	Multi-unit but structured (routines)	Single-unit, within PIA's reach
Impact on IT's role	Too blurred for IT to cover	Too practical and external for IT	IT enters to trace results	IT pushes the frozen innov.	IT steers ordering	IT helps sales and use

customers are directly involved to present their customization requests, but they need to respect certain technical constraints that give more structure to this phase. By converse, the idealization phase at IKEA is much less interactive, because new product ideas are generated centrally by a single unit (IKEA of Sweden), even though this is done without any rigid routine or template, that is, in a rather unstructured way.

The underlying rationale for our focusing on the impact of inter-unit interactions and of routines and structuring on the role of IT is that: (a) if an IT tool does not include or is not accessed by some key units intervening in an innovation phase, its role is potentially reduced; and (b) if an IT tool does not mirror the routines and knowledge bases that sustain the performance of an innovation phase, it can only play a minor role; and clearly, whenever such routines are absent and such knowledge bases are blurred or unstructured, it becomes almost impossible for IT to mirror them.

In fact, our empirical material points to the importance of inter-unit interactions and the strength of routines and structures, in each single innovation phase, which make more or less useful the intrinsic features of the two IT tools we studied. Therefore, we now discuss these two contextual features in each innovation phase (see Table 2 for a summary) in order to better understand how they impact on the role played, in the respective innovation processes, by MIDAS and by PIA (depending also on their technical properties and potentials).

SCA and MIDAS

1. *Idealization:* This phase at SCA is very interactive, with the direct participation of customers. Whereas this contextual feature tends to push MIDAS aside, because it is not accessed by customers, SCA strives to connect the knowledge bits composing a new customized solution with MIDAS's database of existing technical solutions. As this knowledge base is highly structured, MIDAS is important in the later stage of idealization.
2. *Concretization:* This phase is driven more unilaterally by a single SCA unit, which transforms the customers' functional requests into structured technical specifications inside MIDAS, where they can be matched with entries on technical issues previously made also by other SCA units. MIDAS clearly suggests how to design the new customized product, based on the solutions recorded inside it.
3. *Emergence:* In this phase a single SCA unit utilizes MIDAS in order to materially produce the CAD drawing, a structured and routinized task for which MIDAS is perfectly fit.

4. *Introduction:* This phase implies selling the new customized solution to a customer and is therefore highly interactive, with much face-to-face interaction taking place. Besides, the discussions between SCA unit and customer are quite unstructured and cover broad topics, such as costing issues, for which MIDAS was not conceived, and for which it would be inflexible. Therefore, MIDAS is not utilized in this phase.

5. *Diffusion:* This phase concerns spreading to all sister units the new customized solution, especially to those that will physically produce it for the local subsidiaries of the original customer. However, the context is not highly interactive, because sister units simply download the emerged solution (a CAD drawing) and manufacture it.[7] MIDAS is very helpful in delivering to all units a structured knowledge base, in a format that is understood by all of them.

6. *Exploitation:* The context of utilization of the new packaging solution inside the customers' plants is not currently covered by MIDAS, which has therefore no role in, for instance, improving this particular phase.

IKEA and PIA

1. *Idealization:* This phase is characterized by a single unit, IKEA of Sweden, that generates new product ideas on the basis of suggestions collected from surrounding units, but that eventually decides which ones to pursue in a unilateral fashion. Whereas this centralization could favor the use of PIA, in reality the highly blurred knowledge bases involved and the absence of stringent routines puts PIA in the background.

2. *Concretization:* This phase is highly interactive, with the competences necessary to identify concrete solutions to the problems defined in the idealization phase are spread across Ikea's whole supplier network. Being PIA not accessible to external units, it becomes even less useful in this phase. Moreover, interactions are informal and concern so concrete and unstructured issues that PIA is virtually forgotten here.

3. *Emergence:* The context is still very interactive, with few routines and rather unstructured knowledge involved for PIA to drive this innovation phase. But, when tests at suppliers' plants show satisfactory results, the new Lack's technical features can be frozen inside PIA, which accordingly enters the scene

---

[7]If a local adaptation were necessary, the innovation process would start here again from the early stage of idealization, in interaction with a local subsidiary of the original customer.

at the end of this phase, when the new solution has become stable and ready to be introduced to retail units.

4. *Introduction:* The context in this phase sees a single unit, IKEA of Sweden, addressing unilaterally all IKEA's retail units by offering a "frozen" Lack, which is described by a structured list of features included inside PIA and accessible to all retail units. Moreover, the presence of strong routines on how information should be created with PIA makes this IT tool absolutely indispensable during this innovation phase.

5. *Diffusion:* This context includes several units, but with only limited inter-action. The sales success and diffusion of a new Lack depend in fact on local contingencies. Even if PIA does not cover such contingencies, its standard product information nevertheless covers the need for structured knowledge of retail units in search of reasons whether or not to place orders for the new Lack.

6. *Exploitation:* Similar to the previous phase, this phase happens within single retail units (and customer homes) acting with minimal interaction with each other. PIA is conceived for the purpose of covering and contributing to this final innovation stage, particularly because PIA carries standard messages to retail units on how to sell or exhibit the new Lack. Moreover, some of the information produced within PIA, namely assembly instructions, becomes indirectly available to IKEA's final customers, as printed material.

Conclusions and Managerial Implications

By looking at the two innovation processes where MIDAS and PIA are involved, we have been able to present a more fine-grained and in-depth view of how IT tools intervene and analyze the role they play for innovations, such as product development. We saw, in particular, in these case studies, the impact of the innovation context on the role and utility of IT tools, not only in general, but also within single innovation phases. A first interesting conclusion that we can draw from Tables 1 and 2 is that the roles of the two specific IT tools (MIDAS and PIA) seem to be localized on just one or a few adjacent phases of the whole innovation process. Is this a rule or just a coincidence? Further investigations are necessary to tackle this aspect that clearly emerges from the above comparison. However, we argue that this pattern is strictly associated to how the IT tool's specific functions relate to the innovation context (and object), thereby delimiting also the scope and domain of usability of a certain IT solution.

Tables 1 and 2 also show that there is a minimal overlap between the innovation phases sustained by MIDAS and by PIA: this depends not only on the rather different technical features of these two IT tools, but also on the different contexts in each single innovation phase. More precisely, we showed how the ability of an IT tool to sustain a certain phase depends on the *match* between its internal technical features and the context of that phase, in terms of inter-unit interactions, routines, and knowledge structures. The difficulty in expressing general judgments on how fit IT is for innovations is compounded by the fact that even technically very similar IT tools are exposed to contexts that vary both *in time* — from one innovation phase to another, or even from one innovation cycle to another within the same firm — and *in space,* from one firm to another.

The fact that two IT systems observed in this paper do not cover all phases of the innovation process opens the question of how to sustain the whole process by using IT. Shall firms use many single separate IT tools or a whole large integrated system? Neither approach is best a priori. On the basis of our theoretical framework and from the two empirical investigations it seems that what really matters is matching each single phase (i.e., its context and object) with the right IT tool and building in inter-phase coordination between tools if many are utilized. This calls consequently for a deep understanding of the innovation process, both as a whole and in terms of its specific phases, each one with different IT requirements. Managers should choose single IT tools (or a whole system) depending on their potentials, and in order to fit the single innovation phase they should sustain and not overlap with each other (MIDAS and PIA could be good examples in this direction). At last, different IT systems should also be integrated in order to mirror the way the innovation phases are interrelated within the whole process. The critical aspect is, in fact, that as different phases are connected and interdependent, so have also to be the single IT tools. A large integrated system or a collection of single separate IT tools can both satisfy these conditions.

A further complication is that the actual performance of IT tools is affected also by the ways the context changes and interplays with each innovation phase. That is why the understanding necessary to create and use IT tools in the innovation process, should stretch also to cover the details of the context where innovation unfolds. In particular, innovation contexts characterized by *intensive interactions* with external units need to be matched by IT tools that take these units into account, at least the most important ones. In some cases, the contribution of such external units is so strong that some of these even need to be granted access to the focal IT system. Incidentally, this is what IKEA is doing while further developing PIA, which will soon be accessible to a restricted set of key suppliers that have pivotal roles during the concretization and emergence phase of innovation processes. Besides this interactive dimension of the innovation context, the presence of favorable routines and of structured knowledge bases seems also to be a condition for IT tools to play a major role in each innovation phase.

In conclusion, in order to create or use IT tools to sustain innovations, a firm needs to understand the innovation process — its different phases and how they relate to each other and to their contexts. This holds especially true for complex IT systems that should cover the whole innovation process. In this paper, although concerned with the whole innovation process, we have mainly focused on innovation development, but much more research needs to be done on the phenomenon of innovation diffusion, transfer, and adoption. The importance and role of IT as an innovation transfer mechanism is still an open issue on many researchers' agendas (e.g., Hansen, Nohria, & Tierney, 1999; Maltz, 2000; Dewett & Jones, 2001). This issue is particularly critical for large organizations such as MNCs, which are characterized by a geographically dispersed network of specialized subsidiaries that interplay with local customers and suppliers, and whose competitive strength is increasingly based on the ability and efficiency in leveraging innovations from one unit to another.

References

Alavi, M., & Leidner, D. E. (2001). Review: Knowledge management and knowledge management systems: Conceptual foundations and research issues. *MIS Quarterly*, 25(1), 107–136.

Andersson, U., & Forsgren, M. (1996). Subsidiary embeddedness and control in the multinational corporation. *International Business Review*, 5(5), 487–508.

Andersson, U., Forsgren, M., & Holm, U. (2001). Subsidiary embeddedness and competence development in MNCs – a multi-level analysis. *Organization Studies*, 22(6), 1013–1034.

Andersson, U., Forsgren, M., & Holm, U. (2002). The strategic impact of external networks: Subsidiary performance and competence development in the multinational corporation. *Strategic Management Journal*, 23, 979–996.

Baraldi, E. (2003). *When information technology faces resource interaction: Using IT tools to handle products at IKEA and Edsbyn*. Ph.D. thesis, Department of Business Studies, Uppsala University.

Bartlett, C. A., & Ghoshal, S. (1987). Managing across borders: New strategic requirements. *Sloan Management Review*, 28(4), 7–16.

Bartlett, C. A., & Ghoshal, S. (1989). *Managing across borders: The transnational solution*. Boston: Harvard Business School Press.

Bessant, J., & Buckingham, J. (1993). Innovation and organizational learning: The case of computer-aided production management. *British Journal of Management*, 4, 219–234.

Brown, S. L., & Eisenhardt, K. M. (1995). Product development: Past research, present findings, and future directions. *Academy of Management Review*, 20(2), 343–378.

Cantwell, J. (1989). *Technological innovation and multinational corporations*. Oxford: Basil Blackwell.

Cohen, W. M., & Levinthal, D. A. (1990). Absorptive capacity: A new perspective on learning and innovation. *Administrative Science Quarterly,* 35(1), 128–152.

Davenport, T. H., & Short, J. E. (1990). The new industrial engineering: Information technology and business process redesign. *Sloan Management Review, 31*(4), 11–27.

Davies, A., & Brady, T. (2000). Organizational capabilities and learning in complex product systems: Towards repeatable solutions. *Research Policy, 29*(7–8), 931–953.

Dewett, T., & Jones, R. G. (2001). The role of information technology in the organization: A review, model, and assessment. *Journal of Management, 27*, 313–346.

Doz, Y. L., Santos, J., & Williamson, P. J. (2001). *From global to metanational: How companies win in the knowledge economy*. Boston, MA: Harvard Business School Press.

Forsgren, M., Johanson, J., & Sharma, D. (2000). Development of MNC centers of excellence. In: U. Holm, & T. Pedersen (Eds), *The emergence and impact on MNC centers of excellence — a subsidiary perspective* (pp. 45–67). London: Macmillan.

Frost, T. S. (2001). The geographical sources of foreign subsidiaries innovations. *Strategic Management Journal, 22*, 101–123.

Ghoshal, S., & Nohria, N. (1997). *The differentiated MNC: Organizing multinational corporation for value creation*. San Francisco: Jossey-Bass.

Grant, R. M. (1996). Prospering in dynamically-competitive environments: Organizational capability as knowledge integration. *Organizational Science, 7*(4), 375–387.

Gupta, A. K., & Govindarajan, V. (1991). Knowledge flows and the structure of control within multinational corporations. *Academy of Management Review, 16*(4), 768–792.

Håkansson, H., & Snehota, I. (1989). No business is an island: The network concept of business strategy. *Scandinavian Journal of Management, 5*(3), 187–200.

Håkansson, H., & Snehota, I. (1995). *Developing relationships in business networks*. London: Routledge.

Håkansson, H., & Waluszewski, A. (2002). *Managing technological development. IKEA, the environment and technology*. London: Routledge.

Hansen, M. T., Nohria, N., & Tierney, T. (1999). What's your strategy for managing knowledge? *Harvard Business Review, 77*(2), 106–116.

Hedlund, G., & Rolander, D. (1990). Action in heterarchies – new approaches to managing the MNC. In: C. A. Bartlett, Y. Doz, & G. Hedlund, (Eds), *Managing the global firm*. London: Routledge.

Huber, G. P. (1990). A theory of the effects of advances information technologies on organizational design, intelligence, and decision making. *Academy of Management Review, 15*(1), 47–71.

Kanter, R. M. (1988). When a thousand flowers bloom: Structural, collective, and social conditions for innovation in organization. *Research in Organizational Behavior, 10*, 169–211.

Kogut, B., & Zander, U. (1992). Knowledge of the firm, combinative capabilities, and the replication of technology. *Organization Science, 3*(2), 383–397.

Kogut, B., & Zander, U. (1993). Knowledge of the firm and the evolutionary theory of the multinational corporation. *Journal of International Business Studies, 24*(4), 625–645.

Maltz, E. (2000). Is all communication created equal? An investigation into the effects of communication mode on perceived information quality. *Journal of Product Innovation Management, 17*(2), 110–127.

Martinez, J. I., & Jarillo, C. J. (1989). The evolution of research on coordination mechanisms in multinational corporations. *Journal of International Business Studies, 20*(3), 489–514.

Nelson, R. R., & Winter, S. G. (1982). *An evolutionary theory of economic change.* Cambridge, MA: Harvard University Press.

Normann, R. (1971). Organizational innovativeness: Product variation and reorientation. *Administrative Science Quarterly, 16*(2), 203–215.

Rosenberg, N. (1994). Path-dependent aspects of technological change. In: *Exploring the Black Box.* Cambridge: Cambridge University Press.

Spender, J. C. (1996). Making knowledge the basis of a dynamic theory of the firm. *Strategic Management Journal, 17*(Winter Special), 45–62.

Simon, H. (1977). *The new science of management decision.* Englewood Cliffs, NJ: Prentice-Hall.

Teece, D. J. (1986). Profiting from technological innovation: Implications for integration, collaboration, licensing, and public policy. *Research Policy, 15*(6), 285–305.

Tidd, J., Bessant, J., & Pavitt, K. (2001). *Managing innovation, integrating technological, market and organisational change.* Chichester: Wiley.

Van de Ven, A., Polley, D., Garud, R., & Venkataraman, S. (1999). *The innovation journey.* Oxford, NY: Oxford University Press.

Chapter 14

Ignorant Internationalization? The Uppsala Model and Internationalization Patterns for Internet-Related Firms

Mats Forsgren and Peter Hagström

Introduction

Firms invest abroad. Ever since Hymer's (1976/1960) seminal study the research focus has very much been on how firms overcome their liability of foreignness vis-à-vis their competitors in overseas markets. The answer to the question *why* firms can go abroad has fundamentally been put down to such firms possessing a firm-specific competitive advantage (Buckley & Casson, 1976; Dunning, 1977; Caves, 1982).

Another influential strand of research has instead occupied itself with the process of internationalization, i.e. *how* does internationalization evolve over time. Traditional theories of internationalization behavior of firms take their cue from the historical experience of manufacturing firms. Carlson (1966) was one of the earliest scholars to make the observation that firms intending to invest abroad suffer from lack of knowledge about how to conduct business in a foreign market. His primary area of inquiry became the decision process itself after having formulated the hypothesis that firms tend to handle this risky problem by trial and error and by gradual acquisition of information about foreign markets. This empirically based reasoning gave rise to an — what was to become the dominant — internationalization process model with several variations. Essentially, this theory(-ies) makes two predictions:

(a) firms internationalize through increasing commitments to foreign markets,
(b) firms choose new markets sequentially according to their perceived proximity.

The former is a story of incremental learning in a given foreign market. The latter builds on subjective perceptions (subject to the Chandlerian (1986) restriction of existing technology permitting the maintenance of relevant administrative structures across borders) determining the choice of which specific geographic markets to enter.

The resultant process has been seen to be slow and deliberate, seemingly flying in the face of recent experience, in particular as it pertains to the internationalization of Internet-related firms in the second half of the 1990s. Then, there was no shortage in the business press of accounts of how these firms expanded internationally and that at what was a breathtaking speed. Although a more sober atmosphere lately has replaced the "irrational exuberance" associated with rapidly expanding equity markets, the question still remains whether or not these new firms behaved differently when internationalizing from what the old models would have us expect. Anecdotal evidence often made Internet-related firms represent something totally different from traditional multinational enterprises.

The most well-known model of internationalization behavior, the so-called Uppsala Model, has been claimed to be very general and therefore applicable to many different firms and different situations (Pedersen & Petersen, 1998). A reasonable task in order to develop the model, therefore, is to confront the model with data from more "extreme cases," that is data from firms other than those firms through which the model was originally induced. In line with this the purpose of the chapter is to scrutinize and discuss more in depth some of the basic assumptions behind the Uppsala Model of internationalization by confronting these assumptions with data from internationalization in some Internet-related firms.

The chapter first reviews the theoretical constructs associated with the Uppsala Model focusing on the key concepts of learning and knowledge. Then, the internationalization experiences of selected Internet-related businesses are reviewed. Eight firms (two web design firms and six consumer retail firms) were singled out for a richer empirical setting. Interestingly, two of the firms, and probably the best-known ones at the time, Boxman and Dressmart, have since gone bankrupt. This way we also avoid the standard empirical problem of only sampling successful, i.e. surviving firms, which should add to the validity of our findings.

The third section of the chapter juxtaposes the predictions of the internationalization model with observed behavior. Some counterfactual experiences cast doubt over the continued relevance of the model, whereas other behavior can be accommodated within the realm of classical explanations. Since this inquiry does not constitute a "test" of any propositions but is rather an *inductive* investigation, the paper concludes with a brief discussion of possible new internationalization patterns.

The Arduous Process of Internationalization

Carlson's (1966) reasoning laid the groundwork for what later has become known as the Uppsala Internationalization Process Model (Johanson & Wiedersheim-Paul, 1975; Johanson & Vahlne, 1977). It primarily deals with knowledge acquisition, i.e. learning. Central issues concern how organizations learn and how this learning affects their subsequent investment behavior (Johanson & Vahlne, 1977, 1990). A basic assumption of the model is that lack of *knowledge* about foreign *markets* is a major obstacle to internationalization, but that this obstacle can be overcome through learning about foreign market conditions. The firm's own *current operations* are the main source of this kind of learning. In turn, this reasoning leads to a second assumption of "learning by doing" (cf. Lindblom, 1959; Johnson, 1988). Investment *decisions* and actual investment *commitments* are made incrementally as uncertainty is successfully reduced. The more the firm knows about a foreign market, the lower the perceived market risk will be and, consequently, the higher the actual investment by the firm in that market tends to be.

The core concepts of the model are *market commitment, market knowledge, commitment decisions,* and *current activities.* All tangible and intangible assets that a firm accumulates in a specific geographical market make up its *market commitment.* This is a matter both of the sheer amount of resources committed and the degree to which they are committed to a specific market (cf. Johanson & Vahlne, 1990). The latter refers to the relative ease or difficulty of transferring resources to another market. For instance, well-established local customer relationships tend to be idiosyncratic to a particular geographic market.

Market knowledge is taken to stem from experience of foreign markets. Hence, the critical knowledge is on the whole tacit in nature. As such it is highly dependent on individuals and therefore difficult to transfer to other individuals or other contexts (cf. Johanson & Vahlne, 1977). This also constitutes a third, basic assumption of the model (cf. Forsgren, 2002). It is individuals, e.g. the sales subsidiary personnel, who learn about the problems and opportunities present in a particular market. Knowledge acquisition is then seen here as very much of a 'bottom-up' process. Learning is initiated when a problem is encountered in the current operations and ends when a satisfactory solution is found; a "bounded rationality" approach (cf. Cyert & March, 1963).

A given level of market knowledge and market commitment at a certain point in time will then affect the commitment decisions and how activities are carried out in subsequent periods. In turn, these decisions and activities will influence the later stages of market commitment and market knowledge in an incrementally evolving spiral.

On the basis of the three basic assumptions and four concepts above, the model predicts a pattern for firms' internationalization behavior. This pattern is characterized by two main aspects:

1. Investments in a given country are carried out cautiously and sequentially as a result of incremental and concurrent local learning.
2. Firms start (and continue to) invest in one or a few neighboring countries rather than investing in distant markets and/or several markets simultaneously. "Closer" markets are those that are perceived to be close, i.e. markets about which the extent of knowledge and the "comfort level" are higher. These are markets located at a shorter *psychic distance*, which may diverge from straight geographic distance (cf. Johanson & Vahlne, 1990).

With the above terminology in place, the stage is set for a description of the internationalization process of young, Internet-related firms.

Recent Internationalization Experience of Internet-Related Firms

Eight Internet-related firms were investigated concerning their internationalization from the respective launch of the businesses to the end of year 2000. The sample of firms is by no means random as the relevant population was found to be impossible to identify. First, the phenomenon is new as postulated by our inquiry; a fact that implies that generally accepted groupings or listings of relevant firms are yet to emerge. Second, there is no officially accepted definition of this type of firms making them hard to classify. Rather than using an arbitrary definition of the population, a decision was made to ensure variation in the sample, and to select firms that are known to have been actively engaged in internationalizing their businesses.

The firms under consideration are Bokus, Boxman, Buyonet, CDon, Dressmart, SEB, Framfab, and Icon Medialab. The first six firms have sold consumer products or services over the Internet, and the last two firms are web-design consultancies. All businesses were launched in 1995 or later. Two firms, Boxman and Dressmart have gone bankrupt since the investigation started and the consultancies have gone through major restructuring, i.e. downsizing. This is an advantage as the common drawback of only studying successful firms is somewhat mitigated. Firms only needed to demonstrate short-term survival instead of the long-term staying power normally associated with firms drawn from official sources or the like.

Primarily for practical reasons, all the firms are of Swedish origin. Data collection was made easier. However, Sweden is also known for an exceptionally early and high Internet penetration rate (together with the US and other Nordic countries) although the top rankings may vary somewhat depending on source. Fact remains that Sweden is a good place to start since we are interested in a longitudinal study.[1]

Both primary and secondary data were collected. Much of the data gathering was carried out by Masters' students working under supervision on their final theses at the Stockholm School of Economics.[2] Both the sheer volume and overlap of data and of data sources have assured substantial triangulation. The reliability of the material is judged to be fairly high. The validity of the studies is clearly not very high, and that goes especially for the external validity. The findings are thus best interpreted as exploratory (cf. Yin, 1984), generating hypotheses instead of attempting to falsify them.In view of space constraints, only highlights from the case study firms are presented below.

Bokus

The online bookseller Bokus went live in August 1997. It was modeled on Amazon.com and the ambition was to become a regional alternative to the same Internet store. The first funding came from a couple of business angels.[3] The ambition to expand internationally required additional funding and Bokus turned to a High Street competitor (similar to Barnes and Noble). The parent company (KF Media) purchased 45% of the stock in Bokus in March 1997. The company outsourced its distribution and computer systems as well as all invoicing and payments. Bokus held no stock, but left that to the publishers. The hired Chief Executive Officer had extensive experience from the industry, but not from operating an international company. To a large extent, Bokus relied on external

---

[1] An additional benefit is the possibility of this experience having a trail-blazing quality, meaning that similar patterns may occur in other markets as they mature in terms of Internet usage.

[2] Bergman (2000), The Broadening of Competencies of Internet Consultancies; Johansson and Lindblad (2000), Border Breaking Bits — Internationalization of Virtual Distributors; Mörn and Cedervall (2000), The Internationalization Process of an Internet Retailer — A Case Study of Boxman; and Tersmeden and Törnell (2000), The Internationalization of Bokus, Boxman, Buyonet, CDon, and Dressmart.

[3] The founders were Kajsa Leander and Ernst Malmsten, who later went on to start Boo.com.

consultants for market knowledge. The board contributed with experience from logistics and mail order.

The first international subsidiary was established in Finland 1 year after commencing operations. A local office with local customer service was set up only to promptly be withdrawn when local fixed costs started to mount. All activities except for a single country manager were pulled back to Sweden. The leaner model was employed for subsequent establishments in Denmark (1 month after Finland) and Norway (another 9 months later). The company put down its choice of markets to enter as a function of first, the extent of Internet usage and second, the structure of the local markets.[4] Proximity, in a wide sense, was seen as concern only after that. KF Media had bought another 47.5% of Bokus in January 1999, and their corporate strategy had a clear Nordic focus.

In the beginning of 2000, 50% of Bokus was sold to Bertelsmann and the company began to operate under the Bertelsmann trademark of bol.com. That foray into a larger international market never took off and the Bokus name was relaunched in May 2002. That fall KF Media repurchased Bertelsmann's shares and withdrew from *all* foreign markets.

Boxman

Boxman's Swedish website for selling CDs opened in December 1997. A venture capital firm financed the startup with the explicit ambition to expand the product range which also include videotapes and computer games. In addition, the company had an explicit strategy of internationalizing quickly in order to build a brand name and to exploit first-mover advantages. During the third quarter of 1998 Boxman placed a new tranche of shares with private investors and opened green-field subsidiaries in Norway, Denmark, and Finland. The model was to hire a local country manager, who in turn hired around 4–8 people to man a local site for customer support, adaptation of the product range, and payments. The computer systems and logistics were outsourced as were some corporate payments. The choice of countries was first and foremost contingent on the degree of Internet maturity. These countries also served as trial markets before the larger markets of France, United Kingdom, and Germany were entered in the period March–May 1999. Less mature and bigger markets also meant heavy spending on marketing, not least since generic marketing activities were required. In August 1999, the Dutch subsidiary opened for business.

---

[4]Finland does not have minimum price rules for books as do Denmark and Norway.

Boxman went bankrupt and the trademark (only) was acquired by a new firm that was launched under that name in 2002. The "new" Boxman operates in the Swedish market only and is in the business of renting movies over the Internet.

Buyonet

The raison-d'être of Buyonet was a patented software that allows the company to track whether or not a customer had received a functioning copy software online. In June 1997 Buyonet began offering standard software from its first, Swedish site in 10 languages and accepting payments in 10 currencies. By December 1998 the number of languages had increased to 12 and currencies to 20. One year later, Buyonet handled 20 languages and 22 currencies for customers in around 120 countries. All major software companies have licensed their products to Buyonet except Microsoft, which has limited its licensing to the US market only. Buyonet's only foreign subsidiary was established in April 1998 in Seattle, Washington. The main rationale for this was to avoid European value added taxes, since electronically stored and delivered services are exempt if they come from outside the European Union. The US office handles local customer support, while the rest of the world is dealt with from the head office in Gothenburg. A US partner, Netsales, is responsible for storage and transport as well as for delivery of any complementary physical items.

Initial funding came from a local Gothenburg family. It was supplemented in 1999 with a full-fledged venture capital firm, which with two purchases brought its share of the company up to 30% by August. The internationalization strategy has largely been left up to management, subject to board approval. Buyonet has decided not to invest in any generic marketing. In fact, marketing expenses have been kept to a minimum. Maintaining its Swedish link, Buyonet is from 1999 operated by Mirror Image Internet out of Woburn, Massachusetts; a firm 99% owned by Xcelera Inc. (formerly Scandinavian Company) incorporated in Grand Cayman, British West Indies.

CDon

The Swedish Media conglomerate Modern Times Group (MTG) founded and funded the online compact disc (CD) retailer CDon in February 1999. It opened shop in Sweden, Norway, and Denmark on the same day. Degree of Internet penetration and geographic overlap with MTG's other activities motivated the choice of markets to enter. The latter criterion meant that a Finish site was delayed until a year later and was quickly followed by sites in the Netherlands and Estonia.

CDon has relied rather heavily on MTG for market knowledge and has outsourced distribution, invoicing and payments, logistics, and web traffic to other MTG subsidiaries. The intention has been to keep fixed costs low and to primarily spend on marketing. Activities are clearly geared toward the respective local markets and the green-field sites are adapted to local tastes and market conditions, e.g. price levels. The local subsidiaries are largely left to grow organically.

CDon pulled out of Estonia and the Netherlands and focuses on the four Nordic countries complemented by a "EU site". At the end of 2003 CDon was the second largest online retailer of CDs and DVDs in the Nordic region and the most visited Internet retail site of all categories in Sweden.

Dressmart

The business idea behind Dressmart was to sell good quality, brand name clothes to young middle-aged male professionals. This target group was thought to consist of people with little time on their hands for shopping clothes and people who would not be very price sensitive. The company began operating in April 1999 backed by SEK 6 million from a venture capital firm and a government pension fund. The financial backers had a very clear strategy of rapid internationalization and openly declared that they would change the management team if this strategy could not be implemented according to schedule. Consultants, who had been involved in the internationalization of Boxman, were extensively used by Dressmart. By August 1999 Merrill Lynch had also invested in the company and was committed to help Dressmart raise the money needed for its international expansion.

Dressmart prepared each market entry well with extensive help from outside consultants. The business idea hinged on shipping directly from the manufacturer/distributor who owned the brand name so it became very important to build up networks of supplying firms. Dressmart also adapted its product range to fit each market and had a strong local presence to offer what was felt to be vital customer support. From the beginning Dressmart spent a staggering 60% of turnover on marketing, chiefly for building the brand. Other activities were outsourced to the greatest possible extent.

The choice of which countries to enter was guided by degree of Internet maturity and then by market size. From August to October, 1999, Finland, Norway, Denmark, and the Netherlands got Dressmart green-field subsidiaries. The larger markets the UK, Germany, and France followed between October 1999 and January 2000. A plan for entering the US was never implemented as the company began to get restless investors during the late spring. A protracted battle to stay in operation ensued until finally Dressmart went bankrupt during the fall of 2000.

SEB

Financial services are commonly perceived to be an extremely internationalized business. However, this pertains mainly to business-to-business transactions. Retail banking, personal insurance, and brokerage for individuals are still very much of a local business with local brands. SEB is one of the major Swedish banks with about a fifth of the Swedish savings market. It was the first bank to launch an Internet banking site in the country in January 1996. During the first couple of years SEB was typically identified in the press as the largest Internet bank in the world as measured by the number of accounts. SEB's vision for its e-bank is for it to become the leading player in Europe for online personal savings and investments. The strategy is to internationalize quickly by exploiting its "first-mover advantage". SEB has developed a proprietary platform for both fixed and mobile Internet; a platform they believe is ahead of anything the competition has. SEB handles its activities almost exclusively in-house.

The early internationalization strategy for the e-bank has in practice been derived from the corporate strategy. In practice, the SEB e-bank has entered geographic markets when the parent company made acquisitions that allowed the e-bank a local brand name. Thus, SEB has been operating e-banks in Estonia and Latvia since 1999 and in Denmark, Germany, and the UK since 2000. Only the last market entry was not linked to a local acquisition. With a local physical presence, customers are seen as more likely to trust SEB and access to local payments systems, ATM networks etc. are made easier. This was also the reason for rather quickly pulling out of the UK. SEB's Internet customers in the remaining markets doubled from approximately 800,000 in 2000 to more than 1.6 million in 2003.

Framfab

Framfab was established as an Internet consultancy in 1995. They developed one of the main Swedish portals ("Passagen") for Telia and were responsible for the first live Internet presentation of a new car the following year (Volvo's C70). The firm grew organically as well as through acquisitions. The international expansion began during 1999 during the last 8 months of which Framfab grew from a domestic firm with 270 employees to one of Europe's biggest Internet consultancies with 750 employees in four countries. It is listed on the stock exchange.

A key concept at Framfab is that of a cell. Company policy dictated that no single office should have more than 50 employees. Projects can, however, be staffed with people from more than one cell. Not surprisingly, the approach to integrating acquired firms was quite relaxed in that they were accepted as an additional cell among all the others.

Framfab went through 1 year of frantic internationalization largely relying on its own devices. In May 1999 one firm with 49 employees was acquired in Denmark and one with 20 employees in the UK. One in France (41 employees) followed in September. In December there were acquisitions in Germany (105 employees) and in the US (15 employees). The last acquisitions were in Norway (25 employees) in February 2000 and in May in the Netherlands (135 employees). Framfab used its own shares as payment in all instances. This currency ceased to be viable after the fall in equity values in the late spring. One green-field site was established, in Italy in February 2000. Frantic restructuring allowed the company to remain in business. In the beginning of 2004 Framfab had 420 employees in Sweden, Denmark, Germany, Switzerland, the Netherlands, and in the UK.

Icon Medialab

Icon Medialab opened its first overseas office within months of its founding; in Madrid in August 1996. It developed a rather strong corporate culture and took great care to integrate acquisitions. For instance, where possible, offices were laid out and furnished to look similar around the world. Icon Medialab used a matrix organization along the dimensions of physical location and competence areas. The company is listed on the stock exchange.

Internationalization proceeded both through acquisitions and the establishment of green-field subsidiaries. Icon Medialab did not use consultants or other advisors to any significant degree. From August 1996 until October 1999 Icon Medialab opened 11 offices[5] abroad. In parallel, from November, 1997 through April 2000 13 international acquisitions were made.[6] By 2001, Icon Medialab had wholly owned subsidiaries in 19 countries. Icon Medialab's aggressive growth strategy was funded by a rising share price as long as that lasted. The subsequent financial pressure forced a merger with a Dutch consultancy, Lost Boys, in January 2002. The Swedish main subsidiary went bankrupt. The new merged company operates under the umbrella of Icon Medialab International incorporated in Sweden. Corporate headquarters are located in Amsterdam, the Netherlands. Of the "old" Icon Medialab subsidiaries in Sweden, Italy, Spain, Portugal, the US, and Swizerland remained at the end of 2003. Subsidiaries in the Netherlands, the UK, and Germany operated under other names.

---

[5]Spain, US, UK, Malaysia, Denmark, Finland, Germany, Belgium, Germany, Germany, and Spain.
[6]Finland (11 employees), Germany (7), Norway (25), Norway (25), France (16), Italy (20), UK (15), Netherlands (40), US (100), France (5), Norway (50), UK (80), and Spain (142).

New Internationalization Patterns?

At first sight, the general predictions of the Uppsala Internationalization Process Model do not seem to hold up that well when confronted with the experience of eight Internet-related case companies. Rather than slow and incremental, the process seems to be fast and discontinuous. Regarding choice of markets, it appears as if most firms did enter markets at a relatively short psychic distance. However, rather than cultural affinity or reduced uncertainty, the main reason given was the maturity of markets in terms of Internet usage that determined which markets to enter. If we believe the firms, then the observed pattern is just spuriously correlated with psychic distance. Market potential (size) was also unanimously put before any notion of psychic distance when motivating market choice.

Even though we have seen substantial variation among firms, one thing that they do have in common is an explicit internationalization strategy. Whereas the prediction was one of firm growth "spilling over" the home country borders irrespective if any such decisions had been made or not (cf. Johanson & Vahlne, 1990), every case firm not only claimed an internationalization strategy but that international growth was a top priority.

The case firms do exhibit substantial variation in other aspects of their internationalization behavior, however. Boxman and Dressmart stand out in terms of making market commitments among the six business-to-consumer firms. They also forced the pace of internationalization to a greater extent than the other consumer market firms. CDon and SEB displayed a more moderate expansion pattern; one that is more in line with the traditional predictions. It is noteworthy that these two cases represent Internet business within bigger, more established firms. Bokus seem to fall somewhere in between, also having been bought by an established firm during the period under scrutiny. Buyonet is arguably more similar to an exporter in that the only subsidiary outside Sweden owes its existence to the wish to avoid paying European value added tax.

The web consultancies made the greatest market commitments both in relative and absolute terms. The need to secure scarce resources/competencies was on the agenda in addition to international expansion. This is evident from Framfab's and Icon Medialab's propensity to use acquisitions as a means for their international growth. Rather than the more passive, reactive learning allowed for in the model, we can see how these case firms take a much more proactive stance.[7] By acquiring a local firm the slow process of personal, experiential learning (Johanson & Vahlne, 1977) can be replaced by "grafting" (cf. Huber, 1991) knowledge into the

---

[7]Of course, there is a strong element of opportunism here as well, since there must be firms to acquire.

firm. Why wait if there is a unit that already possesses the required knowledge that can be readily acquired? Obviously there are alternatives to only learning from one's own, current activities. However, this is not to say that this is always a successful strategy. The ability of the acquiring firms to assimilate the knowledge inherited in the acquired firms can be limited, and therefore create difficulties in later stages of the internationalization process. Still, this strategy implies a faster internationalization process than predicted by the received model, at least in the beginning of the process.

In addition, there is a problem with assuming that experiential learning and incremental behavior necessarily go hand in hand as is done in the Uppsala model. Not only can firms learn through making acquisitions, experience of making acquisitions is likely to equip the firm to be able to move even more quickly than it otherwise would be inclined to do (cf. Barkema & Vermeulen, 1998). Hence, there may be a negative relationship between experiential learning and incremental behavior.

Another complication for the Uppsala model relates to the basic feature that firms are said not to invest abroad if they assess the risk of investing as intolerably high (cf. Johanson & Vahlne, 1977). However, it is quite possible that the firm experiences not investing abroad as even more risky and intolerable. This can be the case when the general uncertainty about the future of the industry is high in combination with a feeling that a first-mover advantage is crucial. Such a situation can force the firm to invest abroad, even if it considers the adventure an extremely high-risk project due to lack of market knowledge. The action would then be based on a conviction that if the firm does not take the step now, there will be no second chance in the future (Forsgren, 2002). Consequently, the first step in the internationalization process can sometimes occur much earlier than predicted by the Uppsala model.

The speed of internationalization is moreover fueled by the desire to exploit economies of scale (Shapiro & Varian, 1999). One of the salient features of Internet technology is its scalability. The production costs for serving an additional geographic market are very modest. Costly production activities, such as distribution and payments, are typically outsourced reducing the need for investment in those activities.

The marketing costs have been seen to be substantial. Building a brand is expensive, in particular in consumer markets when generic advertising also is required. Internet savvy may also have to be taught in some markets. A somewhat curious possibility is that firms may actually reduce their physical market presence once they have well established customer relationships, i.e. improved market knowledge can lead to less market commitment. Bokus pulled back from Finland and Buyonet handles its international customer support out of

Gothenburg. It is not too far-fetched to imagine a situation when, say, SEB closes the branch network after having acquired and reassured the local customer base. The importance of initial local presence is further underlined by SEB finding itself having to exit the UK market.

A different twist to the story is that some firms do not build up home-market knowledge before they go abroad (Oviatt & Phillips-McDougall, 1994). Boxman is a good example of such a strategy. It had an explicit intention to establish operations abroad quickly in order to build a brand name presence and exploit first-mover advantage. This strategy has first of all an impact on the amount of time lapsed before first going abroad, but tell us less about the speed of the further internationalization process. It has been suggested, though, that the time of the first step and the speed of the internationalization process are related. The reason for that would be that investing abroad in fact requires de-learning of certain routines and procedures acquired in the home market but of little relevance abroad. Therefore, no or limited knowledge from operations in the home market could actually constitute an advantage as there is not much to unlearn (cf. Autio, Sapienza, & Almeida, 2000).

Another way of reducing the uncertainty associated with investing abroad not allowed for in the Uppsala model is mimetic behavior (cf. DiMaggio & Powell, 1983). Firms may imitate actions taken by other firms if these actions are seen to have been successful and/or legitimized some other way (Levitt & March, 1988). The point is that both radical and quick action may be taken under these circumstances without having to wait for experiential accumulation of one's own knowledge. There is no good reason why this general mechanism should not be applicable to internationalization.

The standard interpretation of imitation is that firms tend to follow typically one leading firm in the industry in order to reduce uncertainty by imitating a successful recipe (Haunschield & Mimer, 1997). A closer look at the case firms instead reveals that there is no apparent leader to imitate. The Internet-based concept was relatively new and the "industry" not old enough for any single leading firm to emerge. Still, the cases give the impression of a more or less pronounced "following-the-herd" behavior among the firms. The firms feel that they need to internationalize, and internationalize fast, because that is what other Internet-based firms do or should do. So, here we seem to have an interesting case of imitation without any leading firm to imitate. It seems like some kind of nervousness and expectations evolve among firms in a new industry that lead to a "following-the-herd" behavior like screaming jackdaws at dusk. Similar to "follow-the-leader" behavior, it is an attempt to reduce the uncertainty of the individual firm. The difference, though, is that the behavior is not based on experiential knowledge of any firm, only on expectations, and in that sense it deviates even more from the Uppsala model. The consequence, though, is again a faster internation-alization process, at least as long as this is what the herd, as a group, appreciates as the appropriate behavior. Indeed, the case firms themselves stressed the momentum that built up when explaining the commonly ferocious international-ization behavior of Internet-related firms.

The case firms also demonstrate another important aspect if we want to under-stand internationalization behavior. In the Uppsala model, the crucial actors in the firm are the ones that acquire and hold market knowledge. They shape the inter-nationalization process of the firm in accordance with their own learning, risk, and opportunity perception.[8] The cases show quite strongly, though, that other stakeholders also can shape the internationalization behavior. The "forgotten" stakeholder category is the owners. In particular, venture capitalists demanded a more rapid internationalization process than that motivated by the level of market knowledge of the firm in order for them to be able to profit quickly and in rich measure from their investment. Unlike the "grafting strategy" above it is not pri-marily an attempt to avoid the "experiential knowledge imperative", but rather to disregard it. The non-listed firms also put this factor at the top of their list when explaining their urgency in implementing internationalization strategies.[9] The sit-uation for Framfab and Icon Medialab were not too dissimilar in that the value of their shares was contingent on continued international expansion. Any delay tended to lead to lower share values, in turn making acquisitions more costly as the preferred mode of payment were the same shares. There are strong incentives in both these cases for internationalization that cannot afford to wait for experi-ential knowledge to build up.

The Uppsala model concerns prediction of firm behavior. This also means that to the extent the conditions prevail assumed in the model, it also has managerial implications. It is interesting to note, though, that the model was originally launched as understanding actual behavior of firms, rather than suggesting suit-able norms for how to invest abroad. Paradoxically, though, one may argue that an important strength of the model is more related to its normative implications than to its predictions of what firms actually do. On one hand, the cases suggest that there are factors missing in the model that shape the internationalization process of firms. These factors must be considered if we want to build a more full-fledged model of internationalization behavior. On the other hand, at least

---

[8] The Uppsala model assumes that the holders of market knowledge are the same individuals as those responsible for, and having the ultimate influence over, investment decisions. For larger organizations this is a questionable assumption (Forsgren, 2002).
[9] Recall the ultimatum put to the management team in Dressmart, see 2.5 above.

some of the cases suggest that if the firm had applied a more cautious, incremental strategy based on successive building up of market knowledge it may have been more successful or avoided bankruptcy. It is also interesting to observe that the managerial dimensions of the Uppsala model has been focused lately in research that actually tries to relate economic performance to incremental behavior. (cf. Drogendijk, 2001). Our concern here with Internet-related firms highlights another important aspect of internationalization not dealt with explicitly in the Uppsala model: namely the importance of establishing and developing business relationships. One crucial factor behind the reason for a firm taking on an incremental, time-consuming internationalization behavior is the fact that exploring foreign markets is actually about investing in specific customer (and supplier) relationships within a foreign business network rather than surmounting economic, institutional, and cultural country barriers. Investing in relationships also means demands to manage these relationships by learning gradually about the counterparts' capabilities. These aspects are fundamental insights from business network theory that can be used to infuse new elements into the Uppsala model. An interesting issue, then, is to what extent Internet-related firms, which extensively manage their customer relationships through Internet, are condemned to follow the same rules or not. Or expressed otherwise, how easy is it for these firms to exploit the sheer size of their customer network (by avoiding too much investments in specific relationships) and therefore conduct a faster internationalization than would otherwise be possible? A reasonable answer to that question is that Internet-related firms also differ in that respect, for instance in the sense that a publishing firm has a higher possibility to conduct an "arms-length" relationship with customers while a consultant needs to build up and invest in such relationships more carefully and on one-to-one basis.

Conclusion

The Uppsala Internationalization Process Model has been the subject of — and has withstood — much empirical testing during its quarter-of-a-century existence (for overviews see, e.g. Johanson & Vahlne, 1990). There has, however, been less scrutiny of the basic theoretical tenets of the model (Hadjikhani, 1997; Forsgren, 2002).[10] This chapter has the ambition to do a bit of both. Far from conclusively proving anything, we have called the model into question on theoretical as well

---

[10]Some notable exceptions are Anderson (1993), and Barkema et al. (1996), and Pedersen and Petersen (1998).

as on empirical grounds. Although the attractiveness of the model in large part has rested on its simplicity and incorporation of a dynamic view of internationalization, it seems less well suited to the context of Internet-related firms.

In particular, the model's central tenet of incremental learning has been scrutinized and found wanting. A telltale example is when a firm is ignorant about the market conditions. Then the risk of investing abroad is great, and the model predicts that the firm is unlikely to want to follow through with the investment. If, however, the firm finds the risk associated with *not* investing abroad even greater, then the ignorant firm will invest. The cost of not investing would then be forgone first-mover advantages of the kind discussed above.

The case firms that most closely resemble this scenario would be Boxman and Dressmart. Since they were the ones to go bankrupt, perhaps there is more to be said about incremental market learning after all.

References

Anderson, O. (1993). On the internationalization process of firms: A critical analysis. *Journal of International Business, 24*(2), 209–232.

Autio, E., Sapienza, H.J., & Almeida, J.G. (2000). The effects of age at entry, knowledge intensity, and imitability on international growth. *Academy of Management Journal, 43*, 909–924.

Barkema, H., & Vermeulen, F. (1998). International expansion through start-up or acquisition: A learning perspective. *Academy of Management Journal, 41*(1), 7–26.

Barkema, H.G., Bell, J.H.J., & Pennings, J.M. (1996). Foreign entry, cultural barriers and learning. *Strategic Management Journal, 17*, 151–166.

Buckley, P.J., & Casson, M. (1976). *The future of the multinational enterprise.* London: Macmillan.

Carlson, S. (1966). *International business research.* Uppsala: Acta Universitatis Upsaliensis.

Caves, R.E. (1982). *Multinational enterprise and economic nalysis.* Cambridge: Cambridge University Press.

Chandler, A.D. (1986). The evolution of modern global competition. In: M.E. Porter (Ed.), *Competition in global industries.* Boston, MA: Harvard Business School Press.

Cyert, R.D., & March, J.G. (1963). *The behavioral theory of the firm.* Englewood Cliffs, NJ: Prentice-Hall.

Di Maggio, P.J., & Powell, W.W. (1983). The iron cage revisited: Institutional isomorphism and collective rationality in organization fields. *Administration Science Quarterly, 48*, 147–60.

Drogendijk, R. (2001). Expansion patterns of Dutch firms in Central and Eastern Europé: Learning to internationalize. Tilburg University, Tilburg: Center Dissertation Studies.

Dunning, J.H. Trade, location of economic activity and the multinational enterprise. A search for an electric approach. In: B. Ohlin, P.O. Hesselbom, P.J. Wiskman (eds), *The international allocation of economic activity*. London: MacMillan.

Forsgren, M. (2002). The concept of learning in the Uppsala internationalization process model: A critical review. *International Business Review, 11*, 257–277.

Hadjikhani, A. (1997). A note on the criticisms against the internationalization process model. *Management International Review, 37*(Special Issue), 1–23.

Haunschield, P., & Miner, A.S. (1997). Modes of interorganizational imitation: The effect of outcome salience and uncertainty. *Administrative Science Quarterly, 42*, 472–500.

Huber, G.P. (1991). Organizational learning. The contributing processes and the literatures. *Organization Science, 2*(1), 88–115.

Hymer, S. H. (1976/1960). *The international operations of national firms: A study of direct investment*. Cambridge, MA: The MIT Press (previously unpublished doctoral dissertation, MIT, 1960).

Johanson, J., & Vahlne, J.-E. (1977). The internationalization process of the firm — A model of knowledge development and increasing foreign market commitments. *Journal of International Business Studies, 8*, 23–32.

Johanson, J., & Vahlne, J.-E. (1990). The mechanisms of internationalization. *International Marketing Review, 7*(4), 11–24.

Johanson, J., & Wiedersheim-Paul, F. (1975). The internationalization of the firm — four cases. *Journal of Management Studies, 12*, 305–322.

Johnson, G. (1988). Rethinking incrementalism. *Strategic Management Journal, 9*, 75–91.

Levitt, B., & March, J.G. (1988). Organizational learning. *Annual Review of Sociology, 14*, 319–340.

Lindblom, C.E. (1959). The science of muddling through. *Public Administration Review, 19*(Spring), 79–88.

Oviatt, B.M., & Phillips-McDougall, P. (1994). Towards a theory of international new ventures. *Journal of International Business Studies, 25*, 45–64.

Pedersen, T., & Petersen, B. (1998). Explaining gradually increasing resource commitment to a foreign market. *International Business Review, 7*, 483–501.

Shapiro, C. & Varian, H. R. (1999). *Information rules*. Boston, MA: Harvard Business School Press.

Yin, R. K. (1984). *Case study research: Design and methods*. Beverly Hills, CA: Sage Publications.

Subject Index